GO
SLOW

GO SLOW

THE LIFE OF

Julie London

Michael Owen

CHICAGO
REVIEW
PRESS

An A Cappella Book

Copyright © 2017 by Michael R. Owen
Foreword copyright © 2017 by Arthur Hamilton
All rights reserved
First edition
Published by Chicago Review Press Incorporated
814 North Franklin Street
Chicago, Illinois 60610
ISBN 978-1-61373-857-3

Library of Congress Cataloguing-in-Publication Data

Names: Owen, Michael, 1962–
Title: Go slow: the life of Julie London / Michael Owen.
Description: First edition. | Chicago, Illinois: Chicago Review Press,
    [2017] | Includes bibliographical references and index.
Identifiers: LCCN 2016048585 (print) | LCCN 2016049827 (ebook) | ISBN
    9781613738573 (cloth) | ISBN 9781613738580 (adobe pdf) | ISBN
    9781613738597 (epub) | ISBN 9781613738603 (kindle)
Subjects: LCSH: London, Julie, 1926–2000. | Singers—United
    States—Biography. | Motion picture actors and actresses—United
    States—Biography. | Television actors and actresses—United
    States—Biography.
Classification: LCC ML420.L866 O94 2017 (print) | LCC ML420.L866 (ebook) |
    DDC 784.42164092 [B] —dc23
LC record available at https://lccn.loc.gov/2016048585

Typesetting: Nord Compo

Printed in the United States of America
5 4 3 2 1

To my wife, Libbie Hodas, with love for helping me
get to the heart of the story.
And to my late mother, Johanna Owen,
for her lifetime of encouragement.

Go slow, ooh, ooh, honey,
Take it easy on the curves.
When love is slow, ooh honey,
What a tonic for my nerves.

—"Go Slow" by Russell Garcia and Ned Kronk

Contents

Acknowledgments

I N "LONELINESS AND SOLITUDE," the first chapter of his 1963 collection *The Eternal Now*, philosopher and theologian Paul Tillich
made the compelling statement that "the mystery of a person cannot be
encompassed by a neat description of [her] character." During the years
it took to research and write this book about the life and career of Julie
London, I came to understand Tillich's words more fully.

Each person I spoke with about Julie gave me another facet of her
character to consider, and for their assistance I am forever grateful.
Thoughts and memories, either in person or via phone conversations
and e-mails, came from the following: James Austin, the late Don
Bagley, John Bähler, Colin Bailey, Bob Bain, Jim Bawden, Chuck
Berghofer, Hal Blaine, Dennis Budimir, Buzz Cason, Gene Cipriano,
Edwin Greines Cohen, Lee Evans, Robert Fuller, the late Russ Garcia,
Murray Garrett, the late Snuff Garrett, the late Dick Gauthier, Terry
Gibbs, Arthur Hamilton (who was also kind enough to write the fore-
word to my book), Enid Harlow, Harry Hawthorne, Bones Howe,
the late Johnny Mann, Leo Monahan, Dick Nash, Dave Pell, Bucky
Pizzarelli, Emil Richards, Lyle Ritz, Tony Russell, Jill Schoelen, Karen
Schoemer, Cal Sexton, Joe Sidore, Maynard Sloate, Al Stoffel, Kevin
Tighe, Lenny Waronker, Peggy Webber, Tom Williams, Mari Wilson,
and Julie's daughter and granddaughter, Lisa and Ryann Breen. My
sincere thanks to all of you.

I particularly want to express my appreciation for three individuals whose kindness and interest in the project went beyond the norm. Linda Wheeler Lackey was Julie London's friend for more than thirty years. From the moment we met in Palm Springs in 2011, Linda has encouraged me to tell Julie's story. Cynnie Troup and Bob Bayles were endlessly generous with their time and provided me with access to a wealth of material that had been in storage since Julie's death. Cynnie regaled me with funny stories and was a gracious host on my visits to Los Angeles. Bob, who's married to Cynnie's sister Ronne, shared many rare images and audio recordings and helped in other ways too numerous to mention.

Thank you as well to Lynn Todd, who provided fascinating information on the history of the Peck family, much of it written by her mother, Jeanne Woodson Labadie, the daughter of Julie London's aunt Ethel Woodson (née Peck).

A special debt of posthumous gratitude to Julie's longtime friend Dorothy LaPointe Gurnee, who compiled nearly forty scrapbooks on the lives and careers of Julie and Bobby Troup.

My thanks also go out to the following people, who shared information, resources, contacts, and/or words of encouragement along the way: Gene Alvarez, Polly Armstrong (formerly of the Stanford University Library, Department of Special Collections), Marilee Bradford, Elliot Brown, Professor Keen Butterworth, Steven Cerra, Frank Collura, Ned Comstock (Cinematic Arts Library at the University of Southern California), Professor Richard Crawford, Michael Cuscuna, Professor Mike Evans, Carmen Fanzone (American Federation of Musicians, Local 47), Michael Feinstein, James Harrod, Chad Hemus, my brother-in-law Glenn Hodas, Phyllis Kessel, Arthur Krim, Jaime Lennox (San Diego State University), Shane MacDonald (the American Catholic University History Research Center and University Archives), Ron McMaster, Daniel Moyer, Mark Quigley (UCLA Film & Television Archive), Michael Rabkin and Chip Tom, Bill Reed, Lauren Rogers (University of Mississippi, Archives and Special Collections), Brett Service (Warner Bros. Archives, School of Cinematic Arts, University of Southern California),

Maurice Summerfield, Steve Taravella, Richard Thompson (San Bernardino County Historical Society), Janice Torbet (San Francisco Public Library), Mel Vapour (East Bay Media Center), and to my friends at the Library of Congress: Mark Eden Horowitz, Loras Schissel, and Ray White (all of the Music Division), and Karen Fishman (Motion Picture, Broadcasting, and Recorded Sound Division).

And a final thank-you to the folks at Chicago Review Press who brought *Go Slow* to fruition: senior editor Yuval Taylor, project editor Ellen Hornor, and copyeditor Julia Loy.

Foreword

WE WERE SEVENTEEN TOGETHER. I borrowed my brother's car to take her to our senior prom. She was always singing. We tried to outremember each other, reciting the lyrics of once-popular songs. Her favorite word was *warm*. I was just beginning to write, and she was a great audience for anything I brought to her.

Michael Owen, in his marvelous memory of her, brings her back into my life (and into yours), accurately describing her years as a film actress, television performer, and nightclub and recording star. She was all those things but never wanted to be any of them. She just loved to sing, almost to herself. Her voice was a whisper.

Three or four years after high school, she called and told me she was married to actor/producer Jack Webb, who was planning to produce a television series called *Pete Kelly's Blues*. Julie asked me if I was still writing songs and if I had written any blues songs. I lied and said, "Of course." She invited me for dinner the following Thursday night—which gave me four days to write three blues songs.

Jack liked what he heard and put me under contract. (I think it's important to tell you that, at that time, I was delivering prescription drugs for the Horton & Converse pharmacy, earning fifty bucks a week—so you can imagine how Julie changed the course of my life.)

A few weeks ago, the National Recording Preservation Board of the Library of Congress sent me a certificate honoring the selection of Julie

London's recording of "Cry Me a River" to the National Recording Registry.

We remained friends throughout her life. I still hear her voice in my head. I can still see her. She is still seventeen.

Arthur Hamilton
Writer of "Cry Me a River"
Beverly Hills, California
July 2016

Prologue

Spring/Summer 1955

"YOU OPEN IN THREE weeks!"

Julie London had done everything she could possibly think of to forget about her upcoming nightclub debut. She heard what her boyfriend, songwriter and pianist Bobby Troup, was telling her. She just didn't want to deal with it. Two months earlier he had persuaded her to make a few demos in the hopes of getting her a recording contract. She laughed and said she just enjoyed singing songs she liked among friends. Besides, she was about to resume the acting career she had abandoned a few years earlier. Why in the world would anyone want to hear her sing? Relieved when the recordings were quickly rejected, Julie was certain that Bobby's nagging attempts to convince her she could also have a career as a singer had finally—thankfully—come to an end.

But Bobby Troup was a man in love. Julie London's lifelong lack of confidence in her abilities as a performer was offset by his undying belief in her talent and his persistence in trying to make her realize just how special she was. Without her knowledge he had arranged for Julie to perform at an intimate venue on Hollywood's La Cienega Boulevard—the 881 Club, a place she had recently told him she'd want to sing in . . . if she ever wanted to sing in public. To Julie London "if" meant no; to Bobby Troup "if" was just another musical obstacle that required a key change to overcome.

Twenty years later, with her singing career largely behind her, Julie London joked that she had prayed she'd break a leg before opening night.

Julie's parents and many of her friends were among the customers packed into the tiny club on the evening of Wednesday, June 8, 1955. "I was so scared I walked across the street to the Encore, where Bobby was working," she later told celebrity journalist Pete Martin for a *Saturday Evening Post* profile, "and I had a couple. But they didn't help. . . . I had butterflies so bad I thought I would die." Upon her return she nervously paced around the small dressing room until club owner John Walsh peered around the door and said, "It's about time for us to do a show."

Cautiously, Julie made her way onto the darkened stage. As her hidden accompanists launched into Cole Porter's "From This Moment On," a single spotlight was directed onto her face and the long reddish-brown hair that fell around her shoulders. Julie opened her mouth to sing. Only "noise" emerged. "All the faces blurred and ran together," she recalled. A petite, curvaceous woman, she was simply dressed in a tight black turtleneck sweater and black skirt, sorely disappointing those who recalled her glamorous fur-and-jewel-bedecked image from photographs taken during her acrimonious divorce from actor Jack Webb. Everyone in the opening-night audience acknowledged that Julie was gorgeous, but there were some who hoped to be witnesses at a spectacular public failure. Was she really a singer or was this merely a blatant attempt to capitalize on Webb's success as Sgt. Joe Friday in the hit radio and television series *Dragnet*? Julie was as aware of these questions as anyone else.

As the opening number continued, additional spotlights gradually revealed her musicians to be guitarist Barney Kessel and double bassist Ralph Peña, similarly outfitted in black turtlenecks and black pants. The music the duo made had a rare subtlety, and Julie's voice had a haunting, unaffected quality, even if she couldn't remember all the words to the songs. "The audience thought it was cute," recalled a member of the audience. "Everybody started feeding her the lyrics from their tables." By the end of the brief set, which closed with an up-tempo rendition of George and Ira Gershwin's classic "'S Wonderful," Julie was relaxed enough to discover she could ad-lib and make fun of herself. "The only thing I remember I said is, 'I've got a frog in my throat. You'll have to wait till it hops out.' It doesn't sound like much, but they laughed."

Those who hoped for a car wreck instead found themselves at the beginning of a unique musical story. The striking combination of Julie's whispered voice, her provocative figure, and the subtle instrumental accompaniment captured crowds at the 881 Club for ten weeks, far longer than the original two the understandably wary club owner had agreed to. Critics raved and audiences were delighted, but a small club in Hollywood could take her only so far. And really, she thought, wasn't this all just another lark, one of a series of accidents that had shaped what she laughingly called a career? Still, she *had* come a long way from being just another girl running an elevator on Hollywood Boulevard . . . and even further from her obscure beginnings as a child of the Great Depression. Once again the doors had opened for Julie London.

1

God Bless the Child

*I was kind of a wallflower... too moodily mature for
my age.*

—Julie London, *TV Guide*, July 15, 1961

B EFORE THERE WAS JULIE LONDON, there was Nancy Gayle Peck.
Born amid the economic prosperity of the 1920s, her fortunes
would change as a child of the devastating Great Depression that followed.

Her story begins in Stockton, California, a bustling city of more
than forty thousand along the San Joaquin River, a major trade
route that brought the agricultural products of the state's fertile
Central Valley to its economic and trade center in San Francisco.
The band at a local vaudeville performance was playing "It Had to
Be You," a popular romantic ballad. In the audience that day was a
twenty-five-year-old California-born salesman named Jack Peck and
twenty-year-old Josephine "Jo" Taylor, originally from Indiana but
a recent arrival—with her mother and stepfather—from Arkansas.
The pair locked eyes across the crowded room, quickly bonded over
their shared love of music, and fell in love. On November 14, 1925,
the couple was married by a Stockton justice of the peace and began
their new life together.

———◦∞◦———

The first Pecks arrived on the shores of Virginia from England in the eighteenth century. Some drifted north in search of arable land, settling and tilling the soil in the northeastern section of what became the state of Ohio. A descendant of one of these adventurous souls was Jack Peck's grandfather Sedley, a man "quick to take advantage of all offered opportunities." When gold was discovered in California in the late 1840s, Sedley became a wagon master, leading arduous journeys west to become one of the "first of the '49ers to stake a claim" there. Sedley Peck's adventures became part of the stories he told his family, tales that lured all eight of his children to the promised land of the Golden State by the last decade of the nineteenth century.

For more than twenty years after his arrival in California, Sedley's son Wallace eked out a hardscrabble existence as a miner in a series of inhospitable Southern California desert boomtowns with evocative names like Calico, Havilah, Isabella, Panamint, and Ballarat, which popped up and just as quickly disappeared in the wake of significant silver and gold discoveries in the late nineteenth and early twentieth centuries.

While Wallace Peck struggled, his brothers prospered as cement contractors, laying down building foundations, streets, and sidewalks throughout burgeoning Southern and Central California, becoming pioneers and leading citizens in the city of Compton. Their success lured Wallace from the mines to Los Angeles, where he joined the family business. Within a few years, his own financial gains allowed him to move his wife, Elizabeth, and their three children to a ten-acre ranch in the newly laid-out San Fernando Valley town of Van Nuys.

Much like Sedley Peck, however, Wallace cherished dreams, and in 1913 he traded the Van Nuys property for land one hundred miles north, on the Cottonwood Ranch, south of Bakersfield in Kern County, hoping to strike it rich as a farmer. It was a costly deal. He quickly discovered that most of the land was worthless alkaline soil and filed a lawsuit to recover his losses. Weakened by a bout of pleurisy, Wallace fell ill again after returning to Kern County from Los Angeles over the snowy Tehachapi Mountains and died of pneumococcal meningitis at the age of fifty-two in December 1914.

Wallace had been a baritone soloist in the local Methodist church, and his son, handsome and blue-eyed Jack Peck, had inherited his father's fine voice as well as a "natural ability in salesmanship" from his mother, Elizabeth. After a hitch in the navy during the First World War, Jack returned to Bakersfield, where he married briefly, found employment at a department store and in the local oil industry, and led a second life as a vaudeville performer.

By the time he and Jo Taylor met in 1925, Jack had followed *his* dreams further north to the Stockton portrait photography studio of Fred Hartsook, part of a successful chain scattered throughout California. When Jo became pregnant, Jack opted for a better position as a photographer in the Hartsook branch in Santa Rosa, fifty miles north of San Francisco. Ten months after their wedding, the Pecks' only child was born at a local maternity home at six o'clock on the evening of September 26, 1926. The family's stay in Santa Rosa with their daughter, whom they named Nancy Gayle, was short lived. (Nine years later, the name Julie Peck was added to the birth record, presumably for legal reasons when "Julie London" began her acting career.) By the end of the year, the Pecks had moved south to the city of San Bernardino, where Jo's mother and stepfather lived and where Jack quickly found a position at another photography studio.

Gayle (the family quickly stopped calling her Nancy) naturally became a frequent subject for her parents' cameras. Whether as a chubby-cheeked toddler posed in a wicker chair in Jack's studio, her head covered with a bonnet or with ribbons in her hair, or outdoors as a smiling, curly-haired little girl, dressed in a jaunty cowboy outfit while seated on a pony, she was very feminine and unguarded.

Summers were often spent with Jack's sister Ethel and her family on picnics and trips to the mountains above San Bernardino or in the warmth and fun of beach towns along the California coast. Gayle's older cousin Jeanne remembered how Jack Peck held his tired daughter in his lap at the end of the day, telling her impromptu "marvelous, hilarious bedtime stories" populated by fantastical animals.

What mattered most in young Gayle's life was the music that surrounded her parents. The musical genes of the Peck and Taylor families were strong: one of Jo's cousins was the songwriter, vaudeville performer, and music publisher (William) Tell Taylor, composer of the 1910 popular standard "Down by the Old Mill Stream." So as Gayle listened to records or watched as her mother and her friends sang in four- and five-part harmony while sitting on their living room floor, she absorbed the music through her pores. For three years during her childhood, Jack and Jo Peck hosted an informal radio show on San Bernardino station KFXM ("The Voice of the Sunkist Valley"), broadcast from street-level studios in the elegant California Hotel. While her parents were on the air, Gayle spent most of her time in the restaurant next to the station, eating green peas served to her by a friendly waitress. Occasionally, she would be invited into the studio, and it was here, at the age of three and a half, that she made her public singing debut with an imitation of Marlene Dietrich's German accent in a performance of the iconic "Falling in Love Again."

"Our whole family kind of leaned toward jazz," Julie recalled, and her mother's bluesy voice could often be heard in San Bernardino–area nightclubs and theaters, where she sang to supplement the family's income. "In those days, there were no such things as babysitters, so if my mother worked in a club, I went along and slept in the checkroom, under the coats. But I didn't sleep. I'd listen to the music." By the time Gayle turned nine, her voice was distinctive enough to amaze talent scouts auditioning participants for a statewide radio contest. She didn't make the cut, but her mother sang "I Can't Give You Anything but Love" in a live "Salute to San Bernardino" broadcast on radio station KHJ from a theater in downtown Los Angeles. Although Jo's performance caught the ear of actor Conrad Nagel, the program's emcee, she failed to pick up the $500 first prize.

The first half of the 1920s had been a golden age for San Bernardino. Its agricultural output, particularly the vast orange groves that covered much of the city's acreage, and the establishment of Route 66, which ran directly through the city on its way to the Pacific coast, led to a 200 percent population increase during the decade. But San Bernardino, like the rest of the United States, was hit hard by the Great Depression. "It was pretty much a lost decade," wrote one local historian.

The economic struggles of the Peck family during the 1930s meant frequent changes of address, and Jack's mother occasionally became the fourth member of a household that was devastated when he lost his job at the Platt photography studio. As Jack's failure to find work continued, he became discouraged with himself and his future. His disappointment was reflected in changes in Gayle's physical appearance. The open-faced, smiling child of early photographs became the young girl who sometimes turned her face away from her father's camera with a clearly troubled mien. "There wasn't anything" for a while, but she insisted she didn't suffer; though her parents sometimes didn't eat, "they made sure" she did.

By the late 1930s, the local economy had rebounded under the programs of President Franklin Delano Roosevelt's New Deal, subdivisions began to replace many of San Bernardino's orchards and crop lands, and the impending war in Europe bolstered the region's manufacturing and industrial concerns. Jack Peck's self-confidence and the family finances rebounded when he was hired as a salesman for the Simon Levi Co., a large Southern California wholesale grocery and liquor distributor. He remained with Levi, moving up the ranks to become a sales and credit manager, until the family's departure for Los Angeles a few years later. The proximity to liquor, however, aggravated Jack's tendency toward alcoholism, an affliction that probably began during his naval service; on at least one occasion during the 1930s, he was arrested for public drunkenness and reckless driving.

Gradually, life improved for the Pecks, and by the end of the decade, Jack's salary and the value of the San Bernardino house he had purchased were comparable to, if not higher than, those of many of his neighbors.

⸻⸮⸰⸮⸻

Gayle Peck spent much of her childhood surrounded by the musicians who congregated around her parents. This early isolation left her with a feeling of discomfort around her peers, and her years in San Bernardino were not particularly happy ones for an introverted girl who often lived in a world of her own making. "People thought my mother was a snob," said her daughter Lisa. "She was shy." Gayle had few friends, but Caroline Stagg remained loyal from the day they met in elementary school. To Caroline, who knew Gayle better than anyone, she was "a gentle, quiet girl without much self-confidence." On weekends Gayle's parents drove the girls to dances at the San Bernardino Auditorium or in the mountains near Crestline, but her parents never worried about her and boys. "I wasn't what you'd call madly popular. I was sort of old for my age and didn't fit."

When given the opportunity to perform, however, she came out of her shell to become more than the typical girl next door. Gayle sang in front of local big bands, was chosen as a candidate for her school's Mardi Gras queen, and often appeared on the radio. San Bernardino was a popular spot for advance screenings of new movies, and Gayle became part of the onstage entertainment at local theaters on Saturdays before the lights dimmed and the projector started. Her repertoire spanned popular ballads like the First World War–era "There's a Long, Long Trail A-winding," Irving Berlin's "God Bless America," and hits of the day such as "By the Waters of Minnetonka" and "All Ashore." It was good teenage fun but not the makings of a career.

2

Dream

F RUSTRATED AND MISERABLE as she advanced through Arrowview
Junior High School, Gayle's restlessness continued when the family
moved to Los Angeles in 1941. After developing a severe case of hives,
doctors put her "on every special diet known to man," without providing any visible relief for the incessant itching and swelling. When a
specialist recognized the symptoms as potentially psychological and made
the radical suggestion to keep Gayle out of school, the hives quickly
disappeared. Emboldened by the solution to one problem, the fifteen-
year-old asked her parents if she might leave school permanently. They
agreed, but on one condition: Gayle had to prove she wouldn't be a
financial burden.

The Pecks lived in a tiny, one-room apartment at the Marathon
Arms, a nondescript three-story building in East Hollywood, located a
few blocks from the campus of Los Angeles City College. The thirty
units of the Marathon Arms were occupied by other solidly lower-
middle-class Angelenos: telephone operators, bookkeepers, salesmen.
One of their neighbors was Dorothy LaPointe, a twenty-year-old elevator

7

operator at Roos Bros., an upscale clothing store on Hollywood Boulevard. Dorothy suggested that Gayle's looks—even though she was still a
teenager—would make her a natural fill-in while she went on vacation.

If contemporary photographs are any indication, it's not surprising
that Gayle Peck was able to fool people into thinking she was significantly older. The gawky child of the 1930s, who gazed abstractedly away
from the camera's lens, had undergone a remarkable transformation.
The skinny waif had blossomed into a curvaceous fifteen-year-old who
was well aware of the good looks she had inherited from her parents.
She got the elevator operator job by telling the hiring manager she was
nineteen, yet it still took the paychecks of all three members of the Peck
family to "put food on the table and pay the bills."

Her looks soon caught the attention of another pair of eyes. The circumstances of her first encounter with Jack Webb are best described
by his biographers:

> One 1941 evening when Jack was living with [his friend] Gus
> and [his grandmother] Gram on Marathon Street, the two young
> men decided to visit a malt shop on the opposite side of Vermont
> Avenue. On their way they approached two girls talking in front
> of a large apartment house.

(No exact citation is given for this specific sequence of events, but it
appears at least as plausible as other published versions of the meeting,
including one in which Jack spilled a soda on Gayle at a La Cienega
Boulevard jazz club.)

Immediately struck by her alluring figure, strawberry blonde hair,
and striking blue eyes, Webb probably "had one look at her and had
to have her." Quiet and unsure of herself, Gayle was attracted not only
to Jack's smiling, boyish qualities but also to his palpably intense determination to become something better than his circumstances might have
dictated. When they met, the twenty-one-year-old Webb was living in

a duplex less than two blocks away and was barely earning a living as a clothing salesman at a local department store.

Gayle was always a responsible young woman, and her parents didn't object to the six-year age difference between their daughter and her new beau. The pair had a lot in common besides their current occupations. A love for music and movies meant there was much to listen to, watch, and talk about, including their budding thoughts of becoming actors. Even after Japanese airplanes attacked the Pacific Fleet at Pearl Harbor, Hawaii, on December 7, 1941, life for many Americans—including Gayle Peck and Jack Webb, caught up in their youthful romance—continued much as usual. Gayle's job at Roos Bros. meant she was just steps from the famous corner of Hollywood and Vine, and there were plenty of inexpensive entertainment options for two young people looking for fun. Located within blocks of the store were the Egyptian, Pantages, and Paramount Theatres, as well as the elaborate Grauman's Chinese Theatre, and numerous small clubs where Gayle and Jack could enjoy the hot sounds of jazz. Carefree months of movies, music, and trips to San Bernardino to visit Gayle's old friends were finally interrupted by the call of the US government, which asked Jack Webb to serve his country in the army air corps.

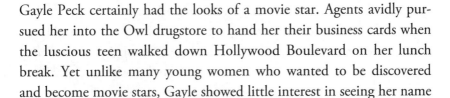

Gayle Peck certainly had the looks of a movie star. Agents avidly pursued her into the Owl drugstore to hand her their business cards when the luscious teen walked down Hollywood Boulevard on her lunch break. Yet unlike many young women who wanted to be discovered and become movie stars, Gayle showed little interest in seeing her name on a theater marquee.

That indifference changed on an otherwise routine day in 1943, when Gayle opened the gates of the elevator at Roos Bros. The woman who walked in didn't merit a second glance during the short ride, and when Sue Carol introduced herself as an agent, Gayle had no idea that Carol was also the wife of movie star Alan Ladd. On the lookout for new talent, Carol suggested that she could get the beautiful young woman a screen test. Gayle thought it was a joke, but when the agent came back to the store a few weeks later to ask where she'd been, she realized that Carol hadn't been kidding. With the encouragement of her parents and the advice of actors who worked at Roos Bros. between jobs, the sixteen-year-old decided to take a chance and signed a contract with Sue Carol.

One of her new agent's first comments was that the name Gayle Peck lacked pizzazz; the teenager needed a moniker that had "movie star" written all over it. The origins of how "Julie London" was chosen are lost to time, although the potential publicity of seeing and hearing the name of the British capital amid the patriotism of a world at war can't be discounted as a factor. Decades later Julie jokingly told Canadian journalist Jim Bawden that she "could have killed sweet Sue" after she saw Gregory Peck's name on a Sunset Boulevard theater marquee.

The newly minted actress took a few acting classes but found that studying—even for a subject she enjoyed—was far too much like school. After failing her first screen test, she gained some stage experience via a brief run in the two-a-day vaudeville of entrepreneur Sid Grauman's *Highlights of 1943* and through occasional jobs as a singer. The most memorable of these stints was with a Southern California dance band led by violinist Matty Malneck, whose hits as a songwriter included "I'll Never Be the Same" and "Goody, Goody." Julie had fun taking the Red Car line down to Long Beach to perform—and even made a few (alas, undiscovered) recordings—but it all came to an abrupt end when someone discovered she was only sixteen. Thoughts of becoming a professional singer were later dashed by a booker who told her, after an audition, that she should "learn to be a stenographer."

Between shifts running the Roos Bros. elevator, Julie earned extra money working behind the counter in the menswear department, where she met *Esquire* pinup photographer Henry Waxman, who—as many others had been—was struck by Julie's sensual face and figure. He persuaded her to pose for him, and the provocative, full-page color image was published in the popular magazine's November 1943 issue. She was barely seventeen, and the picture of the supine, luscious young woman, her apparently naked body covered only by what appears to be a wet, gold-colored piece of cloth—strawberry blonde hair fanned around her head as she stares abstractedly into the distance—is stunningly erotic even more than a half century later.

The *Esquire* photograph was quickly distributed to army camps and naval bases across the United States, although Julie insisted in the accompanying article that she would rather be "a one man wallet girl" than "a regiment's favorite pin up." To the typical GI, Julie London was just another girl whose image was meant to remind him of what he was fighting for; to a lonely Jack Webb, who saw the picture pinned to a wall in his Del Rio, Texas, barracks, it was a reminder that this gorgeous girl might be waiting for him when he returned to California.

They had seen little of each other during his period in the service, only an occasional date when he was on leave in Los Angeles. At seventeen Julie was more "infatuated with the idea of being in love" than with the reality of any one man. For Jack Webb, by contrast, the love he felt for Julie London was real, and the image he retained of her sustained him during his hours away from home. They began to correspond more frequently, and when he boasted to his bunkmates that he had dated the beautiful pinup, their ridicule turned to envy when he showed them her letters.

Julie's career in motion pictures was launched in late October 1943, when a second, successful screen test led to her first movie role in the jungle-exploitation adventure *Nabonga*, one of the many five-day quickies churned out by the prolific Producers Releasing Corporation (PRC), located on what was derisively referred to as Hollywood's Poverty Row. Producer Sigmund Neufeld signed Julie to play the daughter of an embezzler whose plane crashes in the African jungle loaded with a cache of stolen jewels, a role that she acquired more for her physical attributes than any necessary acting skills.

A seventy-minute low-budget jungle movie isn't the most auspicious way to begin a career, but it had its compensations other than money, including the chance to work with Olympic swimming champion turned action movie hero Buster Crabbe. Costumed in a form-fitting sarong and adorned with a tropical flower in her hair, most of the actress's screen time in *Nabonga* is limited to watching in mock horror as Crabbe and veteran heavy Barton MacLane tussle in front of fake jungle scenery or gasping as the gorilla (actually stuntman Ray "Crash" Corrigan in a monkey suit) mauls yet another supporting actor.

The highlight of *Nabonga*, if one has to be found, is a ten-minute sequence of playful dialogue where the young actress reacts with a combination of vivid teenage petulance and naïveté at the thought of giving up the baubles, bangles, and beads she's kept from her father's thievery. It's a quality Julie would more fully develop in her next significant movie role. Lauded by one movie industry trade magazine as "an eye-filling blonde," another complained that all she did was "slink around . . . and mouth an occasional phrase in pidgin English."

Thirty years later, when reminded of *Nabonga*, Julie could only joke about PRC's threadbare style and note that after adding this picture to her résumé, the only movie work she could get was as an extra. The first of these bit parts was in *Janie* (1944), a Warner Bros. wartime teenage romantic comedy directed by Michael Curtiz (*Casablanca*), where she earned $125 a week for appearing in a few crowd scenes.

While *Nabonga* attracted scattered crowds to movie houses in the winter and spring of 1944, Julie joined the casts of USO Camp Shows, which toured throughout Southern California, and entertained the troops at the Hollywood USO, experiences that were of more help to her career than her initial foray into the movie business. Her relatively carefree teenage days came to an end when truant officers from the Los Angeles school district finally caught up with her, and she was forced to return to high school.

With money from her salary running the elevator, the occasional bit part in a movie, and some help from her parents, Julie enrolled at the private Hollywood Professional School (HPS) on Hollywood Boulevard, about a mile east of Roos Bros., to study dramatics. Her brief time at HPS was more significant to her future than its limited extent indicates, for sitting next to Julie during one of her classes was a young man named Arthur Hamilton, who had ambitions of becoming a songwriter.

Impressed when he learned that his classmate had sung with a band, Hamilton recalled that no matter where she went, her stunning looks attracted attention, yet she remained unaffected. The pair dated during the last months of the school year and attended the senior prom together, but their strongest connection was music. "We sang each other songs, made up song games, and talked about what she was going to sing and what I was going to write."

After graduating from HPS in the summer of 1944, Julie made the rounds of the movie studios but could find her only steady work at Roos Bros. She found comfort in a normal life. "In pictures I made $250 a week, but the $19 weekly from the department store seemed more important to me. It represented security, because there seemed to be thousands of stunning girls hotly pursuing movie stardom and very few interested in running elevators."

Julie London and Jack Webb resumed dating after his discharge from the army air corps in January 1945. His passion for the movies was rekindled, and the pair spent a lot of their time together sitting in theaters; for Jack, it was like going to school, and Julie remembered they would "sometimes sit through double features twice so Jack could see a certain bit of business."

During this period Julie landed parts in a few local radio programs but remained more interested in a big-screen career. One of her fellow radio actors was Peggy Webber, a young woman from Texas who later became one of Jack Webb's favorite actresses on his radio and television programs. In 1945 Webber thought he was just "a college boy, somebody [Julie] was in school with." When the actress later spotted Julie and Jack necking, she thought, "Gee, there must be a serious something going on!"

Frustrated by his lack of opportunities in Los Angeles, Jack Webb moved to San Francisco, where he got a job as a radio announcer at

KGO and found some success with *Pat Novak for Hire*, a hard-boiled
detective show he starred in and wrote with his friend Richard Breen.
Occasionally, Julie traveled north to spend time with Jack, but she
wasn't ready to accept his offer of a long-term commitment. Even after
his return to Los Angeles, Julie continued to demur when Jack asked
her to marry him.

It was another chance encounter with an elevator passenger—producer
Walter Wanger—that led to Julie signing an $82.50 per week term con-
tract with Universal in late January 1945. Her first job for the studio was
three weeks of barely visible work as a palace maiden in Wanger's *Night
in Paradise*, a Technicolor extravaganza starring Merle Oberon. Intended
as a follow-up to the producer's 1942 hit *Arabian Nights*, the expensive
production suffered from extensive shooting delays and wasn't released
until the spring of 1946. (Prior to landing the Universal contract, Julie
spent a few days on the 20th Century Fox lot as a chorus girl in *Billy
Rose's Diamond Horseshoe*, a lavish Technicolor musical starring Betty
Grable, which was released in May 1945.)

Julie enjoyed shuttling between the store and the movie studios as
the war years wound down and peacetime normality resumed, and her
employer—during a period when women were still filling many jobs
previously held by men—was happy to let her take time off to follow
her big-screen dreams. Her work at Universal attracted little attention
from studio executives, but she was popular enough to be paid $1,000
to appear in *On Stage Everybody*, a low-budget musical adaptation of
a short-lived radio talent show. She made the most of her brief scenes
as the cousin of the movie's star, a minor-league Judy Garland clone
named Peggy Ryan. Given her first opportunity to play a real character,
the young actress showed a flair for comedy as she mocked the fake
upper-crust accent of Ryan's bland boyfriend (Johnny Coy). Helmed by
veteran Universal director Jean Yarbrough, *On Stage Everybody* opened in
July 1945 to largely tepid reviews, but Julie was singled out for showing
"some promise as an ingénue."

Julie didn't perform in any of the musical numbers in *On Stage Everybody*, but it didn't take long for someone at Universal to recognize that she had potential as a vocalist. A cute sequence in *Solid Senders*, a short subject released in late 1945 under the studio's long-running *Name Band Musicals* umbrella, showed a curly-haired nineteen-year-old Julie singing "The Boy with the Wistful Eyes" to the significantly older actor Jimmie Dodd.* (He became famous a decade later as the star of television's *Mickey Mouse Club*; his theme song for the show would play a significant part in Julie's singing career.) Ability was there, but her generic singing voice was indistinguishable from that of many girl singers of the 1940s and lacked the unique, breathy qualities that would make her famous a decade later.

Julie's time at Universal had yielded little of note (during this period she also made *Science Spins a Yarn*, a short industrial film about the artificial fabric rayon, in which she appeared as the all-American daughter of actor Regis Toomey), so the actress had few expectations when she learned that Universal had loaned her services to independent producer Sol Lesser. The result of that deal—*The Red House*, released in February 1947—turned out to be the significant break she had hoped for. Lesser, whose career had taken off two decades earlier with a successful series of movies starring a young Jackie Coogan and an equally profitable group of Tarzan pictures, had acquired the rights to an eerie novel by George Agnew Chamberlain serialized in the *Saturday Evening Post*. In Julie London, Lesser believed he had found the perfect young actress to play the part of a mature-for-her-age high school student named Tibby Rinton. Decades later Julie laughingly called it "strictly type-casting!"

She always retained fond memories of making *The Red House*—or *No Trespassing*, as the movie was called during production—especially

---

* The Don Raye and Gene de Paul song had originally appeared in Universal's 1941 Abbott and Costello comedy *Keep Flying*.

the weeks of location work in April 1946 in the rural Tuolumne County towns of Sonora and Columbia, California. Delmer Daves, the movie's writer and director, had a good rapport with the cast, particularly its young quartet of protagonists. The San Francisco–born Daves, author of the screenplays for *The Petrified Forest* (1936), *Love Affair* (1939), and Sol Lesser's successful wartime musical comedy *Stage Door Canteen* (1943), was determined to make *The Red House*, only his fourth movie as a director, an effective picture, even under the constraints of a low budget.

Julie and her young costars—Lon McCallister, Rory Calhoun, and Allene Roberts—spent a lot of time together, both away from the city and when the cast and crew returned to Los Angeles. Captured by the lens of the ever-present publicity photographer, they enjoyed canoe trips, roller skating, listening to music on a jukebox, and horseback riding. The older stars weren't so much fun. Edward G. Robinson, whose marquee name brought in much of the financing from United Artists, and Judith Anderson, who played Robinson's sister in the film, were always battling during their scenes together.

The plot of *The Red House* revolves around farmer Pete Morgan (Robinson) and his ultimately futile attempts to keep his ward (Roberts) and her friend (McCallister) from snooping into the mysterious structure that lends its name to the movie's title. Julie's supporting role isn't central to the story, but her scenes—largely variations on the themes of playacting and dreaming—are among its most memorable. With Daves's help, she was able to create a sharply edged portrait of a young girl longing to escape from the dreariness of her rural life. "I want to clear out of these hills when I get married," she tells McCallister, and spend the winters in the city "with two station wagons and a limousine." By the movie's end, however, it's clear that her stylish outfits and hairdos only help Tibby Rinton *act* the part of an adult; behind the facade of maturity is a petulant child whose longings ultimately lead to a tragic end.

Aided by crisp black-and-white cinematography by three-time Academy Award nominee Bert Glennon and a spooky score by Miklós Rózsa,

The Red House performed well at the box office.* *Life* magazine, in a contemporary feature article, noted Julie's skilled performance as a "predatory bobby-soxer." One reviewer even dubbed her "a potential Lana Turner," while another said she handled her part "with the ease of a practiced siren." The voluptuous young actress was prominently featured in many of the movie's advertisements, and Julie joked that it wasn't "a bad comeback for a kid of 21."

That comeback seemed secure when, prior to her twentieth birthday, Julie signed a $200 per-week contract with Sol Lesser. (Adjusted for inflation, this equals approximately $2,500 in contemporary dollars.) The producer spent the next few months searching for properties to reunite the young actors from the movie's cast, but none ever moved beyond the initial development stage.

The financial success of *The Red House* and Julie's obviously provocative sex appeal in it prompted Universal to call for her services again, and Sol Lesser loaned her back to producer Walter Wanger. Her ten-week $7,500 contract (about $80,000 today)—more money than Julie had ever made in her life—provided her with a potentially juicy role as Susan Hayward's scheming younger sister in the Civil War epic *Tap Roots.*

It was an exciting, yet frightening, moment for Julie as she boarded an American Airlines chartered DC-4 with her mother at Los Angeles's Mines Field in the early morning hours of May 31, 1947. Among her fellow passengers on the journey, her first out of California, was the glamorous, intimidating Hayward; leading man Van Heflin; and Whitfield Connor, an Irish-born, Broadway-trained actor making his feature debut, with whom Julie would share most of her scenes. The

---

* The movie fell into the public domain when its copyright lapsed in the 1970s. Praised by critics for its psychological complexities—apparent even in numerous low-budget home video editions—*The Red House* was given a proper restoration and reissued on DVD to acclaim in 2012, while Rózsa's score was captured in a new recording by the Royal Scottish National Orchestra.

flight arrived in Tennessee early the following morning. From the airport the passengers were delivered in limousines to Asheville, North Carolina, and the historic Battery Park Hotel, located at the entrance to the Great Smoky Mountains National Park. The expensive production got underway at the vast Biltmore Estate of the Vanderbilt family a few days later, with veteran director George Marshall (*Destry Rides Again*, 1939, with Marlene Dietrich) filming a love scene between Julie and Whitfield Connor set on the banks of the French Broad River, which bisects the grounds.

Julie London often wondered whether Jack Webb, whose ardor for her was equaled only by his relentless drive to succeed, was really the right man for her. The ups and downs of the couple's relationship had become fodder for Hollywood gossip columnists, and as every prospective marriage date passed without a ceremony, it seemed unlikely that the budding stars would ever tie the knot. "I was very much under the impression that he was madly in love with her," recalled Peggy Webber, and Jack wasn't deterred by Julie's latest refusal to marry him before she left for North Carolina. Surprised and touched by his sudden arrival on the location set, a tearful Julie finally accepted his engagement ring and promised they would get married after she returned to California with the company in late June to begin studio work at Universal.

On July 17, 1947, as the *Tap Roots* shoot reached its conclusion, a beaming Julie London—still dressed in her costume as a Southern belle—and an awkwardly smiling, skinny Jack Webb posed for photographers on the set as they formally announced their engagement. Two days later the pair climbed into Jack's beat-up Buick convertible and drove to Las Vegas where, in a small ceremony without the presence of their families, they were quickly married. The newlyweds checked into the lavish new Flamingo Hotel on the Vegas Strip. According to a Universal Studios press release, Julie's matron of honor, English actress Edna Best, discovered that Julie and Jack had been given the hotel's presidential suite, recently occupied by Bugsy Siegel, the notorious gangster who had been murdered in Los Angeles a month earlier. Best quickly had the hotel staff change the couple's room while the ceremony was underway. An atmosphere like that was no way to start a marriage.

3

Bouquet of Blues

Jack was married to Dragnet *not me.*

—Julie London to journalist James Bacon, 1957

JULIE'S CONTRACTUAL COMMITMENT to finish *Tap Roots* meant the postponement of a longer honeymoon, and with little money to spare for a place of their own, she and Jack spent the first month of their marriage living in the apartments of his friends. (Although she received a good salary at Universal, Julie likely gave a significant amount of it to her parents—a pattern that continued for the rest of their lives.)

With time the young couple was able to rent a small, three-room bungalow in the same duplex on Marathon Street where Jack had lived when the pair met years earlier, yet the new surroundings couldn't smooth the rough patches that had quickly developed in their relationship. Restless at the stark contrast between Julie's developing career and his own lack of employment, Jack frequently took out his frustrations on his young wife, their quarrels becoming so intense at times that he eventually moved into a local hotel. Julie struggled to understand how it could have gone wrong so quickly.

Without much thought for the consequences, by the spring of 1948—just nine months after their wedding—Julie London and Jack Webb had unofficially separated.

———∞∞∞———

While her marriage teetered on the brink of collapse, Julie's acting career appeared to be moving forward. Universal's publicity office sent her to Pennsylvania with three of her *Tap Roots* costars for the movie's gala world premiere at Philadelphia's Goldman Theatre in July. Five weeks later she and Jack—temporarily reconciled—drove to San Francisco for an appearance at a charity event that coincided with the movie's opening there.

The promotional efforts proved singularly unsuccessful. *Tap Roots*, an adaptation of a bestselling novel by James Street about a Mississippi family whose hatred for slavery prompts a rebellion against the state's secession from the Union, turned out to be little more than a derivative, poor man's *Gone with the Wind*. One critic lambasted the entire cast, damning them as not being "good enough actor[s] to make you care" about their fate. Julie's appearance in the movie garnered little attention, largely because the majority of the love scenes she had filmed with Whitfield Connor had been cut after audiences at early screenings rated them as "very blah." While her fleeting moments—including a humorous "fiddlesticks!" that recalls Scarlett O'Hara—shielded her from the criticism heaped on Susan Hayward and the rest of the cast, Julie was provided with little opportunity to display the burgeoning sexuality and impetuosity visible in her vivid performance in *The Red House*.

The *Tap Roots* failure could not have come at a worse time for Julie London's career. For nearly a decade, the motion picture industry had operated under the terms of a consent decree. It had been created to mediate the studios' alleged monopoly of production and distribution; in August 1948 the US Supreme Court ruled that the decree had largely failed and ordered an end to the system of vertical integration that had allowed the studios to make the movies and subsequently distribute them to theaters under their control. The five largest studios—Paramount, RKO, MGM, 20th Century Fox, and Warner Bros.—were forced to retool their business model, a process that eventually led to the disintegration of the system that had created a galaxy of Hollywood stars.

One of Universal's decisions in the uncertain atmosphere of 1948 was to drop Julie London's contract option. Although she and Jack continued to live apart, he persuaded her to leave Sue Carol for his more powerful agent at the firm of Polan and Rosenberg. The impact was immediate: George Rosenberg negotiated a seven-year deal for Julie with Warner Bros. that began at twenty-six weeks for $300 per week and included options that could potentially raise her salary to $1,500 a week. Despite her disappointment at the final result of her *Tap Roots* experience, the financial security of the Warner Bros. contract and her good notices for *The Red House* were enough to convince Julie to quit her job at Roos Bros. and fully commit to a career as an actress.

Much of producer Jerry Wald's naval aviation epic *Task Force* had already been filmed when Julie reported to the Warner Bros. lot in mid-December to begin shooting six days of uncomplicated sequences with director Delmer Daves and actors Gary Cooper, Jane Wyatt, and Wayne Morris. Not even the reunion with the actor-friendly Daves and a chance to work with Cooper, one of her screen idols, could bring much joy to the holiday season. She had never seriously believed that her marriage would fail, but within days of finishing the *Task Force* shoot, Julie and Jack had agreed to a trial separation. She told the press she wasn't taking any definite steps toward divorce; in her heart she wasn't so certain.

Julie still hoped for a reconciliation as the state of her marriage became gossip-column fodder. After some false starts during the winter and spring of 1949, she and Jack once again began to enjoy each other's company and agreed to give their relationship another try.

Under the terms of her contract, Warner Bros. had put Julie on leave in January 1949 for six weeks without pay. No new roles appeared on the horizon, and her public appearances were limited to studio-arranged publicity stunts in which she "painted" the name on a new fighter bomber or promoted a traffic-safety campaign in downtown Los Angeles. Such was the life of a young actress.

She was finally called back to the studio in late April as a last-minute replacement for leading lady Alexis Smith in *Return of the Frontiersman*, a low-budget western for producer Saul Elkins. Making the picture opposite future movie musical star Gordon MacRae, then just another Warner Bros. contract player, was a welcome break from the turmoil of her personal life.

Illness kept Julie off the set for a number of days during filming. A studio doctor diagnosed a bad cold; in reality it was the onset of the morning sickness she began to suffer after she discovered she was pregnant. With the interests of a child to consider, Julie and Jack worked hard to sort out their differences, and their year-long separation had ended by the time she completed work on *Return of the Frontiersman* in early May.

The couple enjoyed a second honeymoon in Palm Springs and bought a Tudor-style house at 1911 North Serrano Avenue in the upscale Los Feliz neighborhood of central Los Angeles, just three miles and a world away from the homes of their parents back on Marathon Street. The tastefully decorated one-story structure gave visitors the impression that its owners enjoyed a warm and happy relationship, a facade further solidified by the couple's adoption of a devoted dachshund named Patsy. (Julie was never without at least one dog; the ones she later owned with Bobby Troup always had free rein of the house and frequently tore up the carpets and irretrievably damaged the furniture.)

In reality their domesticity was anything but comfortable. Warner Bros., seeing no particular reason to take up Julie's contract option, had dropped her from its roster after production on *Return of the Frontiersman* ended. Julie spent more time promoting her husband's faltering career than trying to revive her own, with little effect on either. "When I got pregnant," she later admitted, "we were completely broke."

In a last-ditch effort to find a way out of their financial difficulties, Jack recalled his recent role as a police laboratory technician in the movie *He Walked by Night*. Out of those memories grew the concept of a radio story that would dispassionately examine the day-to-day work of a Los

Angeles police sergeant named Joe Friday. Thus was born *Dragnet*, which began its run on NBC on the evening of June 3, 1949. As the show's ratings steadily improved, *Dragnet* became an all-encompassing world for Jack Webb, one in which his young wife was allowed no part.

Julie's pregnancy was publicly announced shortly after *Task Force* opened in early October 1949. Once again her brief scenes were peripheral to the main action, and the best that can be said of her role as the wife of a naval aviator, played by Wayne Morris, was that she looked more like an adult on the big screen than she ever had before. (A scene apparently filmed but cut from the final print had Julie's character breaking down under the pressure of not knowing the fate of her missing husband.) Her final moment in the overlong movie, in which Gary Cooper's character implies that Morris had been engaged in extracurricular activity with the wahines on the island from which he had been rescued, gave Julie the opportunity to deliver one of the screenplay's few humorous lines of dialogue: "I've seen pictures of those native girls!" she yells at Morris. "If that's the best you can do, it's a pretty droopy best!"

The promise Julie London had shown as an actress in *The Red House* had yet to be fulfilled, and by the end of 1949, her career had effectively come to a standstill. She chose to turn down a number of roles due to the impending birth of her first child, a difficult pregnancy made more painful by the lack of attention and concern she received from her husband. To relieve her physical pain, Julie had consulted an osteopath as well as a traditional doctor, but Jack couldn't understand why his wife "insisted on going to that damn Chinaman!" On January 11, 1950, while Julie went through hours of labor at a Los Angeles hospital, Jack tried to concentrate on work, rehearsing an episode of *Dragnet*. When word came through that his daughter—named Stacy after Jack and Julie's friend, actor Stacy Harris—had arrived, the suddenly concerned father tore out of the studio to be with his new family.

As a first-time mother, Julie probably didn't notice that the lightly regarded *Return of the Frontiersman* had arrived in theaters in June 1950.

After six years in the business, the B-western was her first leading-lady role, and it gave her a number of good moments as a young woman who helps the sheriff's son (Gordon MacRae) clear his name after he's accused of robbery and murder. She and the five-foot-eight MacRae made a cute screen couple, even if the actress joked that she only took the role to pay for a new set of shutters. One critic dubbed the movie "one of the season's sorriest sagebrush sagas," while another called Julie "as spiritless a heroine as ever rode side-saddle."

The telephone had stopped ringing. The studios seemed uninterested. Julie became frustrated with her career and her life as a wife and mother. Jack neglected his obligations as a husband and father in favor of pursuing his own success, while Julie wondered whether she could—or even should—continue acting.

An opportunity finally arose in July when Julie signed a freelance contract with Universal-International to play one of the female leads in the studio's low-budget adaptation of Dashiell Hammett's *The Fat Man*, the popular radio mystery program from the acknowledged master of hard-boiled detective fiction. The studio had bought the property before the conclusion of a congressional investigation into the author's alleged Communist leanings. By the time the movie was released in May 1951, any reference to his name had been removed from the prints.*

Julie was needed for only two weeks, and the $1,700 she received for the five days she actually worked was enough to splurge on some louvered doors for the house. Filming began on July 31 at Universal Studios under the direction of journeyman William Castle. The director would become known later in the decade for a series of gimmicky horror movies with Vincent Price (*The Tingler, House on Haunted Hill, 13 Ghosts*, etc.), but in 1950 he was retained for his ability to shoot

---

* Hammett spent six months in federal prison for refusing to cooperate with the inquiry. *The Fat Man* was the last movie associated with the author to be released in his lifetime.

quickly and within budget. Starring the rotund actor J. Scott Smart, who continued his portrayal of the private detective Brad Runyon from the radio show, the cast was rounded out by Rock Hudson in one of his early screen roles, Jayne Meadows, and the famous clown Emmett Kelly Jr., making his movie debut. Julie's scenes, including a sequence with Hudson filmed on location at the Griffith Park Zoo in Los Angeles, were completed by August 7, and production ended, under budget, two weeks later.

While *The Fat Man* has moments that reveal Julie's beauty and her innate likability as an actress, it *was* a B-movie, and as such didn't stay long in the theaters, not even in J. Scott Smart's hometown of Buffalo, New York. Private detective Brad Runyon is investigating a murder when we first meet Julie's character—barfly Pat Boyd—in a Hollywood club, poised with drink in hand and cigarette dangling from her fingers. (This was Julie's first on-screen smoking scene, but she was a veteran smoker, having begun as a San Bernardino junior high school student at the age of thirteen.)

Dressed in an off-the-shoulder black satin dress and high heels, Pat gets a long, lingering look from Runyon before he delivers one of the movie's few witty lines: "You're the first thing I've seen in California that lives up to the advertising." (Rosemary Odell's costume design is remarkably similar to the sexy outfit worn by Ava Gardner in the 1945 Universal movie *The Killers*. Since Odell had succeeded that film's costume designer, Vera West, at the studio, it wouldn't be surprising if Gardner's gown had been recycled for an unimportant picture like *The Fat Man*.)

The unlikely pair hit the floor for a stab at a combination boogie-woogie and Charleston, and Smart handles himself well; much better than his partner, who never was much of a mover. In a series of flashbacks, Pat reveals how she met and married an ex-convict (Hudson) who mysteriously disappeared four days after the ceremony. As the movie ends, she takes the detective's advice to leave Los Angeles and return to Kansas, declaring, "I guess I just don't rate being happy," the irony of which was probably not lost on Julie at the moment she delivered it.

The Fat Man marked the end of the first stage of Julie London's career. All she had to show after seven years as an actress were a few good memories and a stack of eight-by-ten glossies. Her decision to turn down a new contract with Universal was an easy one. She was afraid accepting it would ruin her marriage; she had no interest in competing with her husband. "My career didn't mean a thing. I found out having happiness to go home to at night meant more to me than being a big glamour girl with no place at all to head for at 6 p.m."

To anyone who didn't know them well, Julie London and Jack Webb appeared to be the perfect Hollywood couple. There may have been trouble behind the walls of their house, but in their public moments together, Julie was the loving wife, supporting Jack in his newfound success. She was with him at the Pantages Theatre in Hollywood in March 1951 when two big movies in which he appeared, *Sunset Boulevard* and *The Men*, were up for Academy Awards. In late April a dazzling, smiling Julie was by his side in New York, when *Dragnet* was presented with a Mystery Writers of America's Edgar Award. Less than three months later, they hosted a press party at a Hollywood nightclub to mark the debut of his next radio drama, *Pete Kelly's Blues*. (The program, set in a 1920s Kansas City speakeasy, had only a brief run, but Jack's 1955 film adaptation would play a significant role in Julie's transition from actress to singer.)

Dragnet's radio success encouraged Jack to adapt the series for television. This meant more time at the studio for him and more loneliness for his wife and not-yet-two-year-old daughter. Peggy Webber was an eyewitness to Julie's fragile emotional state. "She seemed kind of at loose ends" when the pair met at an elaborate Christmas party held at the home of a *Dragnet* writer. Julie "acted like she wanted to be friends, like maybe she needed somebody to talk to." It was more of the same a few days later when Julie arrived on the *Dragnet* set with a large basket of food, gorgeously dressed in a fur coat and fur-lined boots. "It was a very, very cold night!" Webber recalled. "I thought Jack should be so proud of her, that she was so loyal, that she'd come out at midnight and bring food for everybody. I just recall the generosity of her spirit; she was a very loving person."

Love wasn't enough. The relentless beat of composer Walter Schumann's *Dragnet* theme had begun to resemble a death knell for Julie London's marriage. Not even the arrival of the couple's second daughter, Lisa, on November 29, 1952, could drag Jack away from his obsession with his work. Julie suffered through another difficult pregnancy, and her husband's reaction to congratulations on Lisa's birth was little more than a testy "Oh, yeah, diapers in every bucket in every room of the house!"

To give themselves room to spread out, the couple had recently moved to the family-friendly suburbs of the San Fernando Valley and a twelve-room ranch house at 3936 Ethel Avenue in Studio City. Yet if the houses were getting "better and better" as a result of Jack's success (when *Dragnet* went on the air he was making $150 per week; four years later, he was earning more than ten times that amount), the marriage was getting increasingly worse. While Jack spent days on end at the studio, Julie aimlessly roamed around the property, sunned herself at the pool, played with her daughters, and watched the servants work. The situation deteriorated to the point where they weren't even able to stand each other's company long enough to eat together.

April 1953. It was another typical day. Jack left for work, telling his wife he'd be home for dinner; when he telephoned later to tell her he had to stay late, she said fine. It wasn't unusual. He didn't return for six weeks. Julie didn't know what to do. There were rumors that Jack may have been seeing other women, but she had no proof. A friend insisted that Jack "really wanted to be married" to Julie, but "once he found how much work he had to do, he began to resent having to spend time with babies at home and all of that. He just wasn't ready to settle down."

Julie tried to mask her pain and sadness. After Jack finally returned, she tried to deflect reporters who had gotten another whiff of juicy Hollywood scandal by saying that she remained optimistic about her marriage. "I believe we ironed out our troubles and understand each other better than ever." The words had little effect, and photographs taken during the brief reconciliation show two people struggling to present a united front for the camera while clearly uncomfortable with being in the same room and bored with each other's company.*

Julie London and Jack Webb formally separated less than two months later. She hired S. S. Hahn, one of the country's top divorce attorneys, to file the August 14, 1953, complaint, which claimed incompatibility and charged Webb with cruelty. Julie asked the court for the division of an estimated $3 to $4 million worth of community property and sole custody of the couple's two daughters, three-year-old Stacy and nine-month-old Lisa.

She never thought this would happen. The shock of the divorce caused her to put more than twenty-five pounds onto her petite frame as she worried about her family's future. (Screenwriter Anne Edwards, who befriended Julie in London during the making of *A Question in Adultery* four years after the divorce, wrote in her 2012 memoir that Julie "claimed [Jack] was often violent, and that even separated by so many thousands of miles, she found herself looking over her shoulder, fearful he would appear.") The physical discomfort was compounded by overwhelming embarrassment and anger when the *Dragnet* theme was chanted at her by people she passed in the street. To avoid the noise and the prying press, Julie decided to go to Europe, where she intended to make a temporary home in Paris while the divorce made its way through the courts.

Julie toured the sights of Paris, Rome, and London, but her loneliness and unhappiness were magnified by memories of what had gone

---

* The photographs used for a September 8, 1953, *Look* magazine profile of Jack Webb come from this session. The full contact sheets from photographer John Vachon's work are in the Prints and Photographs Division of the Library of Congress in Washington, DC.

wrong. One day, as she and the girls sat under a tree in a Paris park to get some relief from that summer's stifling heat and humidity, her mind drifted back to thoughts of home and an "old-fashioned American peanut-butter sandwich." Julie later recalled that she had "sentenced [herself] and [her] children to an exile of wandering." Boarding the *Queen Mary* on October 1, she left for New York.

Decades later Julie's daughter Lisa insisted that Jack Webb had broken her mother's heart. It was a devastated Julie London who arrived at the Los Angeles Superior Court on November 25, 1953. Yet with a plush mink stole wrapped around her shoulders and a pink chiffon scarf tied around her throat, she was the height of fashion as she told Judge James G. Whyte that her husband's career "gave him no time for marriage." Asked to describe a typical day at their house, Julie replied that Jack ignored her attempts to talk about music and isolated her by turning on the television, even when others were present. She reluctantly described his "habit of talking down to me as if I were three years old. He'd tell me something ten times when I'd already understood the first time."

The divorce—which under California law included a one-year waiting period that gave the parties time to reconcile—was quickly granted and the property settlement approved. The forty-page financial agreement stated that in exchange for full visitation rights, Julie was to receive $150,000 in cash and an equal amount in securities of Dragnet Productions, a new white Cadillac, jewelry and furnishings valued at $50,000, and $21,000 in annual alimony and child support. Webb also agreed to take out a $150,000 life insurance policy with his ex-wife as the sole beneficiary. (A sizable sum in current dollars, equaling over $4 million in cash, securities, life insurance, and goods and nearly $200,000 in alimony and child support.)

A rash of insinuating articles with titles like How Julie London Cried Herself a Bankroll, $18,000 a Year Julie London's Price-Tag on Love, and How Julie London Gave Jack Webb the Business sealed her image in the public mind as a gold digger—the scheming woman who had squeezed America's hero Jack Webb out of his last dollars. It would be the only thing many people remembered about Julie London for years to come.*

---

* See also the first issue (November 1953) of *Playboy* magazine, which featured a harangue against alimony titled "Miss Gold-Digger of 1953."

4

A Place in the Sun

We were two people who lacked confidence.

—Bobby Troup to columnist Erskine Johnson, 1958

JULIE FOUND TEMPORARY SOLACE in the warmth and isolation of Palm Springs, the California desert resort town of the stars located one hundred miles southeast of Los Angeles. Bitter at the failure of her marriage, when newspaper reporters asked her to comment on rumors that her ex-husband was already contemplating a new wife, she angrily replied that she wasn't interested and didn't care what he did.

Her past continued to encroach on her present and her future as she restlessly wandered back and forth from the desert to Los Angeles. When Jack made one of his infrequent visits to see Stacy and Lisa, Julie made it a point to be absent. She didn't want to spend more than a moment in Jack's company, yet she was reluctantly forced to interact with him just months after the divorce when she took him to court for failing to create a trust for her from his share of the $5 million proceeds of the sale of *Dragnet* to the Music Corporation of America.

She was in limbo—scared and insecure. Reduced to being identified solely as Jack Webb's ex-wife, Julie struggled to recover her sense of individuality. It seemed that no one knew that Julie London had ever existed. Jack was famous; she barely registered a shrug. It was "a crushing, frightening and challenging experience" to have her ego and reputation so publicly battered. She even wondered what she could possibly talk about if another man asked her for a date.

She needn't have worried. Even with her troubles hanging like a dark cloud over her head, it wasn't long before Julie began to attract new admirers. During the early months of 1954, she dated numerous men—trombonist Phil Gray, bandleader Charlie Barnet, baseball player John Beradino, and former Stan Kenton arranger Pete Rugolo—in brief relationships "marred by a feeling of disloyalty" to Jack Webb.

Julie revealed her uncertainty about postmarriage life in an interview in the 1970s. "Everyone who has gone through a divorce will tell you the same thing," she reflected. "There's a period when you have to rediscover yourself. It takes time to regain your self-confidence and feel whole again." Music remained a source of pleasure. To take her mind off her situation and to get a night on the town after the recent stormy weather had kept her cooped up in the house, she accepted an offer from her friend Kae Saunders to join her at a local nightspot. Their destination was the Celebrity Room, a small club on La Brea Avenue in Hollywood, where Bobby Troup, a thirty-five-year-old songwriter, pianist, and singer, was leading his popular trio. It was Wednesday, March 24, 1954.

As Troup made his way through his friend Johnny Mercer's hip tune "Jamboree Jones," he looked up from the piano keys and saw a beautiful woman walk into the club and sit down at one of the tables. He couldn't take his eyes or his mind off her as he stumbled through Mercer's lyrics while finishing the number to a round of applause from the audience in the small room. Bobby knew Kae and her husband, pianist Herm Saunders, so he felt secure when he sat down at the women's table during intermission. Much like the self-deluded protagonist of his song "You're Looking at Me," he was "certain his charms couldn't fail" with the woman who introduced herself as Julie Webb. When she sarcastically responded to his thanks for coming to see him by saying she was only there to see his guitarist, Howard Roberts, Bobby's ego was shattered.

He dragged himself back to the piano to finish his set, convinced he'd struck out. As he was packing up, Julie walked over to the bandstand. To his surprise she asked if he'd like to join a small group of friends that was meeting at her house at two in the morning. For hours everyone sat around Julie's living room, smoking, drinking, and listening to one record after another. As the sun rose, Julie languidly eased herself off the cushioned fireplace hearth and approached the piano. Herm Saunders was tinkling away at a favorite melody. Her inhibitions removed by copious amounts of alcohol, Julie began to sing.

> Sit there and count the raindrops
> Falling on you.
> It's time you knew
> All you can count on is the raindrops
> That fall on little girl blue.

As Bobby heard Julie pour out Lorenz Hart's poignant lyrics, he was stunned once again. Oddly, the song's impact on Julie's future happiness never appears to have led her to record "Little Girl Blue," but Bobby recognized its effect and put out his own affecting version on his 1955 Bethlehem album *The Distinctive Style of Bobby Troup*.

Bobby Troup was always charming and persuasive, and his interest in Julie was obvious, although the idea of a serious relationship so soon after her divorce made her extremely uncomfortable. "Stop brooding" about lost happiness, her father advised. Bobby took Julie out to the posh Hollywood nightspots where celebrities often mingled—Ciro's, the Mocambo—and she began to feel more at ease with the situation and the handsome musician sitting next to her at the small tables. She quickly discovered that her new beau had led an eventful life before their paths crossed.

Robert William Troup Jr. was born in Harrisburg, Pennsylvania, on October 18, 1918. He had a music-filled childhood: his father had run the Lancaster branch of the family's popular music store, founded by Bobby's grandfather John. At twenty-two, Bobby graduated Phi Beta Kappa with a degree in economics from the Wharton School of Business at the University of Pennsylvania. It was there that he began his songwriting career with "Daddy," a slightly risqué tune he wrote for the university's Mask and Wig show, which bandleader Sammy Kaye unexpectedly turned into a number-one hit in 1941. This early success, followed by "Snootie Little Cutie"—recorded by Tommy Dorsey, with vocals by a young Frank Sinatra—gave Bobby the money to purchase a brand-new, green convertible Buick, a car that played an integral part in the writing of his best-known song.

Commissioned into the US Marine Corps, he was ordered to the segregated state of North Carolina, where he became the recreation officer at Camp Lejeune's Montford Point depot, home of the all-black Fifty-First and Fifty-Second Defense Battalions. In December 1944 Captain Troup was put in charge of the Sixth Depot Company—another all-black unit—and was deployed to the island of Saipan in the South Pacific.

In May 1942 he married Cynthia Hare, a Pennsylvania debutante, and the couple's two daughters, Cynnie and Ronne, were born during his enlistment. Upon his discharge from the Marines, Bobby decided to try his luck as a songwriter in Los Angeles. The couple loaded up the now not-so-new green Buick, deposited the girls with his mother, and departed along the Pennsylvania Turnpike for California in early February 1946. As they approached the US 66 junction from US 40 in East St. Louis, Cynthia began noting the towns they passed through on a map. The phrase "get your kicks on Route 66" played around in her head. Inspired by what she told him, a tune and lyrics began to take shape in Bobby's head as the odometer measured the miles.

Arriving in Los Angeles a few days later, Bobby ran into former Tommy Dorsey promoter turned agent George "Bullets" Durgom. They made the rounds of song publishers, performers, and nightclubs, trying to sell Bobby's tunes, including the new one, which he had dubbed "(Get Your Kicks on) Route 66." Durgom introduced him to the popular singer and pianist Nat King Cole, who heard the song's potential and encouraged its completion. Cole's recordings of "Route 66" and "Baby, Baby All the Time" in March and April 1946 for Capitol Records became hits and launched Bobby's career in earnest.

Troup became a popular performer at Southern California piano bars and made his major recording debut under his own name for Capitol in 1953. His understated singing and laid-back, cool style (Cynthia Troup dubbed her husband the "poor man's Nat Cole") gave him a loyal following, but by the time he met Julie London, Bobby Troup—who had been separated from his wife for nearly six months—had become increasingly frustrated by the direction of his career. The great songwriter Johnny Mercer joked about the level to which his friend had descended in his liner notes to Troup's 1955 all-Mercer album for Bethlehem: "I love each crummy room he works."

Opposites do indeed attract. The ebullient, enthusiastic Bobby and the diffident, reserved Julie made an unlikely pair. She happily introduced him to her parents before leaving for a previously scheduled European holiday with composer David Rose (known for "The Stripper") and his wife. Smitten, Bobby made his feelings known by presenting her with a St. Christopher medallion engraved with the words JULIE, JULIE, JULIE. Sailing aboard the French Line's SS *Liberté*, Julie arrived in England on June 23, en route to the French Riviera. Europe was grand—she wrote to Bobby in July from the famous Le Provençal hotel in Juan-les-Pins, telling him of shopping and sunbathing, although saving her most descriptive phrase for the four hours she spent losing thousands of francs ("my big downfall") at a Cannes casino—but Julie was soon lonesome once again. She longed to come home to her children and the new man in her life, who made her feel "like a girl again, like a woman out of limbo."

Bobby, eager to help Julie stage her professional comeback, offered a suggestion: What about singing? The entertainment business had changed since her retirement. An actress who sang might have more opportunities. The combination could expose Julie to the right people in Hollywood.

It was a difficult sell. Julie had always been a "living room singer" like her mother. She could be counted on to enthusiastically join in the fun around the piano once the alcohol began to flow, but she quickly fled if asked to entertain. Bobby had to come up with a solution that made Julie comfortable, one that gave her the feeling she was singing with friends. He invited the musicians who had backed him on his first Capitol recording sessions to Julie's house—trombonist Bob Enevoldsen (who probably doubled as the arranger); saxophonists Bill McDougal, Newcomb Rath, Jack Dulong, and Don Davidson; double bassist Harry Babasin; and drummer Don Heath—to rehearse a song she liked in an arrangement made especially for her. What he kept hidden was that two record company executives had been invited to listen. Once that information was revealed, Julie became too frightened to perform and stayed behind the closed door of her bedroom until everyone left.

In his desire to persuade Julie to sing in public, Bobby alternated between sweet talk and bullying. She resisted and frequently got angry. It was a tug-of-war. He couldn't tell her what to do. She couldn't pull herself away from his charm. Despite their inability to come to an agreement, each day seemed to bring them closer together. Bobby's adoration was soon on full public display. Capitol Records released his recording of the heartfelt "Julie Is Her Name" in late 1954, and the song's head-over-heels lyrics ("Who has got a mouth just made to be kissed, / Eyes to set the coldest heart aflame") surely delighted and frightened her. Jack Webb had never so openly expressed his feelings. Could this nice guy be for real?

5

Cry Me a River

I was a has-been that never was.

—Julie London, 1968 radio interview

JULIE LONDON'S DIVORCE FROM Jack Webb became final on December 3, 1954. Her new status as a single woman coincided with published stories that she had grown tired of idleness and was "kicking the idea around" of reviving her acting career. Jack had fired her agent George Rosenberg years earlier in the wake of a dispute over *Dragnet* profits, so she'd need new representation to get her name before studio casting directors again. Henry Willson, the agent who had successfully shepherded the career of Julie's *Fat Man* costar Rock Hudson, arranged interviews for the actress with executives at Columbia and Universal-International. None were "terribly anxious" to hire her, although she did manage to land a small television role in an episode of the NBC anthology series *Armstrong Circle Theatre*. Ironically, "Hit a Blue Note," which aired on December 14, 1954, told the story of a jazz trumpeter (played by Walter Matthau) trying to return to the big time.

Bobby Troup made his first album for the New York–based Bethlehem Records in January 1955 at Radio Recorders on Santa Monica Boulevard in Hollywood, an independent studio popular with labels that lacked local facilities. Always on the lookout for a way to promote Julie's talents, Bobby convinced Red Clyde, the label's West Coast head of artists and repertoire (A&R), to pay for her to make a four-song demo.

If for no other reason than to humor Bobby and get him off her back, Julie reluctantly agreed to the session. She walked in the front door of Radio Recorders on the afternoon of March 2, 1955, with Bobby, his current trio of guitarist Howard Roberts, double bassist Bob Enevoldsen, and drummer Don Heath, along with the versatile reedman Buddy Collette. Examining the recordings in the light of what was shortly to come, "Don't Worry 'Bout Me" is notable for its sparse, guitar-only accompaniment and as the first instance in which Julie ends a song by hitting an unexpected note. Yet only the nineteenth-century Negro spiritual "Sometimes I Feel Like a Motherless Child," where her mournful voice is accented by the haunting sound of tom toms, displayed anything that stood out from the crowd of contemporary girl singers. She showed little disappointment when Bobby told her that the label's executives were unimpressed by what they had heard and had no interest in signing her to a recording contract.

Back in Palm Springs, Julie pondered her options. She desperately needed and wanted to do *something* with her life. How was she going to make a name for herself again when she was so frequently paralyzed by the fear of performing?

When Bobby told her that John Walsh had agreed to put her on the bill at his swanky Hollywood club, sans audition, Julie felt relieved. At least that part of the process of being in the spotlight again could be avoided. How, though, was she was going to find the courage to sing before an audience, provided anyone even bothered to show up? "As shy as the smallest bud in a field of roses," Julie needed reassurance that it wasn't all a joke.

More important, she needed to feel at ease with her musical surroundings. There wasn't time to work up full band arrangements; besides, working with a large group on the small stage of the 881 Club wasn't feasible. Julie may have been uncertain of herself as a singer, yet she already knew what she wanted: not to ride on Bobby's coattails again by using his quartet and to find a combo that replicated the comfort of singing at home by not overwhelming her delicate vocal instrument.

Opting to eschew the piano-trio format, Julie began her unique musical journey by thinking back to a musician she had first encountered when she was seventeen: guitarist Barney Kessel. A native of Muskogee, Oklahoma—where Julie's mother had lived as a child—Barney had arrived in California in the summer of 1942. The following year he met Julie's parents and soon was coming by their house, where he'd play his guitar and the teenage Julie would sing. "I sensed how sensitive she was," he later said, "and what wonderful diction she had." Julie told Barney that it was the gifted vocalist Jo Stafford's "clarity of sound" that inspired her singing style.

Whether strummed or plucked, the guitar resonated well opposite Julie's untrained voice. Although pop and jazz vocalists had been accompanied by the instrument in the past—most notably Bing Crosby with Eddie Lang and Peggy Lee with her husband, Dave Barbour—the guitar's role had changed as the swing era gave way to modern jazz. Thanks to the likes of Charlie Christian, Les Paul, and Kessel himself, the instrument had become more than a timekeeper in the rhythm section.

By 1955 Barney Kessel had gained a significant presence on the West Coast jazz scene. His Charlie Christian–influenced playing landed him gigs with the legendary saxophonists Charlie Parker and Lester Young, a slot in pianist Oscar Peterson's trio, and his own series of recordings on the Contemporary label, which featured his arrangements and compositions. He was so in demand that Julie had "a heck of a job" convincing the skeptical musician to accompany her, even for $250 a week, twice what Julie earned. "My bar bill was more than that," she later joked.

The second member of her original duo was the accomplished, Nevada-born double bassist Ralph Peña, whose résumé included work with saxophonist Jimmy Giuffre and trumpeter Jack Sheldon. The role of the bass was more vital than usual; without a drummer to keep the time, Julie needed a solid grounding to keep herself on track. With the accompaniment set, work began on a set of tunes that the singer called ones she "just happened to remember the words to!" During the few days of rehearsals Julie had at hand before she was to make her debut, a series of largely uncomplicated "head" arrangements were devised to provide her with a comfortable key and to avoid straying too far from the melody.

Yet Julie's emotional insecurities flared time and again. "I was scared to death, mad at myself for being talked into it, and mad at Bobby for pushing me. . . . I was sure I would fall flat on my face." She awoke on the morning of opening night with a host of physical ailments. She frantically ran to doctors and the hospital, where she was examined for a lump on her breast and was treated for laryngitis and cold sores on her lip.

She was astonished that she made it. "It was frightening, especially because I knew so many people that were involved in entertainment and music. It was very scary to sit down and sing the first song on opening night and see everybody that I knew that were terribly good—and I wasn't terribly good."

John Walsh, the silver-haired former singer who ran the 881 Club, was a shrewd publicity seeker. He had run many small clubs in Los Angeles, including the chic Café Gala on Sunset Boulevard, where Bobby had once been among the musicians who entertained at the well-known hotspot where celebrities and members of the Hollywood gay crowd could congregate beyond prying eyes. Whether Julie made a fool of herself or not, the potential financial bonanza of having the ex–Mrs. Jack Webb—the "gold digger" of recent memory—on his stage was worth the risk.

With little publicity beyond word of mouth, the curiosity seekers who filled the candlelit club for the first few weeks were quickly replaced by audiences captivated by Julie's appealing shyness. It wasn't an act—more like a convivial evening spent at Julie's house, hearing her sing some favorite numbers around the piano with a group of friends. "I sneaked in about a week after she opened," said Bobby, "and the place was packed every night. It had never done that kind of consistent standing-room business before. So about the fourth week I was driving her home and I said, 'What further proof do you need that you are good?' Even then she wouldn't admit it." A psychological breakthrough finally came on the night when Jack Webb showed up with his new wife, actress Dorothy Towne. "I was afraid it might throw me," Julie said. "But it didn't. . . . I realized it was truly over."

The next fateful encounter occurred as the 881 Club engagement neared its end. Si Waronker, a forty-year-old Los Angeles native, was a well-known music contractor at 20th Century Fox. In early 1955 Waronker and Jack Ames of Sunland Music, a Los Angeles–based record distributor, had formed a small independent record company that released a few singles and albums to little notice. Adding singers to the Liberty Records roster was a smart commercial business move. One of the first vocalists Waronker was interested in was Bobby Troup, and when he and a music industry colleague went to see him perform at the Encore, the pianist told them he was still under contract to another label. As always, Bobby quickly sensed another opportunity. Why not go across the street and see Julie?*

Si Waronker never forgot what he saw and heard that night. "We were lucky to walk in just as the show was starting," he recalled decades later. The artful way the spotlight focused on Julie's face and figure, the subtle guitar and bass accompaniment—each made an indelible impression on the former child musical prodigy. Yet it was Julie's voice and her way with a song that really made him sit up and take notice. "The lyrics poured out of her like a hurt bird." After the show Si returned to the Encore to ask Bobby to arrange a meeting with Julie. The Bethlehem demos had left a bad taste in her mouth, Bobby said, and it would be hard to convince her to record again. But the team of Bobby and Si was hard to resist, and after Julie met with Si at her house, she was once again convinced—just as she had been more than

---

* Bobby's deal with Bethlehem Records must have ended quickly, since his LP *Bobby Troup and His Trio* was released by Liberty around the same time as *Julie Is Her Name*.

a decade before when she decided to make her first screen test—that she had little to lose by giving it a try.

During her marriage to Jack Webb, Julie had helped her former Hollywood High School boyfriend Arthur Hamilton secure a job writing songs for her husband's production company. They remained friends after her divorce. "I would attend parties at her home [and] play new songs I had written." Shortly before the end of the ten-week run at the 881 Club, Hamilton came to visit and told her about a song he had written that was supposed to have been sung by Ella Fitzgerald in Webb's forthcoming movie version of *Pete Kelly's Blues*.

"Webb called me into his office," Hamilton remembered, "and told me that several people connected with the film felt that no one would 'believe' Ella singing the word 'plebeian' in the bridge of the song. He told me to change it." Over the next three days, Hamilton wrote fourteen new bridges. "Dissatisfied with all of them, I went back to Jack and told him. He said, 'I'll be a sport. Just play the one you think came closest.' After an embarrassing pause, I said 'No.' He said, 'Why not?' I said, 'Because I know you will think it's good enough, and you'll try to convince me to use it, but I know it will spoil the song.' Jack said, 'Okay, smartass, the song is out of the film.'"

Intrigued, Julie asked him to play the song Jack had so abruptly dismissed. In its haunting melody and coolly defiant lyrics, she heard echoes of her troubled relationship with her ex-husband. It was a different sort of torch song. *She* was the scorned woman now independent enough to reject the man who had abandoned her to a life of uncertainty and tears. *She* could tell him that it was his turn to "Cry Me a River." Julie told Arthur that she was about to go into the studio to make a record and asked if she could use the intriguing new number. Hamilton agreed, thinking that she was being nice because she felt bad that her ex-husband had thrown the song away. But "Cry Me a River" had another meaning for Julie: it was a catharsis, a way for her to release the emotions she had been holding back for years. If it was done correctly, it could provide a very public measure of revenge on Jack.

Certain that her small voice would be "lost in the shuffle" of clinking glasses and audience chatter, Julie dismissed the idea of recording her performances at the 881 Club. Instead, Julie, Bobby, Si Waronker, Barney Kessel, and bassist Ray Leatherwood convened at Western Recorders on Sunset Boulevard to replicate the songs from her live set in the quiet of the studio. (Leatherwood, a veteran of the Tommy Dorsey and Les Brown big bands, had replaced Ralph Peña midway through the 881 Club engagement.) As the tape machines began to roll on the evening of August 8, 1955, Julie needed more than a little liquid lubrication to loosen up her vocal chords.

To compensate for Julie's inability to project her voice above a whisper, audio engineer John Neal asked her to move ever closer to the microphone, which accentuated the smoky, naturally breathy quality in her voice. The result, aided by the addition of a subtle echo to the recordings, was a sound that enticed listeners to move closer to their speakers and suggested the illusion that Julie was singing only to them. It would become the trademark of many of her best records. (An echo was added to the Bethlehem demo recording of "A Foggy Day," but it's possible this may have been done after someone at Bethlehem recognized how effective it had been on "Cry Me a River.")

Work continued until 3:30 the following morning and was completed later that evening. All the songs the trio recorded had been the familiar standards Julie had sung at the club. With time enough for one more track, Julie suggested that they try "Cry Me a River." Although Arthur Hamilton had helped Kessel and Leatherwood learn the basic chords of the song, they didn't have any music at hand for the largely unfamiliar tune. That wasn't enough to deter the expert duo, who rapidly devised the unique bass guitar introduction to Julie's enigmatic vocal, which was laid down to everyone's satisfaction in one or two takes.

Promotion for the completed 12" LP, aptly entitled *Julie Is Her Name*, began with the distribution of prerelease copies to disc jockeys at radio stations around the country. While there's no evidence that record company payola greased any palms in the case of Julie's record—although one of those disc jockeys, Bill Ballance of Los Angeles's KNX, *was* paid to write the liner notes for *Julie Is Her Name*—the guys who spun the discs in the 1950s had a significant influence on what went over the airwaves. Unexpectedly, many of them became enthusiastic about one number on the album—and it wasn't any of the dozen standards. Convinced that "Cry Me a River" had the potential to be a successful record, Si Waronker decided to release the melancholy tune as a single in September 1955. The disc was quickly added to radio playlists, listeners immediately responded with calls to hear the song over and over again, and by early October Liberty was taking out advertisements to tout the surprise hit single.

Yet East Coast music "experts" who came out to California had turned thumbs down on Julie. While her voice had a "degree of warmth and intimacy," they judged it "too soft and not distinctive enough to make a record success." They were soon eating their hats. The critics raved about "Cry Me a River." *Variety* enthused that the song packed "plenty of emotion," and *Billboard* congratulated Julie for displaying "a load of show-wise poise" for someone new to the scene. Demand for copies of the single—in both 45- and 78-rpm formats—was so strong that Liberty, without the resources of a major label, was hard pressed to fill the orders that rushed in. (By 1955 78-rpm discs were being phased out in favor of the 7", 45-rpm single, but there was still enough of a market for them that "Cry Me a River" and its follow-up were released in both formats.)

"I remember the excitement when [the record] really started to connect," remembered Si Waronker's son Lenny. Liberty executives knew they had a hit on their hands when a nearly note-for-note cover version of "Cry Me a River" by vocalist Kitty White was quickly released by

Mercury Records, a recording that resulted in a lawsuit alleging copyright violation. Other discs by singers Jill Corey (Columbia) and Eileen Barton (Coral) soon followed, and Liberty felt compelled to protect its sales by taking out another advertisement to remind disc jockeys that Julie's was still the original, definitive success.

To Julie's surprise the "unknown song recorded by an unknown singer on an unknown label" quickly climbed up the charts. It entered the *Billboard* Top 100 in early November 1955, reached its peak of number thirteen a month later, and stayed on the charts for twenty weeks, until March of 1956. The success of "Cry Me a River" was only slightly lower in *Cash Box*, which had predicted the record's success ("if this one gets a start, it'll be a smash"). During the song's fifteen weeks in the magazine's Top 50, it topped out at number eighteen. By the fall of 1955, the single had reportedly sold one hundred thousand copies, a number that jumped to eight hundred thousand by the following spring. A year later the jazz magazine *Down Beat* claimed that sales of "Cry Me a River" had passed the one million mark. (Although that figure is still repeated today, anything approaching accuracy in record sales didn't begin until 1958, with the institution of a certification program by the Recording Industry Association of America.)

It was an exciting and unusual time. Julie London's arrival as a singer occurred at a transitional moment for the music business. When "Cry Me a River" began to be noticed in the summer of 1955, its biggest competition came from recordings by pop singers like Gogi Grant, Jaye P. Morgan, Joni James, and Patti Page, and the Four Aces' disc of the lachrymose title song from *Love Is a Many Splendored Thing*. Julie's subtle, erotically caressing voice and the minimalist production values of her first record were a sharp contrast to these pedestrian, overproduced sides.

At the other end of the music spectrum, rock 'n' roll was just beginning to make its presence felt on the charts. The likes of Chuck Berry, Bill Haley and the Comets, and Fats Domino were visible, although the purchasing power of teenage record-buyers had yet to become a significant influence on the types of performers signed to record deals and the kinds of music being recorded.

What *was* the secret of the song's success? Julie insisted that it wasn't because she was a singer. She just opened her mouth and "let the sounds and the words come out." She suggested that Arthur Hamilton's unusual use of the word *plebeian* caused listeners to do a double take when they heard the record and made them want to hear it again. Lenny Waronker, who learned a lot about the business from his father and became a significant record producer in his own right during the 1970s, had another idea. Because of Liberty's small size, the label needed a gimmick, something that would make their product stand out from the competition. "Sound was a big deal" for Si Waronker, so he decided to emphasize the technical aspects of the recording process with evocative slogans. Phrases such as "Spectra-Sonic-Sound" were prominently displayed on the covers of early Liberty releases, right under the company's Statue of Liberty logo. They had no basis in the mundane realities of audio engineering but could be effectively marketed to the predominately male record-buyers of the 1950s who were eager to show off their fancy, high-fidelity sound systems.

Another, more visceral gimmick became the stock-in-trade of Julie London's recording career. Liberty's first five singles were released without picture sleeves—a rare commodity in 1955 for any record company, let alone a label as new and lacking in funds as this one—and "Cry Me a River" was no exception. But Si Waronker knew that marketing Julie's first record needed a different approach. He hired photographer Phil Howard to take a series of shots of Julie for publicity purposes.

Two of these photographs were used in advertisements to promote "Cry Me a River." The first, published in the October 15, 1955, issue of *Cash Box* and reprinted the following week, shows Julie in a close-up, her head tilted and her eyes looking down and away from the camera. The second, which appeared in the November 19, 1955, issue of the same publication, is a three-quarter-length pose and reveals what was cropped from the album cover: Julie wearing a pair of not-very-sexy, elbow-length white gloves.

In addition both photographs are in black and white. The full impact of the image—the emphasis on what Waronker called the "dirty appeal" of Howard's photographs—was only delivered when the full-color cover of *Julie Is Her Name* was displayed on record store shelves and in window displays. It was only natural to highlight a beautiful woman's face, but what if Julie's records could be marketed by going one step further, to show more of her body, to draw the male gaze to the parts of her voluptuous figure that men's magazines of the period were able to display on their pages? With the three-quarter-length image cropped to just below the top of Julie's dress, the focus of the eye goes to her cleavage, her tantalizing reddish-gold hair, and her bare golden-skinned shoulders.

Prominent music critic Ralph J. Gleason found the image so over-whelming that he wondered what could be done for an encore. "Anything more powerful would undoubtedly be banned." The provocative, sometimes subliminal message of Julie London's album covers became the primary sales point for her records, far outstripping any emphasis on their musical contents.

Even with the focus on the visual and Julie's jokes about her lack of technique, the range of mood on the singer's first LP is a testament to her innate feeling for lyrics and her ability to make songs her own. The weeks of regular singing at the 881 Club prior to the recording had smoothed out the rougher patches in her voice that were so evident on the Bethlehem demos. A melancholy mood permeates most of *Julie Is Her Name*, and many of the more downbeat tunes, in addition to "Cry Me a River," echo—deliberately or not—her relationship with Jack Webb. While songs such as "I Should Care," "Say It Isn't So," and "Gone with the Wind" veer from depression to hope in the space of their thirty-two bars, the record isn't entirely suffering and lament. Julie's innate cheerfulness and the joy of a new relationship is evident in bright performances of "I'm in the Mood for Love" and "I'm Glad There Is You," and an easy, lightly swinging style is displayed on the loping "Easy Street" and in the subtle rhythmic twists of "No Moon at All." The album's penultimate track, David Raksin and Johnny Mercer's "Laura," is an exception to Julie's disdain for much of her recorded output. She was the first woman to record the haunting ballad, and sixty years later its opening moments of unaccompanied singing retain their power to hypnotize.

"Miss London," wrote one critic, "has that rare combination of simplicity, the ability to tell a story and even supply added meanings between the lines." The "tight rein" she kept on her emotions, wrote Ralph J. Gleason, "might erupt at any moment into violence. . . . Her singing is so tight that what emotion does come through is more intense by virtue of escaping the restraint."

Julie's newly minted success as a singer didn't go unnoticed by the major movie studios. She was offered a screen test by 20th Century Fox, and she hoped that a positive reaction to *The Fighting Chance*, her first big-screen appearance in four years, would seal the deal. Filmed over a couple of weeks in late May 1955, as Julie braced herself for the reaction to her nightclub debut, and released in early December, *The Fighting Chance* turned out to be just another B-movie. Even with Julie's name in the ascendant alongside two frequent Republic Pictures marquee names—rugged Rod Cameron and diminutive former child actor Ben Cooper—the film sank without a trace.

Directed by western specialist William Witney, Julie was cast as Janet Wales, a gold-digging model (perhaps a sly reference to the press comments surrounding her divorce) who picked up tips at Hollywood Park Racetrack to supplement her meager salary. The paltry few who saw *The Fighting Chance* on the lower half of neighborhood bookings could be forgiven for thinking that the role wasn't much of a stretch for Julie, since her image as a gold digger was still fresh in many minds. After four years of "retirement," her rustiness as an actress was obvious, particularly in the few scenes where the uninspired screenplay offered a glimmer of character development. It was clearly beyond Julie's ability to make the unsympathetic Janet Wales as nasty as she should have been, although at least one critic who attended a preview showing thought that the audience's applause "when she gets her comeuppance" showed a "convincing portrayal."

She had little time to dwell on the movie's failure. To successfully promote her records meant Julie had to conquer another fear: singing in front of a large live television audience. The medium's popular variety shows had a major influence on record sales. Julie devised a solution to the problem that eased her worries: she became one of the first singers to insist on taping her songs in advance of the broadcast. Although this made her more comfortable, it launched a stream of jokes at her expense. The negative comments didn't put a dent in her popularity, and her performances of "Cry Me a River" on NBC's *Tonight Show*—then hosted by comedian Steve Allen—in October and the New Year's Eve episode of the *Perry Como Show* (where she also sang "Easy Street") caused her agent's telephone to ring off the hook with lucrative offers.

As the whirlwind year of 1955 came to an end, a spirited bidding war broke out among the owners of New York nightclubs for the right to host Julie's East Coast concert debut. A new supper club on Manhattan's Upper East Side, the Cameo, won the battle against established venues such as the Blue Angel and the Copacabana. As Julie prepared to walk onstage before the capacity crowd on opening night, January 5, 1956, she felt as nervous as she had six months before.

Perched on an upholstered white stool and dressed in a strapless, full-skirted white gown that accentuated her ample cleavage, she looked out at the packed, intimate venue. "I was sure everyone could hear my knees knocking!" Backed by the talented guitarist Al Viola—a member of Bobby's trio and soon to become one of Julie's musical mainstays—and East Coast bass player Whitey Mitchell, Julie thrilled the critics. She used her voice "seductively," commented the *New Yorker*, "and since she has what seems to be an instinctive sense of phrasing, her deliveries of rhythm songs, ballads, and blues numbers are all quite compelling in their way." *Billboard* noted that Julie was a "bewitching paradox as a performer. Her looks are on the spectacular side, her voice is subtle and sexy, but her manner is surprisingly shy and girlish." In *Down Beat* Nat Hentoff wrote that Julie's physicality "made the warm new Cameo room hot and triggered vernal daydreams among a large section of the male nighttime populace," although it was her ability to "really [tell] a story with each song" that made her stand out. "She inhabits the lyrics," he continued, comparing Julie to Jeri Southern, another vocalist "who realizes the value of open spaces."

Sharing equal billing with Bobby for the engagement, Julie largely stayed with her repertoire from the 881 Club but added his 1946 song "Baby, Baby All the Time," which Liberty had just released as her second single with Arthur Hamilton's spectral "Shadow Woman." Both were among the first results from a series of late 1955 sessions with arranger Russ Garcia. (A third item, the dramatic "I'll Cry Tomorrow" from the eponymous Susan Hayward movie, was released on a four-song EP later that year.) She also delved into some as-yet-unrecorded material, including Cole Porter's "What Is This Thing Called Love?" and "Get Out of Town." (The former would appear on *Julie Is Her Name, Volume 2* in 1958; it took until 1965's all-Porter album *All Through the Night* for Julie to record the latter. An additional song, "It's Only a Paper Moon," never made it to disc.) By far the most important of the new numbers was her boyfriend's poignant 1949 tune "Lonely Girl," with the composer accompanying Julie at the piano and singing the first verse. It was the beginning of her career-long promotion of Bobby Troup's work. She would go on to record or perform more than thirty numbers from his catalog, far more than any other songwriter.

The successful engagement was extended through the end of January, yet Julie remained self-deprecating and joked that every time she listened to Ella Fitzgerald she wondered what she was "doing in the same business.'Her unfailing modesty didn't keep a who's who of celebrities—baseball star Joe DiMaggio, movie icon Errol Flynn, and crime novelist Mickey Spillane—from packing the Cameo to catch Julie's erotic whisperings.

Following a three-day gig as part of an unlikely vaudeville bill at the four-thousand-seat State Theatre in Hartford, Connecticut, Julie returned home for a triumphant two-week run at the tiny Interlude club on the Sunset Strip with Al Viola and bassist Bob Enevoldsen.

The publicity from her nightclub and television appearances had resulted in a significant increase in her record sales. "Cry Me a River" was now outmatched by an even greater success as the *Julie Is Her Name* album made its way up the charts. It spent sixteen weeks in the Top 15 at *Billboard*, reaching number two, but the ultimate prize—a number-one LP—came in *Cash Box*, where *Julie Is Her Name* remained on the charts for nineteen consecutive weeks. On February 11, 1956, Julie's debut album remarkably knocked off Frank Sinatra's *In the Wee Small Hours of the Morning* and the *Oklahoma!* movie soundtrack for the coveted top spot. It sustained its popularity and held the top position for two additional weeks until succumbing to the soundtrack for *The Benny Goodman Story*.

Goodman, the still-popular bandleader of the swing years, was another of the celebrities who had jammed the Cameo to see and hear this new vocal sensation. The clarinetist praised the "rather rare and welcome simplicity" of *Julie Is Her Name* and recommended it as one of the ten records everyone should have to start a jazz library. Unsurprisingly, Julie was stunned by the praise and the success. "I thought somebody was kidding me." A year earlier she had been searching for something—anything—to bring herself back to life. Now, told that she had a hit single and a number-one album, she could only shake her head and laugh. What did it all mean and could it continue?

She had little time to think too much about the future. Her datebook was filling up. Shortly after the release of *Julie Is Her Name*, she had spent a few weeks in Tucson, Arizona, shooting a B-level crime drama for producer Howard W. Koch. The movie, *Crime Against Joe*, opened in May 1956 as the bottom half of double features. Although it has the merit of being the first of her movies to exploit her singing success in its promotional campaign, the generic melodrama has little to recommend itself since Julie doesn't do much except pine for the blandly handsome star, John Bromfield. While her big scene—a chase down a country lane—is effective, nothing else about *Crime Against Joe* remains in the memory after its brief seventy minutes have unspooled.

The contrast between Julie's uninspired return to acting and the blooming success of her singing debut could not have been starker. Sessions for the follow-up to *Julie Is Her Name* had begun in late 1955 with arranger Russ Garcia but took an unexpected turn one evening when Julie was at Western Recorders, adding her voice to some backing tracks. On the way to his evening gig with Al Viola, Bobby stopped by to ask Julie if she would cut a demo of a song he had just finished. Of course, she said. Al sat down with his Spanish guitar, and he and Julie ran through the lead sheet before the tapes rolled on the touching "Their Hearts Were Full of Spring."

Entranced by the sound of Julie with just a single instrument, Si Waronker suggested that they forget about the overdubs and lay down some additional tracks with Al. Bobby "wouldn't speak to me for two days because I'd taken his guitarist away from him on a Saturday night!" Julie later laughed. It almost led to "a divorce before we got married!"

Si Waronker believed in "selling mood as well as tune," and he liked the idea of records that had a common theme or sound. Twenty-two tracks were ad-libbed that evening, thirteen of which were quickly released as *Lonely Girl*. (Songs that didn't make the cut included "Foggy Night in San Francisco" by Julie's friend Herm Saunders, the 1937 Tommy Dorsey hit "Once in a While," the classic "It Had to Be You," the otherwise unknown "Funny Man," and, ironically, "Their Hearts Were Full of Spring." The others have yet to be located.) The sparseness of Al Viola's accompaniment emphasized the natural, uninflected tone in Julie's voice and the sensitivity of her lyrical interpretations. By approaching the songs without any affectation that could distract from the intensity of emotions, Julie exposed herself to the listener, as the unadorned setting encouraged a focus on how she buried herself in the story.

The themes of finding love ("Fools Rush In"), losing love (a heartbreaking "What'll I Do"), and recalling love's joys and sorrows

("Moments Like This") culminate in a resolution to live with love's memories ("Remember"). *Lonely Girl* was one of the few records of her own that Julie London really had affection for, and surprisingly—given its format—it found an audience. While it didn't match the success of her first album, the disc did reach the top twenty on both the *Cash Box* (number fourteen) and *Billboard* (number sixteen) album charts, even if the reviews were mixed. *Billboard* praised her "powerful wallop," but *New York Times* columnist John S. Wilson grew weary of the lack of variation, calling it "soporific."

Once again the response of radio station disc jockeys prompted Liberty to pull one song from the album as a single in the hopes of boosting sales of *Lonely Girl*. Arranger Pete King, then working with Julie on what would become her third album, added a subtle string and flute backing to the title song. Although *Cash Box* thought it had chart potential ("watch it go"), the tender single, released with a smooth rendition of "September in the Rain," failed to go anywhere. King also worked on another largely ignored single, issued a few months later: the sultry but up-tempo "Now, Baby, Now" and its gentle flipside, "Tall Boy."

———— ∞ ————

Love, not money, prompted Julie's appearances on Bobby Troup's *Stars of Jazz* television program. The show debuted on Los Angeles television station KABC in late June 1956, and by the time of Julie's low-key performances of "'S Wonderful" and "Laura" three months later, it had become a notable local success. The budgets were low and rehearsal time short, but *Stars of Jazz* is fondly recalled by aficionados for its wide range of performers and its dedication to promoting jazz as an art form. *Stars of Jazz* had gone national by the time Julie returned to the program two years later to promote her *Julie* LP with relaxed performances of "Free and Easy" and "Midnight Sun." For all its popularity with the cognoscenti, *Stars of Jazz* struggled to find a network audience and went off the air at the end of 1958.

It *was* the money—reportedly $20,000 for twenty minutes of work—that convinced Julie to return to live performances for a two-week engagement at the ultramodern New Frontier hotel on the Las Vegas Strip. Her opening number as the vocal star of the *Musical Insanities of 1957* was "Laura," a dramatic counterpoint to the noise coming from bandleader Spike Jones's musicians, and it "absolutely brought down the house." Julie's ability to make fun of her stage fright delighted audiences, who heard her deadpan that "there's no need for all of us to suffer." The big money she could make from clubs wasn't enough to offset the physical and emotional discomfort of being onstage. No more, she said. The future held bright thoughts of records and movies to be made.

Julie's third album was the result of the love Si Waronker had for albums with a hook and his keen sense of marketing. "In those days," his son recalled, "people had to go to a record store if they wanted to get something, and if they saw something that looked really good, there was a chance they might buy it." It's no surprise that the elaborately packaged *Calendar Girl* is remembered more for its cover than its music. Although the recording sessions—done at the recently opened studios of Capitol Records in Hollywood—took place from May to September 1956, when Julie could make time during the filming of *Drango*, she not so jokingly told CBS's Edward R. Murrow that "it took longer to shoot the pictures . . . than it did to cut the album."

From the New Year's party girl of Miss January and the not-so-subtle erotic charge of Julie celebrating the Fourth of July with a giant firecracker resting on her thigh to the well-wrapped Christmas package of Miss December, the dozen images that make up the gatefold cover of *Calendar Girl* are a delicious come-on. Those who purchased the record got the full show, a centerfold that really catches the eye. In a riff on her photograph in *Esquire* a decade earlier, Julie lays back, head turned to one side, long tresses spread out around her, with a strategically placed white boa covering her breasts and lower abdomen. Bob Hope joked to a national television audience during Julie's appearance on his NBC show in November 1956 that the album was "a combination record album and *Esquire* calendar. You don't need a turntable to play it—you just look at the picture and your eyeballs revolve!"

The sparse accompaniment of *Julie Is Her Name* and *Lonely Girl* was replaced with a swinging mixture of strings, horns, and reeds courtesy of Pete King, an arranger best known for his lush orchestrations on the popular series of Capitol mood music albums by Jackie Gleason. "I still wasn't fully broken into recording," Julie recalled. "The thought of making a record date with a full orchestra gave me the shivers. . . . When the time came for the first take, I just shut my eyes and hoped for the best."

Most of the album was written to order, remembered Arthur Hamilton:

Julie and Bobby and I were in her living room . . . [trying] to think of all the songs of the month, and came up a few months short of twelve. I asked Bobby to choose two of the remaining months, which he did [February and October]. I then said I would write a song for the month of August—and in a sudden flash of inspiration, I said I would write "The Thirteenth Month"—the month of Remember.

Julie's personality was captured best by those who knew her well. Bobby Troup's contributions stand out: the atmospheric "February Brings the Rain"—its lyrics inspired by the nineteenth-century poem "The Months" by English author Sara Coleridge ("February brings the rain / Thaws the frozen lake again")—and the happy "This October," which replaced "One October Morning," a ballad by Bobby that Julie didn't care for. Arthur Hamilton's ghostly "The Thirteenth Month" and sprightly "Time for August" are similarly impressive. The efforts of Herm Saunders and Dory Langdon, Earl Brent, Pete King and Paul Francis Webster, and Bob Russell are less convincing, with halfhearted lyrics poorly designed to fit the album's theme.

Given Julie's reluctance to learn new material, it's no surprise that her best vocal performances on *Calendar Girl* are delivered on the standards.

A bright "June in January," the Latin-flavored "I'll Remember April," an appropriately drowsy-sounding "Memphis in June," a misty "Sleigh Ride in July," and a jaunty "September in the Rain" all showcase her easy delivery and warmth. Reviews for the album were mixed, and once again Julie's image received top billing, as critics focused on the lush packaging rather than the musical contents: "If you are male and breathing, don't miss this one." Although promoted in the music trade press as a number-one seller, *Calendar Girl* failed to have the impact of Julie's first two albums, only reaching number thirteen at *Cash Box* and number eighteen at *Billboard*.

Even so 1956 was a very successful year for a woman who still was shaking her head in disbelief at how far she had traveled in such a short time. All three of her LPs wound up in the annual *Cash Box* Top Albums chart. It was time to take advantage of that success in another medium.

The cool, detached persona Julie London displayed on her records had begun to catch the eyes and ears of major Hollywood talent, and her next movie would be the most financially successful of her career. Writer/director Frank Tashlin, fresh off the success of the comedy *The Lieutenant Wore Skirts* for 20th Century Fox, was casting a new picture, a musical comedy satire about the record business called *Do Re Mi*. (The movie's title was changed to *The Girl Can't Help It* after Little Richard's raucous performance of a new Bobby Troup song of that name proved extremely popular with studio executives.) The script included a role for a character Tashlin referred to as "The Girl," a reluctant singer whose voice and ethereal image haunts a washed-up talent agent. Tashlin had even described the character as perhaps *being* Julie London.

The popularity of *The Girl Can't Help It* can be attributed to the physical attributes of its star, the buxom Jayne Mansfield, and the movie's significance as one of the first major Hollywood productions to feature rock 'n' roll. However, Julie's three-minute dream sequence, shot in glorious CinemaScope by multi–Academy Award winner Leon Shamroy, lies at the heart of the broad farce about the making of a new singing sensation.

Frank Tashlin was the first director to find an appropriate use for Julie London's spectral voice, a sound he was able to translate into its cinematic equivalent. The laconic Tom Ewell, as Julie's one-time agent and lover Tom Miller, is haunted by her memory and how he ignored her pleas to live quietly in a tract house and sing lullabies to their children. But Miller didn't listen, his new client, jukebox king Fats Murdock (played by Edmond O'Brien), tells him: instead he "pushed her into a career she didn't want."

After a sodden evening on the town, Miller tipsily turns on his hi-fi, where the covers of the singer's first three albums are prominently displayed. As he wanders into the kitchen in search of a nightcap, Julie's voice emerges from the speakers, and she materializes out of thin air to taunt him with "Cry Me a River." As he flees from room to room, she reappears in different outfits—from capri pants to a diaphanous night-gown—and surrounds him with her ghostly sound. After she renders him helpless, Julie vanishes as quickly as she appeared, leaving him both shaken and stirred. (A short sequence with Julie and Edmond O'Brien was filmed but cut from the final release.)

The critical response to *The Girl Can't Help It* was mixed, but it didn't matter. Enthusiastic fans at the Los Angeles premiere in December 1956 mobbed Julie as they tried to get at copies of her records. Audiences lapped it up and landed the picture in the top-thirty box office hits of 1957. Most critics couldn't comprehend what they were seeing. Bosley Crowther of the *New York Times* sneered that the movie was "as meager and witless as a cheap pin-up magazine joke," although *Boxoffice* recognized the "exploitation bonanza" of Mansfield and music and presciently observed that Tashlin's satire of the contemporary music business was aimed not at teenagers but at an *older* audience that could see through the ephemeral songs (i.e., those not sung by Julie London) on display.

"The juxtaposition of the sultry vamp [Julie] and the innocent sex kitten [Jayne]," wrote a Mansfield biographer, is what makes *The Girl Can't Help It* so effective. The "powerful and mature" Julie "acknowledges and uses sex [while] Jayne pretends it isn't there." Julie's vision of sexuality was not Mansfield's cartoonish one, nor was it in the girlish mode of Marilyn Monroe. She recognized that a woman could get what she wanted . . . if she wanted it.

6

The Exciting Life

Music has paved the way for everything.

—Julie London to journalist Mel Heimer, 1957

IN *THE GIRL CAN'T HELP IT*, Frank Tashlin had transformed Julie's reluctance to be in the spotlight into a telling piece of dialogue. A performer needed to be "vitally interested" in her career if she was to make it big. As Julie London began to attract attention as both singer *and* actress, she remained uncertain of whether she really *wanted* to be a star—in *either* world. A nearly nonstop schedule of recordings, movies, and television appearances over the next three years would play a major part in helping her make that decision.

On December 31, 1956, *The Great Man* opened at the Sutton Theater on East Fifty-Seventh Street in New York City. Based on Al Morgan's 1955 novel of the same name, the gritty ninety-two-minute, black-and-white picture told the story of Herb Fuller, a beloved radio personality who, after his unexpected death, is exposed as a lecherous, drunken fake. Morgan's years in the radio business provided the background for the novel and the movie, which unfolds through a series of revealing interviews with the people who had known Fuller on his way up the ladder to success and during his years as a star.

One of those people was Carol Larson, a singer whom Fuller had hired for his show and quickly bedded, turning her into one of his many mistresses ("when he was in the neighborhood"). It was an opportunity for Julie to sink her teeth into a substantial, albeit brief, role, and the positive reaction to her performance did a lot for her confidence. Her music—as much as her looks—won her the part. Eleven months earlier, Academy Award–winning actor José Ferrer had been in the audience one night during Julie's run at the Interlude. Ferrer was in preproduction for his second directorial effort for Universal and was looking for an actress who could convincingly play a singer yet who could also handle the dramatic arc of a woman whose confidence had been shattered by her relationship with the Great Man. Ferrer's wife, singer Rosemary Clooney, suggested Julie might fit the bill. Impressed by her stage presence, he told Julie she would be ideal for the part and offered her a chance to audition.

The director's serious attitude toward his craft rattled Julie's nerves. He was a dynamic contrast to most of those with whom she had worked in the past, who often settled for what they could get from their actors. Ferrer wanted more from the actress than she thought she would be able to give. She was uncertain whether she could find the deep truth of the character until he invited her to spend some time with him at his Beverly Hills house to talk about the role. (The house, at 1019 North Roxbury Drive, was where George Gershwin resided during the last eleven months of his life. Rosemary Clooney owned the property until her death in 2002, and until 1983 George's brother Ira was her next-door neighbor.) A few drinks helped her to cautiously make her way through some of the dialogue Ferrer had prepared for the scene. He also told her that Bobby Troup's melancholy lyrics for "The Meaning of the Blues," which he heard her perform at the Interlude, succinctly captured the situation in which Carol Larson found herself and would make perfect dramatic sense for her to sing in the movie.

Convinced by the director's faith in her abilities, Julie signed a $4,000 freelance contract with Universal for two weeks of work, a deal with an option for at least one additional picture. During the week of rehearsals Ferrer held at his home, he suggested an experiment that she was open to trying. Most actors who played drunks on the screen just weren't convincing; could she take a couple slugs of gin and still read her lines? It seemed an effective gambit, yet in the days that led up to the start of filming, Julie wondered "whether to be honest" and tell him that she couldn't play the role "or just get to the set and let him find out."

Even on the morning of the first day she was to go before the cameras, she was worried. The addition of a little gin to her usual breakfast orange juice bolstered her confidence. By now she had studied her lines so thoroughly that they had become almost second nature; all she needed to do to give an accurate portrayal of Carol Larson was to stay on the edge of getting totally loaded. With Troup on the set to lend moral support when Ferrer called "action," the actress was ready to give the director—and anyone else who was watching—everything she had. One of those pairs of eyes belonged to bandleader Russ Morgan, who played Herb Fuller's cynical bandleader—no friend to Carol Larson—in the movie. Morgan said the cast "burst into spontaneous applause" as Julie finished her dramatic moments.

Julie grasped the opportunity with both hands, and her performance in *The Great Man*—swinging between drunken pathos and sharp moments of clarity—lingers as a rare glimpse of the woman behind the glamorous image. Alcohol had become as much of a crutch for Julie as it had for the character she portrayed. Both a pleasure and a curse, it brought her out of her shell and gave her the courage to perform but also coarsened her personality. Like Carol, who had given herself to the Great Man at the age of eighteen to get away from home only to watch him wander away when he got bored, Julie had hoped for true love from her marriage to Jack Webb. Yet she too was ignored and gradually sank into a miasma of depression and drink.

Aware that Joe Harris (Ferrer, who also starred in the movie) might become the next Great Man, Carol tries to seduce him, as she had seduced Herb Fuller years before. Her unsubtle attempts at flirtation get no reaction from the laconic Harris, and her constant need for the protection of the bottle transforms her from a self-professed "quiet, shy, reserved" girl into a "pretty tough little broad." As she recounts how she initially tricked Fuller by pretending to be blind, and after their affair began, mistakenly thought that she could handle him as she had handled her local high school football team, the drinks come faster and faster. In an effort to show Harris that she "could really straighten up and fly right," she tries to sing along to a radio broadcast of her only hit recording. "I haven't got a bad voice," she lamely adds. As she slurs and stumbles over the lyrics—words she once knew by heart—she falters and fades away. By the end of the interview, the combination of alcohol and devastating memories causes her tough facade to collapse under the weight of her own failures. All too well she knows the meaning of the blues.

It was the potential breakthrough performance Julie needed to move up the ranks to prominent movie roles. Universal took out full-page advertisements in the *Hollywood Reporter* and other industry trade journals to build her up for consideration as Best Supporting Actress in the 1957 Academy Awards. (She didn't get a nomination.) Julie reacted to the hype in typically sarcastic fashion, but she *was* proud of the work, saying that her father had been so taken with what he saw on the screen that he'd forgotten Julie was his daughter.

The studio sent her to New York for a week to promote the movie with a series of newspaper, radio, and television interviews, which concluded with a January 20 appearance on Steve Allen's highly rated NBC variety show. Her powerful portrayal of hard-bitten disillusion in *The Great Man* came as a surprise to at least one critic who had seemingly forgotten Julie's earlier career when he wrote that she "digs into a dramatic role and socks it across with the aplomb of an actress with many years of seasoning." Another writer called her "second to none . . . in the fervor of her performance," but it was to no avail.

Although *Time* magazine called the movie "a corrosive, cynical comment on TV-Radio Row," the behind-the-scenes goings-on of the radio industry held little interest for audiences not located in the nation's large media outlets of New York, Chicago, and Los Angeles. *The Great Man* quickly disappeared into the ether from which it had emanated, rarely to be heard from again except on late-night reruns.

Julie had known actor Jeff Chandler for nearly a decade when he offered her a role in *Drango*, the first project for his new production company. Chandler's recent pictures for Universal had been box office successes, so she eagerly accepted the part even if was another supporting one. *Drango*, jointly credited to writer/producer/director Hall Bartlett and producer/director Jules Bricken, was Julie's third movie to be released in two months and suffered the same critical and financial fate as *The Great Man*.

Shot during the summer of 1956 on location at a Louisiana plantation, at the Morrison Ranch in Agoura, California, and the Samuel Goldwyn Studios, Julie played Shelby Ransom, the alcoholic lover of an unrepentant Confederate loyalist—played by Ronald Howard in his American feature-film debut—who hopes to foment an uprising against the Union troops occupying his territory during the post–Civil War Reconstruction era. Shelby Ransom, like Carol Larson before her, drinks to forget (although this time, Julie stayed sober during the filming). The alcohol only deadens the pain of her guilt when her lover forces her to dupe a Union soldier who had confessed his love for her even though they had just met. Knowing that the young man would soon die, she plaintively asks, "*Do* you know me? Does anyone really ever know another human being?"

Drango contains a number of powerful, melodramatic moments, some excellent performances, a fine score by Elmer Bernstein, and crisp black-and-white cinematography that captures the grittiness of life in a defeated land, but its small scale and serious subject matter failed to attract a wide audience. Once again, Julie's good work went without notice.

Her schedule during the first ten months of 1957 left little time for relaxation. Between recording sessions and movie work, Julie appeared on five television variety shows, two network television dramas, a top-rated quiz show, and a highly popular interview series hosted by one of the most respected journalists in broadcast history.

Plugging one record after another had already grown tiresome, so Julie welcomed the chance to fool the panel on *What's My Line?* with a goofy pseudo-hillbilly accent that confused comedian Ernie Kovacs into thinking she was a man. Her September 13 appearance on Edward R. Murrow's interview program *Person to Person* was less comforting. The broadcast—which caused a delay for the cast and crew of *Voice in the Mirror*, who were expecting Julie for an evening of location filming in downtown Los Angeles—showed Julie at her sprawling suburban ranch house, nervously laughing when asked to account for her success. It was puzzling, she told Murrow. She didn't think she was "really a very good singer at all." The interview was meant to spotlight the normal lives of stars, although viewers must have been taken aback by seven-year-old Stacy Webb. When the host asked her what she did while she was stuck in the house all day, Stacy declared that she watched television and drank a lot, surely a reference to her mother's alcohol consumption that Julie would have preferred to leave unaired.

The small screen also provided Julie with a chance to add a couple of western dramas to her résumé. In "A Time to Live," an episode of the popular western anthology *Dick Powell's Zane Grey Theatre*, Julie played the first of many saloon-singer roles. The bland teleplay was relieved only by Julie's brief renditions of two traditional folk songs, "He's Gone Away" and "Black Is the Color (of My True Love's Hair)." The *Playhouse 90* production of "Without Incident," which aired two months later, benefited from having been shot on location near Tucson, Arizona, although Julie still had little to do beyond growl huskily in her role as "a bad, wild girl" opposite Errol Flynn and Ann Sheridan. The program received scathing reviews, one critic calling Julie's "girl of the Old West" more like Mae West and recommending that the show's stars "should go after their agents with tomahawks."

---⟨∞⟩---

The pleasure Julie took from her increasing visibility and the personal success she felt as a singer and actress ran parallel to her dismay at the publicity surrounding her relationship with Bobby Troup. Rumors about their impending marriage flooded newspaper gossip columns after it was hinted that she had accepted his engagement ring prior to a March 1957 trip to visit his family in Pennsylvania. Although the loss of alimony may have contributed to her decision to remain single, she was also leery of committing herself to any man. Bobby was determined to remain a good father to his daughters, who were being raised by their mother, Cynthia. This meant that Bobby spent a significant amount of time with his ex-wife, a fact that surely contributed to Julie's hesitation. What was freshest in her mind, however, were the memories of having forsaken her dreams of success after marrying Jack Webb. She wanted to make the most of her career opportunities this time around. If marriage had to wait, so be it.

Even with the disagreements over the future of their relationship, Bobby's upbeat personality gradually influenced Julie's outlook on life. She lost of some of the moodiness that had constantly plagued her and became more self-confident in her abilities as a performer. After reacting in the negative to reports that they were seeing other people, Julie denied that she and Bobby were having troubles, yet when asked whether they had made up from their latest spat—the press seemingly reported on one every other week—she admitted they still had a lot to discuss. By late September 1957, she pointedly blamed Bobby for their problems and seemed relieved to announce that "marriage is not for us."

If this turmoil affected Julie and Bobby's personal relationship, it didn't interfere with the vital role he played in her career as chief encourager. Press reports to the contrary, Bobby was anything but the Svengali figure who told Julie what to sing and how to sing it; if he had been, Julie surely would have recorded more of his songs. As it was, of the nearly 375 commercially released recordings she made during her career, only twenty-five were from his catalog, and the majority of her albums had no Bobby Troup songwriting credits.

Julie was "at her breathiest and most sultry" on her fourth LP, *About the Blues*, "seeming to sing not with her vocal cords, but rather to radiate a protoplasmic sound." The record appears to have originally been intended as the follow-up to *Julie Is Her Name*, but numerous sessions at Radio Recorders with arranger Russ Garcia never seemed to result in a satisfactory finished product, even if Julie eventually professed happiness "about the results of an album of mine, musically speaking" for the first time.

Garcia was a respected composer and arranger in the West Coast progressive style, and often merged jazz rhythms with the formality of classical music. These elements are on full display in the arrangements he brought to Julie, which contrasted Julie's "soft, easy approach" with the "screaming brass" of an eighteen-piece band behind her. (The extreme high notes came courtesy of ex–Stan Kenton trumpeter Maynard Ferguson.) The sound was overwhelming and wholly beyond Julie's ability to sing over. She fled the studio and "didn't come back for a week." It was the beginning of a career-long obsession with finding the ideal ambience.

Julie "never recorded with the orchestra," the arranger recalled. After the backing tracks were laid down, she would return to "do her bit." Alone, with a glass of stimulating liquid by her side and a moody atmosphere often provided by just a single light shining on her music stand, Julie found the courage to sing. "Imagine," he reminisced, "the most beautiful girl in the world had no real self confidence."

Like *Calendar Girl*, the concept was good while the end product was less so. Though Julie was often awkwardly shoehorned into the material, *About the Blues* is a stylistic statement that showed she was willing to look beyond minimalism. When she digs into the haunted feeling of the blues and the backing is subtle, Julie's whispers express the evocative, late-night desolation of the genre. On Arthur Hamilton's title track and his "Bouquet of Blues" (two more rejects from *Pete Kelly's Blues*), Bobby Troup's gloomy "The Blues Is All I Ever Had" and "Meaning of the Blues," and the Middle Eastern–tinged "Bye Bye Blues," Julie's "single-purposed intimacy" was "nothing short of miraculous."

The cover image, with Julie at her most gorgeous in a floor-length, gold lamé gown, made news as usual: "The sight . . . will set all eyes agog." Its chart success bettered that of *Calendar Girl* by peaking at number fifteen in *Billboard* and number eleven in *Cash Box*. Julie—perhaps only jokingly—attributed what she maintained was the album's failure to fly higher to its only having twelve songs, which broke the lucky spell provided by the thirteen tracks on her previous LPs.

Liberty was now issuing records at a rapid pace, and Julie's next album, *Make Love to Me,* came out just months later. Russ Garcia was again responsible for the arrangements, and the cushion of strings, with the occasional flute or bongos added for exotic touches, was an ideal setting for Julie's sultry come-ons. The liner notes set the coital mood: "The lights are dim . . . and by chance, it's the maid's night off. The radio plays softly and out of a fragrant haze of perfume, she whispers . . . '*Make love to me.*' So steady the trembling hand, pour the martinis—let your imagination go."

The combination of the eroticism of Russ Garcia and Ned Kronk's song "Go Slow," which Julie called the summation of her style, moving renditions of standards like "The Nearness of You," "Lover Man," and "Alone Together," as well as Bobby Troup's "It's Good to Want You Bad," make the album a full-blown aural lesson in how to please a woman. But few seemed to notice, and *Make Love to Me* was the first of Julie's albums that failed to make the charts.

The striking cover portrait was Julie's first encounter with the Los Angeles photography studio of Garrett-Howard (Murray Garrett and his partner, former Stan Kenton singer Gene Howard). Garrett recalled Julie as "an absolutely gorgeous woman. Her personality and the way she related to people were just incomparable." He felt that her covers had subtly evolved since *Julie Is Her Name*. "When you get an artist like Julie, who is as beautiful as she is talented, it's a challenge to the photographers to try to do something that not only meets *your* standard of photography, but meets *her* standard of performance."

Meanwhile, Liberty Records issued a steady stream of Julie London singles, many of which contained songs unavailable elsewhere. 20th Century Fox had asked her to record the title song for their movie *Boy on a Dolphin*, starring Alan Ladd and Sophia Loren. Although Julie's name is nowhere to be found in the movie's credits, Liberty decided to release the song as a single, accompanied by an alternate take of "Meaning of the Blues." The lack of promotion from the movie gave the atmospheric "Boy on a Dolphin," which featured the overdubbed guitars of Howard Roberts, little chance in the marketplace.

Backed by the studio-based orchestra of Herbert Spencer and Earle Hagen, Julie skipped Gus Kahn's verse in a negligible version of "It Had to Be You," yet the haunting flipside is one of her best obscure recordings. "Dark" was written by a Fort Worth, Texas, college student named Edwin Greines, who said he had Julie in mind during the composition. Greines recalled that the arrangement on the Liberty record was "very similar to my arrangement and feeling, but where I used an organ for color, Liberty used strings, and if I used one instrument, they used a multiple of it." Like "Boy on a Dolphin," this single went nowhere.

The cigarette that Julie so sexily held in her hand on the cover of *About the Blues* was a clue to one of the most significant stages of her career. She often took pains to deny that the gowns, furs, and other frills that made up her glamorous image truly reflected her personality. "I am not my image and I never have been." Yet she rarely failed to eagerly grasp at opportunities to exploit that image in order to keep her name and face in the public consciousness. In 1957 Julie launched her most lucrative endorsement campaign yet when she followed in the smoky trail of ex-husband Jack Webb (who had shilled for Chesterfield and Fatima cigarettes) with a series of distinctive television commercials that would forever make her name synonymous with one product.

Marlboro cigarettes had entered the marketplace in the 1920s and quickly became popular with women and a sophisticated audience. Thirty years later, the brand's market share was in serious decline. Philip Morris, the corporation that owned Marlboro, agreed to advertising changes to reintroduce the brand as a filtered cigarette. Chicago's Leo Burnett Agency signed Julie in an effort to broaden the appeal to men.

She filmed two commercials a year, sensuous thirty-second spots that featured her with an always-anonymous Marlboro Man, often played by veteran character actor Edward Norris. The locations varied—a cozy fireplace, a drive-in restaurant, a swanky nightclub, a recording studio, the deck of a ferry boat—but the actions Julie delivered for her annual $50,000 fee remained consistent. Without much input from the director other than to "give it a lot of warmth," she puffed sexily on her Marlboro, purred the catchy "You get a lot to like . . . filter . . . flavor . . . flip-top box" jingle, reached out to light her companion's cigarette, and settled back to exhale plumes of exotic smoke rings.

A new audience quickly got hooked on the charms of Julie London. Smoking Marlboros was now a masculine pursuit ("Where there's a man, there's a Marlboro"), and a gorgeous woman could be your reward ("Why don't you settle back?") for switching brands. "When Julie sang, men drooled," remarked Burnett creative director Draper Daniels as he watched his company's commercials achieve their stated goal of raising profits at Philip Morris. For Julie her association with Marlboro—lucrative though it was—would eventually prove a double-edged sword.

Julie yearned to plant roots. She spent years thinking about buying a Southern California "dream house" that would reflect *her* tastes. "There was nothing of me in [the other houses]." Yet none of the Beverly Hills or Bel Air properties she looked at could match her dreams of an "early American den and a French Provincial living room." Now, with her lingering feelings of financial insecurity somewhat tempered by recent successes, her plans began to take form. "There was this beautiful place for sale and it was just what I wanted but it was twice too much. Then I thought, why not look up the architect and see if he couldn't build one just like it, for a lot less."

The man responsible for the Beverly Hills house was Paul R. Williams, one of the top residential architects in Southern California. The prolific Williams—nicknamed the "architect to the stars"—had been designing houses for more than two decades, and his refinement and taste were evident in the elegant combination of modern and historical elements in his finished products.

Following a series of meetings at Williams's office on Wilshire Boulevard where Julie described her ideas for the property, an undeveloped lot, filled with scrub but situated on a beautiful knoll in the fashionable Encino neighborhood of Royal Oaks—about five miles west of Julie's current house—was purchased as the site where her dreams of home would become reality. She confessed that she didn't "really need such a huge house, but when I had the plans drawn up I kept remembering the tiny apartment I shared with my parents, and I just had to get a big place."

During the eighteen months it took to clear the site, make numerous design changes, build the structure, and complete the landscaping, Julie was consumed with worry about making enough money to complete the project, which eventually cost $225,000 (about $1.8 million today). She pondered which offers to accept, which to reject, and the impact her decisions would have on her future. She constantly prayed that nothing would happen to negatively affect her career until the house was complete.

The crisis she feared raised its head shortly after work began on the building site. Liberty Records, the company that had brought Julie London to prominence as a singer and that she had almost single-handedly kept afloat since its formation, was on the brink of financial collapse. Rumors circulated that Julie was looking to leave. A rival company, Dot Records, was in discussion with Liberty about a merger. When Dot's accountants examined Liberty's books, they discovered significant, misleading errors in the company's financial reports. The slow distribution of the label's records and the accounting practices of Si Waronker's original partner had left the Liberty president as the sole owner of $800,000 in company debt. In desperation Waronker asked for help and loyalty from his artists. Julie responded with a letter that stated "she would never record with or for anyone" other than Liberty.

Waronker soon declared that his company was not for sale. Although Julie signed a new three-year deal in the spring of 1958—one that presumably paid her more than the $20,000 she had been receiving on an annual basis to date—the contract coincided with a major structural reorganization at the label. While Si Waronker would continue to run the artistic side of Liberty Records, a thirty-one-year-old Arkansas farm boy turned successful record salesman named Al Bennett was brought in as the company's vice president and general manager.

Bennett's job was to get the struggling company back in the black. His answer, although wildly successful, had an immediate impact on Julie London's recording career. During a search through Liberty's unreleased masters, Bennett came across an infectious novelty tune written by Ross Bagdasarian. "Witch Doctor"—released under the songwriter's David Seville pseudonym as a single in April 1958—quickly paid off nearly all of the company's outstanding debts. Eddie Cochran's anthem of teen-age rebellion "Summertime Blues" and another Bagdasarian creation, Alvin and the Chipmunks, sent the company's sales soaring into the stratosphere.

Sensing the direction in which popular music was heading, Bennett, an opinionated, "really strong guy," shifted Liberty's focus over the next few years to a younger audience. It was a trend to which Julie reacted with blunt disdain. Having already declared that she didn't sing rock 'n' roll because she wasn't "that hungry," Bennett—whose listening tastes ran more to "hillbilly and Western records" than to the sultry sounds of Julie London—got another earful when she flatly turned down his request that she record a rock 'n' roll album, an echo of a common refrain from singers whose repertoire was based on the standards.*

---

* That same year the talented yet largely forgotten singer Beverly Kenney, whom Julie praised in a 1957 *Down Beat* interview, performed her self-penned song "I Hate Rock and Roll" on a national television broadcast.

7

Free and Easy

A singer feels, acts and reacts as much as any T-shirted Marlon Brando.

—Julie London to journalist Armand ("Army")
Archerd, 1957

JULIE'S SIXTH ALBUM, released in 1958, was the jazziest of her career thus far. Much of the loose feeling heard in the grooves of *Julie* (originally promoted as *Julie Swings Gently*) was due to the sympathetic relationship the singer had with the record's arranger, Jimmy Rowles, whose subtle, swinging work over the previous decade had made him one of the most in-demand vocal accompanists in the business. For Julie's record the pianist wrote a set of small-band arrangements that successfully moved her away from the usual sultry whisper and into the territory of Billie Holiday, Ella Fitzgerald, and Peggy Lee.

Accompanied by a stellar group of West Coast jazz musicians, including saxophonists Benny Carter, Buddy Collette, and Bud Shank and trumpeters Pete Candoli and Jack Sheldon, Julie gently makes her way through ten standards and swingers, including "Somebody Loves Me," "Midnight Sun," "(Back Home Again in) Indiana," and "Bye Bye Blackbird." Bobby Troup gets her best performances: a clever arrangement of his 1941 hit "Daddy," with Julie playing the gold digger to the hilt, interspersed with out-of-left-field Ray Nance / Stuff Smith–style violin breaks, and "Free and Easy," a relaxed Henry Mancini instrumental from the movie *Rock, Pretty Baby* to which Bobby added lyrics that seem to sum up Julie's new attitude toward life and music.

While *Variety* praised the "hip quality" of Julie's performances and *Billboard* enthused that her "sultry off-beating of 'Daddy' is enough to make any red-blooded deejay rush to his turntables," the album didn't make the charts. Even the cover failed to have a positive effect on sales, although with Julie lounging in an ultramodern high-backed scoop chair, dressed only in a skimpy, baby doll nightie, it was the most provocative come-on yet. (In May 1959 the first Grammy Awards were handed out. Art director Charles Ward was nominated but lost the Best Album Cover award to the creators of the graphics for Frank Sinatra's dramatic *Only the Lonely*.)

If Julie felt positive about the new direction she was taking with her music, she could not have been pleased by what had happened to the movie she had once seen as her first chance to prove herself as a box office draw.

Although *The Great Man* and *Drango* had failed to find an audience, Julie's performances had been noticed by Hollywood executives. Their positive response resulted in an exponential increase in the number of scripts that landed on her doorstep. She had become something of a hot commodity, yet she desperately wanted to maintain a balance between career and personal life. If she agreed to a project, it had to fit carefully around her extensive commitments to recording dates and television appearances, as well as her steadfast reluctance to spend extended time away from home and family.

In April 1957 Julie had accepted an offer from producer Armand Deutsch for a costarring role in an MGM western called *Three Guns*. (The title was changed to *Saddle the Wind* after the wistful song composed for the film by Oscar winners Jay Livingston and Ray Evans.) It was the first time she would be billed as the costar in a major American studio production, so the deal, which included an option for a second movie, paid a relatively low $25,000, an indication of Hollywood's uncertainty about Julie's ability to draw audiences to her movies in the same way she enticed them to buy her albums.

The film's leading men were a study in opposites: Robert Taylor was a rugged, if somewhat stolid, actor who had been under contract to MGM for more than twenty years, while the promising young actor John Cassavetes—in his first project with the studio—had all the strength of youth, as well as a lack of respect for authority. Director Robert Parrish, who had won an Academy Award for his editing work on the 1947 boxing classic *Body and Soul*, was hired to keep the peace.

What really caught Julie's attention was the literate screenplay by Rod Serling, the acclaimed author of the Emmy Award–winning television dramas *Patterns* and *Requiem for a Heavyweight* and future creator and on-screen host of *The Twilight Zone*. In Serling's hands the standard clichés of the Hollywood western were subjected to a penetrating examination of the characters' psyches, including that of dance hall singer Joan Blake, a catalyst in the struggle between the hot-headed Tony Sinclair (Cassavetes) and his even-tempered former gunslinger older brother, Steve (Taylor). The return of one man and his effect on the love triangle, as well as a paragraph about his coming and going "like the wind"—the likely germ of the Livingston and Evans song—are the only things *Saddle the Wind* has in common with the original 1955 *Saturday Evening Post* story by John Cunningham that the movie was based on.

The opportunity was too good to pass up, and the elements seemed to be in place for a successful outcome, even if Julie remained puzzled by her frequent roles in Old West dramas. "Don't breathe it to a soul but I'm scared to death of horses." The eight weeks of shooting took the cast and crew from location work in Colorado's Wet Mountain Valley to studio sets at MGM. From the start, recalled Robert Parrish, there was trouble. "The more wooden [Taylor] got, the more 'Actors Studio' Cassavetes would get, just to annoy him." Cassavetes brought his New York attitude to Colorado and was paranoid about Hollywood.

Character actor Richard Erdman remembered the actor as "a terrific pain in the ass in the beginning." Julie, meanwhile, "was so beautiful it was hard to keep your mind on what you were supposed to be doing."

Taylor was charming, the actress said years later, and his professionalism kept her relaxed in situations where she often felt ill at ease. She wasn't as impressed by the temperamental Cassavetes, who left an indelible impression during the filming of her final scene at MGM. The script called for Julie to slap the actor across the face. Cassavetes responded with an unexpected shove, which knocked the dazed actress into a bunk across the set. Her physical treatment would be joined by an emotional battering from another source.

MGM executives, disappointed by the finished product, demanded rewrites and extensive edits to clarify the relationship of the quarreling brothers. Taylor and Cassavetes returned to the studio in late 1957 to shoot retakes and rear-projection sequences directed by John Sturges. (Julie was unavailable as she was in England shooting another movie; her part was filled by a double who was only seen in long shots.) These reduced the film's running time to a brisk eighty-four minutes and also resulted in the replacement of Jeff Alexander's original score with an equally fine one by Elmer Bernstein.

When *Saddle the Wind* finally opened in March 1958, it was met by shrugs from critics and audiences alike. While the rugged and snow-capped Sangre de Cristo Mountains make a glorious background for a number of sequences, as shot by multiple Academy Award nominee George Folsey (*Seven Brides for Seven Brothers*, 1954), the movie's brief running time left scant room for character development. The result is a sloppy story that leaves Julie with little to do except look good in Helen Rose's period costumes and passively react to the cool Taylor and the crazy Cassavetes.

Even the lonely, haunting title song, a near lullaby once intended to be a "vital facet" of the film, was quickly tossed off with little effect. Julie's only noteworthy moment comes in her reaction to Cassavetes after she sings "Saddle the Wind" to him. While he takes it as an invitation for love, she wants something different, and his kiss painfully reminds her of those she received from the rough-and-tumble men of the saloon. "Gently, Tony. Anything you do for me—do it gently." It's an all-too-brief sequence in which the qualities of tenderness, isolation, and uncertainty displayed in Julie London's recordings are revealed in a big-screen performance.

Although it's implied by the finale that Julie's character goes off into the sunset for a future with Robert Taylor, who had realized that her relationship with his brother was a means of escape rather than love, their characters' connection is unfulfilled since there is nothing in the movie that clarifies their feelings for each other. Screenwriter Rod Serling was blunt about his contribution: "I gave better dialogue to the horses than the actors."

Boxoffice called Julie "surprisingly effective in her few dramatic moments," while *Variety* complimented her for getting "exceptional believability into her part, somewhat hackneyed, as the dance hall girl." Most critics were less kind, including one who deemed her "a pretty cipher with no plausible connection to the rest of the proceedings." Not even Julie's tender performance of "Saddle the Wind" was successful. Paired with Bobby Troup's "I'd Like You for Christmas," a quality song that has never received the attention it deserves, Liberty had released the single during the holiday season of 1957, when the movie had originally been scheduled for release. Without the promotional tie-in, the disc went nowhere.

After good roles and notices in *The Great Man* and *Drango*, Julie's big-screen work on *Saddle the Wind* was bland. Once she completed her work on a movie, she knew that she had no control over the final result. Pondering her options with some trepidation, she and Bobby decided that finding her own scripts and optioning the properties to one of the studios was a good career move. This resulted in the creation of Stalis Productions (the name was a combination of the first names of Stacy and Lisa Webb), which went into negotiations with MGM for a distribution deal for *The Golden Hatchet*, an original screenplay by writer Joe Calvelli.

⸻ ❧ ⸻

Fortunately, a more satisfying movie followed that summer. *Voice in the Mirror*, a compelling drama about alcoholism made under a $40,000, one-picture deal with Universal-International, offered Julie the costarring role opposite Richard Egan, with whom she had shared a brief scene in *Return of the Frontiersman* a decade earlier. (The movie was shot as *This Day Alone* but, as had occurred during the production of *Saddle the Wind*, Julie's singing of the theme song influenced a title change.) The low-budget black-and-white film was under the direction of journeyman Harry Keller, a capable hand who had steered a number of Universal productions during the decade, including *The Unguarded Moment* (1956) with *Voice in the Mirror* screenwriter Larry Marcus. Cinematographer William Daniels had lensed many of Greta Garbo's greatest films and was an Academy Award winner for the gritty police procedural *The Naked City* (1949). Although the subject matter was difficult, Julie was pleased that her sixteen days of filming during August and September of 1957 didn't entail any location work that took her away from home. The streets of downtown Los Angeles, including Bunker Hill, the Lincoln Heights jail—one of the city's main drunk tanks—and a downtown department store on Seventh Street supplied the gritty ambience the picture needed to get its message across.

Julie's character Ellen Burton was "a girl who lives by faith" in her husband, spending most of her energy trying to create a quiet life for him. Jim Burton's (Richard Egan) repeated failures at sobriety put his wife under a constant psychological strain. Unconvinced that his meetings in their apartment with a proto–Alcoholics Anonymous group are proof of his recovery, she's troubled by his actions and scared by the drunks. A nervous breakdown ensues and she pulls a gun on him, saying she'd rather he was dead than continue to drink. Once again the self-doubting actress was certain she couldn't pull off the scene, until the hysterical stream of tears she displayed wouldn't dry up, even after Harry Keller cried "Cut!"

It was the best showcase for her work as an actress since *The Great Man*. The slow-moving yet absorbing drama contains her most fully rounded on-screen performance, one for which she received a number of critical plaudits. *Motion Picture Daily* called her "restrained and effective," while the *Chicago Tribune* said she was "quietly pathetic." The *Boston Globe* praised the movie's emphasis on "sincerity rather than sensationalism." *Variety* called it "hard-hitting" and said that the film benefited from the documentary-style use of real down-and-out locations. If it wasn't up to the level of Billy Wilder's *The Lost Weekend*, "it [stood] firm as a good, small sermon on a large problem." For all those positive qualities, however, the modest picture performed so poorly in its debut week in Los Angeles that Universal scrapped its downbeat advertising emphasis on alcoholism in favor of a more positive—but fruitless—appeal to women.

The title song of *Voice in the Mirror* was the first of Julie's two published writing credits. Although Pete King's moody arrangement of her tune is an effective counterpoint to Bobby Troup's heartfelt, if somewhat awkward, lyrics, the final result is undistinguished. The couple was more pleased that Henry Mancini thought enough of the melody to interweave it throughout his score for the movie. Released as a single with "It's Easy," a humorous tango by fellow Liberty recording star Ross Bagdasarian, it became another in Julie's ongoing string of nonstarters on the charts. In this she wasn't alone: singers of the quality of Rosemary Clooney, Peggy Lee, Doris Day, and Margaret Whiting weren't having any better luck with their singles.

The worlds of music and movies weren't that far apart, Julie thought, and she still saw no reason why she couldn't succeed in both. There was an "inseparable relationship between the two. . . . I go over the words and phrasing, make sure of their meaning and interpretation and then work them over for hours."

That search for the proper feeling was evident on album number seven. *Julie Is Her Name, Volume 2* reached record stores in August 1958 and returned Julie to the guitar-plus-bass format of her debut. Liberty had asked Barney Kessel to provide the arrangements again, but when the label refused to pay him what he thought he deserved for having contributed the unique instrumental backing in 1955, he turned down the gig. His replacement was Howard Roberts, whose guitar sound gave the new album a grittier, funkier groove. Virtuoso double bassist Red Mitchell took over for Ray Leatherwood. (Even the cover photo mimicked the original, although here the décolletage that got everyone talking was covered by the same type of black sweater Julie wore during her debut nightclub performances.)

The album was marketed as a celebration of Julie's third anniversary as a recording artist, and the result showed how she had grown in confidence and was able to put aside—at least in this comfortable setting—some of her fears of recording. Taped over four sessions at Liberty's studios on La Brea Avenue in Hollywood, the twelve tracks are filled with an infectious, subtle swing of loping, relaxed rhythms and tempos. The big-band hit "Hot Toddy" features some fine wordless vocalizing, while upbeat versions of "Too Good to Be True," "Goody Goody," "The One I Love (Belongs to Somebody Else)," and Cole Porter's "What Is This Thing Called Love?" sit side by side with heartfelt ballads like Rodgers and Hart's "Spring Is Here," Irving Berlin's "I Got Lost in His Arms," and the Gershwins' "How Long Has This Been Going On." Most impressive of all is Julie's take on Josef Myrow and Edgar DeLange's "If I'm Lucky," a minor hit for Perry Como in 1946. The recording ranks among her finest for the atmosphere of wistful longing in Julie's voice and her sensitivity to the lyrics, although not nearly as many people took the opportunity to listen, even with Liberty promoting the album as her first to be simultaneously released in stereo and mono versions. (All of the "stereo" releases of her earlier records were rechanneled from the original monophonic tapes.)

Critics and audiences didn't know what to make of *Man of the West* when it premiered in October 1958. To some the film was an excellent portrait of the savagery of the west, while others called it little more than a sadistic gore fest and expressed concern about the effects its brutality might have on audiences.

To Julie the chance to be reunited with Gary Cooper, one of her favorite actors, and to work with the visual stylist Anthony Mann on a literate script by Reginald Rose was hard to resist, even if it was in another western, a genre she never tired of berating. "You stand out in the hot sun for hours at a time . . . the sand blowing in your face and the light reflectors making your eyes squint up. That's for cowboys."

Although movie making in the small, picturesque California town of Sonora was commonplace, the arrival of the 140-member cast and crew of *Man of the West* in February 1958 was still a cause for celebration. For both Julie London and Gary Cooper, it was a return to the site of prior successes: her thriller, *The Red House*, and his Academy Award winner *High Noon*.

The script by Emmy Award–winner Rose (*Ten Angry Men*) was based on *The Border Jumpers*, a 1955 novel by Will C. Brown about a reformed gunman who finds he can never entirely escape his past, no matter how good his intentions. It was a common theme in the work of director Anthony Mann, who came to *Man of the West* with a sterling reputation via his hard-hitting crime dramas of the 1940s (*T-Men* and *Railroaded!*) and westerns of the 1950s (*Winchester '73* and *The Man from Laramie*, both with James Stewart).

After settling in at the local Sonora Inn, eight days were scheduled for filming in the area along the Sierra Railroad Company's right of way, west of the nearby town of Jamestown, on the "Three Spot," an old steam engine maintained solely for use in movies. Heavy snowfall caused delays before the skies cleared and work began. On the first day of shooting, loud noises from the locomotive caused several teams of horses to bolt, and Julie, who was leaning against the back of a stagecoach between scenes, got her skirt tangled in the wheel spokes as the horses took off. Tossed to the ground and dragged along by the horses, she was lucky to escape with minor injuries. Gary Cooper drawled that "women aren't supposed to get the bruises in these westerns."

Julie's dislike for the genre, and her frequent roles as a fallen woman, only intensified thereafter. "Given a choice," she remarked, "I'd rather be fallen in a drawing room than on those plains. . . . Personally, I'm strictly an indoor, sound-stage type. Just about as far as I care to go in this outdoors thing is to sit around the edge of a swimming pool." Frequently at odds with Anthony Mann during the early stages of filming, when she and Cooper repeatedly flubbed their share of lines in a vital sequence where their characters bed down together in a barn, the exasperated director—who had spent four days shooting the scene— exclaimed, "Do it right this time." By the time cast and crew settled in for additional location work at Red Rock Canyon and the Conejo Ranch, actress and director had at least come to a working agreement.

The second-rate Texas-frontier barroom singer Billie Ellis was a woman on a constant search for a better life, one in which she could be more than a road-weary chanteuse doomed to an endless series of appearances before drunken saloon patrons. Julie seemed a natural fit for the role. Described in Brown's novel as a small, blue-eyed, city-bred woman with a "considerable figure" underneath her clothes, Billie—much like Julie—had spent her share of evenings in front of a "mass of smoke-blurred" male faces. Billie's "Girl with the Golden Voice" has an exterior hardness and a flashy beauty that masked an inner loneliness, where "her thoughts are her own, nameless and sad."

In the *Man of the West*, Julie was given the chance to express some of her own loneliness and to translate the wistful, longing qualities of her recordings onto the big screen. The "men I meet all think they have a right to put their hands on me, like it comes with the introduction," Billie tells Link Jones (Cooper). "All those lonely ones, looking for some kind of special thrill. I know what they're gonna say before they say it. Funny part is—inside me—I'm just as lonely as they are."

Billie's clothes parallel her mental deterioration as the downbeat story progresses. Dressed in stage finery in the opening sequences, her outfit implies her status among the upstanding citizens and potential outlaws on the train that leaves Crosscut, Texas, for Fort Worth, carrying Billie, Link, and Link's money. When the train is attacked by a gang of thieves, Billie is left stranded; forced to start walking, she hitches up her skirts and scuffs her fancy shoes before she, Link, and the weak-kneed cardsharp Sam Beasley (Arthur O'Connell) arrive at a supposedly deserted farm.

When the outlaws, led by Link's uncle, the manic Dock Tobin (Lee J. Cobb) see Billie ("Look at the build on her!"), the sadistic nature of these "men of the west" becomes clear. The brutality and realism of the scene that follows is still hard to watch more than fifty years after its creation: in eerie silence, as Coaley (the menacing Jack Lord) threatens to slit Link's throat, Billie is forced to strip down to her petticoat in front of the leering outlaws, a moment luridly publicized in layouts in contemporary men's magazines.

As the movie nears its conclusion, Link discovers that Billie has been raped by Dock Tobin, a scene that left Julie "shaking for days." Link, realizing that the only way he can find peace is to revert to violence, confronts the aging outlaw and shoots him down. (The novel ends with Billie successfully defending herself against the rape and Dock Tobin committing suicide rather than being shot.)

Man of the West ends with Link and Billie presumably headed back to Fort Worth, where he'll return to his family, while Billie says she'll do "what I always do—sing." Yet a version of the script, the shooting schedule, and a behind-the-scenes production photograph reveal sequences that change how the released ending might be viewed, moments in which Billie, although she knows it's wrong, confesses her love for Link and they kiss. These appear to be the scenes that screenwriter Reginald Rose said were cut from the final print due to what he referred to as Julie being "not up to snuff as an actress."

———— ❧ ————

But even a role that was pared down and deprived her character of motivation merited some of the better notices of Julie's career, with the *Los Angeles Times* saying she gave the movie its only "moments of sympathy and pity" and the *Boston Globe* praising her for being the "only bit of beauty." Best of all was the *Hollywood Reporter*, which noted the "heart-tugging fatalism" she brought to the role, an element not often present in this type of genre film. "Miss London's playing makes the woman, for once, all important in a western. As she develops the character you feel that, no matter what the future, this woman never again will hold herself cheaply."

Lamentably, United Artists hated the picture and "dumped it into the grind houses as the top of a double bill," where it had little chance to return its estimated $1.5 million cost. The studio's confusion over how to market *Man of the West* was obvious. Early advertisements for the movie included a prominent blurb that promoted Julie's performance of Bobby Troup's gently loping title song. Negative audience reaction during preview showings resulted in the tune's elimination from the released prints, and the studio suggested that exhibitors "delete all references to the song from publicity and exploitation copy." While the melody is generic and the production clichéd—percussion mimicking the sound of horses' hooves and Julie's vocal drowned in echo—Bobby's lyrics insightfully match Billie's feelings for the laconic Link Jones.

Time has been kind to *Man of the West*: its reputation has steadily improved, and it is now a critical favorite, frequently offered as a significant piece of director Anthony Mann's oeuvre. Indeed it is the best western Julie London ever made, although at the time of its release she referred to it as another example of what troubled her about her big-screen career. "I've agreed to do pictures because they had wonderful scripts, I loved them. . . . But something always seems to happen; they water them down until the thing I loved just isn't there anymore."

Actor Kevin Tighe, who became a friend of Julie's during the years they worked together on the *Emergency!* television series in the 1970s, said he was "always aware of how honest" her singing was. "Even though they dress her in ermine, when she hits the song, it [is] the sensuality of the lyric that guides her through." The contrast between cover image and the contents of an album were never more apparent than on *London by Night*, the singer's ninth LP for the Liberty label.

"Suggestive without going overboard," is how Murray Garrett described his cover photograph, which showed Julie in front of a generic brick wall, one leg thrust forward out of a slit-up-to-there powder-blue strapless dress. Clearly the intention was to depict an upscale lady of the evening, yet the provocative image belies the album's dramatically honest portrait of a woman's path to self-discovery.

Released in December 1958, the sessions for *London by Night* had begun nearly two years earlier, which makes the cohesiveness of the final product—given Liberty's penchant for getting product on the record store shelves quickly—even more remarkable. Abetted by the evocative string-centered arrangements of Pete King, Julie stayed true to the emotions in each of the album's dozen lyrics. Bobby Troup contributed two excellent songs: "Well, Sir," the tale of a brokenhearted barfly sipping her scotch and seltzers (a variation on Billy Barnes's classic "Something Cool"), and "Just the Way I Am," a reflective number that was quite possibly the bluest and saddest he ever brought Julie's way. The touching "In the Middle of a Kiss" showed off the loveliest tones in the singer's voice, while the unexpected rendition of "My Man's Gone Now" from *Porgy and Bess* has an ethereal quality that prevents the listener from lingering too long on the incongruity of singer and song.

The languorous "The Exciting Life" and the intriguing "Pousse Café"—another of Julie's alcohol-laced depictions of failed romance, in which the many-layered drink becomes the equivalent of the emotional partition of a woman's heart and psyche—are sensuality personified. The album's standout song, however, was an anomaly: the sensitive rendition of "Nobody's Heart," a 1942 Rodgers and Hart ballad, was Julie's only studio recording with a solo pianist. Filled with regret and longing, it harks back to the evening when she sang "Little Girl Blue" by the same writers and won Bobby Troup's heart.

Sadly, a fine album was ignored by record buyers, who opted to put the likes of Mitch Miller at the top of the charts. It was a pattern that Julie was becoming accustomed to, although other factors may have influenced the record's fate. *London by Night* was her third LP and sixth overall release of 1958. Was the Julie London market being oversaturated? Or was it perhaps just the natural course of a recording career? There were few singers who could sustain themselves at the heights of popularity.

The February 1959 release of the disastrous *Night of the Quarter Moon* dealt a significant blow to Julie's fragile reputation as an actress. Shot during the previous fall for independent producer Albert Zugsmith, whose diverse filmography spanned science fiction hits like *The Incredible Shrinking Man* (1957) and the troubled production of Orson Welles's *Touch of Evil* (1958), the movie was the first of Julie's $35,000, two-picture deal with MGM. After getting a whiff of the producer's low-market reputation, which became evident as he roamed the set, yelling "We've got to get more sex in this film!" Julie pulled out of her option for a second movie with Zugsmith, *The Beat Generation*, where she was to have played the role of a detective's wife held hostage in her home by a young thug.

If *Night of the Quarter Moon* was ever intended as a serious examination of racial problems in the United States, the final product didn't reflect it. The trite script by Academy Award nominees Frank Davis and Franklin Coen (*A Tree Grows in Brooklyn*, 1946), weak direction by European émigré Hugo Haas, bland cinematography, and generally uninspired performances combine to leave viewers shaking their heads.

The story was loosely based on the sensational Alice Rhinelander case, in which a wealthy New York socialite filed suit to have his marriage to a chambermaid annulled, charging that she had misled him about her racial makeup. (The defendant was acquitted by a jury of her peers in 1925.) As Ginny Nelson, the newlywed wife of a San Francisco society boy whose family objects to the marriage, Julie wore a brunette wig and had her skin darkened to suggest the character's racial origins as a quadroon (i.e., one-quarter black) woman. It's an extremely odd piece of casting, although par for the course with Zugsmith, who filled the movie with his typically oddball collection of actors and nonactors.

Julie's husband was played by twenty-six-year-old John Drew Barrymore, the troubled son of the late John Barrymore and his actress wife Dolores Costello. (Barrymore was also to have been Julie's costar in *The Beat Generation*.) The young actor had just completed another of Zugsmith's exploitation films, *High School Confidential*, which featured Jackie Coogan, Charles Chaplin Jr., and bandleader Ray Anthony, all of whom make brief appearances in *Night of the Quarter Moon*. Rounding out the cast was Agnes Moorehead (as Barrymore's mother), Dean Jones (as his brother), Nat King Cole (as a local nightclub owner), and Marlon Brando's wife, Anna Kashfi.

Given the movie's overall lack of quality, Julie has a few good moments with John Drew Barrymore, who handles his part admirably, and the climactic courtroom moment, when her attorney (James Edwards in one of the film's few respectable performances) tears her dress off her shoulders to reveal her skin color, is suitably effective. On the other hand, the ending, in which Barrymore drops the annulment proceedings and the couple exit the courtroom to an uncertain future, is flat and uninspired and was likely the result of a compromise that the producer made to get the picture into theaters in the racially divided southern United States.

While Julie was singled out for an admirably muted and sincere performance by the *New York Times* and pleasantly surprised the *Los Angeles Times* critic with "hints of emotional depths still to be brought out," these were extremely rare positive responses. The *Chicago Tribune* was damning, calling *Night of the Quarter Moon* "one of the most inept movies . . . ever encountered" and predicting the "total eclipse" of the motion picture industry if there were many more like it. It was such "outrageous bilge," that the *Washington Post* hoped for the deportation of Julie and "everyone connected with this trash." The movie even took a bite out of Julie's singing career: according to the film's pressbook, she was to have recorded the Sammy Cahn and Jimmy Van Heusen title song for commercial release, yet the final print relegates her brief version to the *end* titles, with the consistently more popular Nat King Cole getting the prime slot during the opening shots.

Unfortunately, another movie looming on the horizon would force her big-screen acting career even further downhill.

When Julie arrived at London's Paddington Station on the chilly afternoon of November 12, 1957, she was surprised at the reception she received. Bundled in furs, looking for all the world like a movie star on parade, she stopped to answer questions from reporters and pose for photographs. Could this all be for her? It was a marvelous moment, worlds away from her fruitless escape to Europe just a few years earlier. She had arrived in a celebratory mood. Bobby Troup's latest album, the heartfelt tribute *Here's to My Lady*, had seemingly repaired the damage to the couple's relationship, and he joined Julie's large party—which included her daughters and their governess, Julie's business manager Robert Ginter and his wife, and Caroline Woods (who lived with Julie for a number of years after her 1958 divorce)—on the journey to England aboard the SS *Liberté*.

The press coverage was the work of media-savvy producer Raymond Stross, who had enticed Julie across the Atlantic to play the lead in his movie *A Question of Adultery*, which dealt with the then controversial subject of artificial insemination. The screenplay about a man who files for divorce from his wife, claiming she had committed adultery by being artificially inseminated, seems to have been influenced by *Breach of Marriage*, a 1949 London play based on a number of English and Scottish court cases. The producer had submitted the script to the Production Code Administration (PCA) in the United States, which sought advice from the American Medical Association on the movie's treatment of the subject.

Although *A Question of Adultery* had opened in the United Kingdom in the summer of 1958, Stross's refusal to make the suggested cuts to eliminate "various scenes and lines of dialogue with problems relating to sexual intimacy, questionable comments and over-exposure of cleavage" kept it off American screens until the following spring.The movie was released in the United States without the PCA's certificate of approval, which relegated it to the grindhouse circuit of bottom-basement theaters and drive-ins. Given the impact *A Question of Adultery* had on Julie's future as an actress, it's surprising that she and her manager apparently failed to conduct basic research on Raymond Stross, which would have revealed that the producer had made a name for himself in England with *The Flesh Is Weak*, another low-budget movie about an exploitable subject—prostitution.

In *A Question of Adultery*, Julie played Mary Loring, a former entertainer and the wife of a jealous Grand Prix racecar driver (the bland Anthony Steel). After an automobile crash in which she loses her unborn child and her husband is left impotent, the couple travels to Switzerland, where a doctor impregnates Mary via artificial insemination. Jealous even of an artificial pregnancy, Mark Loring doesn't believe the child is his and files for divorce on the grounds of adultery. Both main characters are almost entirely without personality. Saddled with poor dialogue and an unflattering swept-back hairdo, Julie looked pale and unhappy, and she and her leading man display a startling lack of chemistry. Only the courtroom scenes, buoyed by the appearance of character actor Anton Diffring as a charming ski instructor, are worth watching. The horrendous ending, which fails to take a stand on the issue at hand, seals the movie's fate. (Two different endings had been shot. Catholic countries where artificial insemination was considered immoral, if not illegal, saw the version "in which the birth is ruled to be adulterous.")

Not even the come-ons of the advertising campaign ("This is a picture no man can resist—no woman can afford to miss!") could prevent the disaster that ensued. Greeted with disdain by critics and audiences alike, the (Catholic) National Legion of Decency rated the movie a C (for "Condemned"), based on the "emotional arguments of the sympathetic characters . . . directed toward justifying" artificial insemination. Julie received a few good notices—*Variety* said she brought "grace and charm to her difficult part"—although the negative far outweighed the positive. The *Los Angeles Times* was probably the harshest when it called

Julie the movie's "great weakness . . . her lack of acting ability . . . magnified" by the capable supporting cast.

Liberty's Si Waronker flew in from California to supervise the recording of Bobby's "My Strange Affair," a song written especially for Julie to sing on-screen. Cut at London's IBC Studios in mid-December 1957, the accompaniment by a small group of British musicians, including jazz and classical guitarist Ivor Mairants, guitarist Ike Isaccs, and double bassist Lennie Bush, was heavily influenced by "Cry Me a River." Although slight, "My Strange Affair" is hauntingly effective and was released as the B-side of Julie's sultry rendition of "Come on-a My House," Rosemary Clooney's bouncy number-one hit from 1951. The jokey arrangement of Clooney's version was replaced with a combination of drums, bass, and finger snapping blatantly borrowed from Peggy Lee's recording of "Fever." The subtle sexual undertone of the lyrics seems almost tailor-made for Julie. Clooney's recording is probably the record she's best remembered for; this disc, even though *Cash Box* predicted its success ("jocks are gonna have a field day"), disappeared without a trace.

Two additional tracks from the IBC sessions were paired for what was probably Julie's most obscure single. "The Freshmen" was an innocuous thank-you to Julie and Bobby's friends the Four Freshmen, who had recently recorded "Julie Is Her Name," and was the second—and apparently final—Troup/London songwriting credit. The flip-side, "Tell Me You're Home," a Troup solo credit, is much better. The pleading lyrics ("When you're not here, why try to pretend / The days never start; the nights never end") read like a letter of forgiveness for moments of turmoil in the couple's relationship, and the use of harpsichord and guitar vaguely recalls the Bethlehem demos of 1955. The work of arrangers Dick Reynolds, a former trombonist with trumpeter Ray Anthony's band, and Johnny Mann, whose eponymous vocal group backed many Liberty artists and had its own long run of albums on the label, would appear—often anonymously—on a number of Julie's records through the early 1960s.

When she finally got a look at *A Question of Adultery*, Julie was horrified by what she saw on the screen. Her public image radiated sensuality, yet in private she was a very conservative woman ("the bikini belongs in your own back yard and nowhere else"). Extremely troubled by the explicit direction the movie industry was taking, she said, "It's a funny feeling to be making pictures your own children can't see." (Ironically, *A Question of Adultery* and *Night of the Quarter Moon* were probably Julie's most frequently seen movies, as their subject matter kept both in circulation for years under then titillating titles such as *Infidelity* and *The Color of Her Skin*.)

It took years for her to comprehend the irreparable damage she had done to her career as an actress. Repeatedly denying that she had shot a nude scene for the "continental" version of *Night of the Quarter Moon*, she later called her work in these exploitation pictures something akin to prostitution.* "That's about what it was, to do something that you know was not right or was not well-done to begin with, or maybe is—which is even worse—[a] mediocrity, and still participate, and in the end it's not what you hoped for."

---

* The topless scene was actually done by actress Bobi Byrnes, whose naked torso was also visible in the version of *The Beat Generation* seen outside the United States.

8

The House That Julie Built

We all fail ourselves, don't we?

—Julie London in *The Wonderful Country*, 1959

THE THEME OF LIBERTY RECORDS' promotional campaign for the spring of 1959—"The House That Julie Built"—was an accurate reflection of her status as the label's first star, even as the year she had spent making movies had coincided with the rise of a record-buying public that was increasingly turning away from her type of songs toward pop and rock 'n' roll. As the final year of the decade began, Julie had reached a crossroads. Faced with the task of regaining her standing with music audiences, she had to decide if she should make a return to nightclubs or try to gain more television exposure. Neither prospect was enticing. The combination of her unconquered fear of performing in public and the years that had passed since she'd stepped onto a nightclub stage made her even more nervous than before.

In the end, television seemed a better, less nerve-racking showcase for her talents as singer and actress. Reluctantly, she turned her sights toward the small screen in the hope that the time spent going back and forth to New York to appear on variety shows would result in higher record sales and eventually land her a spot as the host of a regular program of her own.

Garry Moore, Bob Hope, Perry Como, Andy Williams, Dinah Shore, and Pat Boone: Julie appeared on all their popular shows during 1959. She hoped that what audiences—and more important, producers—saw and heard as she traded quips with Hope or sang a duet with Williams was more than a beautiful figure and a sultry personality but a fully rounded entertainer. She also made a second go-round on *What's My Line?*, sporting a panel-stumping hipster accent ("Man, you know, like, I make that scene") and appeared as a last-minute replacement for the McGuire Sisters on NBC's *America Pauses in September* special.

Her most concerted effort to make an impact in the variety show genre was the same network's March broadcast of *Frances Langford Presents*, an hour-long Technicolor combination of two episodes of a proposed syndicated series that had been bankrolled by Langford's millionaire husband and filmed almost two years earlier. Backed by David Rose's orchestra, Julie received a good share of the airtime for a show that was supposed to belong to the star and could take comfort that her songs were among the few entertaining moments of what was otherwise dubbed an "entire mess." Her performance of "Laura" and duets with Bobby on a lyrically rephrased rendition of "Route 66" and with the Four Freshmen on "Now, Baby, Now" paled in comparison to her standout imitation of Judy Garland on "We're Just a Couple of Average Joes." Paired with debonair English actor George Sanders, the comedy number by Bobby and Earl Brent reversed the classic scene in the 1948 musical *Easter Parade* in which Garland and Fred Astaire sang Irving Berlin's "A Couple of Swells" dressed as tramps. Here Julie and Sanders are dressed to the nines while pretending they "don't look down on Rockefeller, / J. P. Morgan or the Astors, / Just because they happen to work for us."

———— ∞ ————

The failure of the Langford project didn't prevent Julie from attempts at another popular and ubiquitous television genre: the crime drama. "If you can work for a couple of years and then get out, you can live on re-runs in years to come." A successful series could have helped offset the ever-growing expenses she was incurring as her lavish house was slowly taking shape, piece by costly piece, on the north slope of the Santa Monica Mountains. It also could have provided the sizable amount of money she needed to raise her two daughters and help support her increasingly incapable parents who, by the spring of 1957, had come to financially rely on Julie after Jack Peck suffered the first in a series of debilitating strokes.

For three months Julie worked on a projected pilot for a weekly series in which her singing would be secondary to a dramatic plot structure. The result was "Maggie Malone," which aired as an episode of *The David Niven Show*, a summer anthology series from Dick Powell's Four Star Productions. She played the title character, a widow who finds adventure and intrigue after she inherits a chic Sunset Strip nightclub from her husband. Between musical numbers Maggie and her business partner, played by film-noir veteran Steve Brodie (*Out of the Past*), confront a racketeer (played by Julie's old friend Stacy Harris) who wants to take over the joint. The clichéd script—a rehash of *Macreedy's Woman*, a failed pilot starring Jane Russell and cowritten by "Maggie Malone" author Richard Carr—spoiled any hope that the program would be picked up for the fall schedule on NBC. Julie's performances of Jimmy Rowles's arrangements of "When Your Lover Has Gone," "Baby, Baby All the Time," and "Let There Be Love" are the show's only redeeming feature. One critic joked that the producers "should have let her sing for the full 30 minutes."

At the age of thirty-two, with a string of financially unsuccessful and largely dissatisfying big-screen appearances behind her, Julie hoped for the best when she boarded a flight to Mexico in October 1958 to begin work as Robert Mitchum's leading lady in *The Wonderful Country*.

Based on the 1952 bestseller by Tom Lea, Julie was cast as Ellen Colton, the lonesome, wayward wife of a US Cavalry major played by Gary Merrill. She falls for Martin Brady (Mitchum), a Texan who fled to Mexico as a boy after shooting his father's murderer and now acts as a hired gunman for a prominent Mexican politician. Robert Parrish, the director of *Saddle the Wind*, had edited the big-screen adaptation of Lea's first novel, *The Brave Bulls*, and asked the writer to pen the screenplay for *The Wonderful Country*. Lea spent six weeks in Hollywood and turned out a script that Mitchum and Parrish liked. It didn't please the financiers at United Artists, who demanded a love interest for Brady, which didn't exist in the novel. Robert Ardrey received screen credit for the final script, although Lea continued to make contributions during the location shooting and had a small role in the film as the town barber.

Shooting began in the old Spanish colonial hill town of San Miguel de Allende, Mexico, and on a set built twenty miles outside Durango, which was meant to replicate old El Paso, Texas. The two-hundred-strong company of cast and crew, with all their equipment and luggage, had traveled more than five hundred miles overnight from Hollywood in two chartered airplanes, five sleeper buses, twelve limousines, and thirty trucks. For Julie the lengthy stay in Mexico, which was extended due to a longer-than-usual rainy season, had its pleasures and its pains.

During the days in Mexico City, between costume fittings and rehearsals, she enjoyed creek-side picnics and toured museums and ancient buildings with daughters Stacy and Lisa. Those carefree moments were interrupted by a recurrence of the flu she had come down with on the flight to Mexico and a close call when she barely escaped injury after a lightning-struck tree fell on her portable dressing room.

As the movie's only significant female cast member, Julie was granted the corner suite in Durango's only hotel. It was quickly apparent that the Mexico Courts was not the "crème de la crème" of properties. Thankfully, the room had windows large enough to provide "relief from the choking stink" of the outdoor toilets nearby. The water and the food were another concern. Mitchum advised everyone to drink a lot of tequila, which didn't prevent Julie and other members of the cast and crew from coming down with food poisoning.

More dangerous to her peace of mind was the wild and wooly town of Durango itself, "full of bars and hookers," according to actor Anthony Caruso, who played a small role in the movie. The atmosphere was catnip to rough-and-ready actors like Mitchum and Charles McGraw, who would "rather be down at the bar getting drunk than getting laid." Mitchum "was awful on those sets sometimes," recalled Tom Lea. "He'd talk bad, very, very, obscene." Julie bluntly called Mitchum "a creep" who walked into her trailer when she was changing clothes. "Get out of here!" she yelled. Mitchum responded, "Nah, I think I'll sit and watch the view!"

Julie flew back to Los Angeles in mid-December, ambivalent about the entire experience. It was "one of the best times" she'd ever had, but it left her feeling guilty about many of the locals in Durango who were "so badly off when you're doing so well." She was exhausted and worried. Not even the more than $70,000 she was making per picture in 1958 (equal to over $600,000 today) could soothe her bleak feelings about the movies she had made over the past few years.

———— ✸ ————

Julie had never "ventured an opinion" or "ever talked to anybody" about acting during her first five years in the movie business. Already discouraged by the experience of making *The Wonderful Country*, she was devastated following her first look at the final product. "All my lovely big screen shots were gone—every last one of them." She lamented that if all her movie footage over the past fifteen years was put together, "there still wouldn't be enough to add up to one presentable part."

The poor response to early previews—which may have included a purported vocal duet between Julie and her leading man—had pushed the United Artists release of the movie from summer to fall 1959. Not even Julie's East Coast promotional trip, the popularity of Robert Mitchum, or efforts to highlight baseball star Satchel Paige's participation to black audiences via ads in *Ebony* and *Jet* could help sell *The Wonderful Country*. Tom Lea blamed Mitchum—who was also one of the movie's producers—for distorting the picture; director Robert Parrish's widow, Kathie, attributed the choppiness of the final product to Mitchum's unwillingness to fight for a better version.

The combination of the laid-back Mitchum and the equally laconic Julie London may have seemed like a winning idea during preproduction, but there is no spark in their scenes together. While there are moments when Julie is able to express some of her character's self-deception, loneliness, and inner pain ("I'm always betrayed by hope"), the removal of a number of her scenes from the released film leave her character with little motivation for her actions. One scene with Gary Merrill, which corresponds to an important section of the novel that explains Ellen Colton's relationship with her husband, would have given audiences a sense of why she would be attracted to Mitchum's gunfighter character.

The Wonderful Country looks and sounds good, largely due to the cinematography of Floyd Crosby (*High Noon*) and the brooding score by Alex North, although Mitchum appears uninterested throughout the entire slow-moving picture. Reviews praised the atmosphere while criticizing the meandering script, which "like so many of today's pictures," strayed "into side-story paths [that] are not too well integrated into the main story." Even with her lack of screen time, Julie was lauded for "being immensely appealing without having a single really sexy scene."

By 1959 Julie had hoped that "something would happen to take away rock and roll." That something hadn't occurred, and the new music had become an unstoppable force and an increasingly large part of the catalog at Liberty Records. "Must Be Catchin'"—from the pen of singer/songwriter Ray Stanley, known for his work with Eddie Cochran, one of Liberty's new big sellers to the teenage market—was Julie's first, tentative attempt to dip her toes into the style. (According to the liner notes on the 1996 European compact-disc compilation *Swing Me an Old Song*, the bass player on "Must Be Catchin'" was Cochran himself, although this attribution is unverified.) For all her resistance, the result is a delightful, albeit largely unknown record. Arranged once again for a trio of bass, drums, and finger snaps in the manner of "Fever," Julie growls her way through Stanley's hipster lyrics to no avail. Young audiences weren't buying it, and her old fans were apathetic.

Alternatively, Julie enjoyed the popular folk-music sound of acts like the Kingston Trio, whose run of top-selling albums was a clear influence on her next album, the delightfully corny *Swing Me an Old Song*. Recorded over three days in late April and early May of 1959 and arranged by pianist Jimmy Rowles for a small jazz combo, the album breathed "new life into many of the more faded sentiments, a feat made all the more pleasant by her commendable sense of humor." (The album—plugged by *Cash Box* as "the swingin'est London yet"—was initially advertised under the title *Julie—the 90s Jazz*.) The laughter extended to the cover—in fact, two variations on the same cover for the stereo and mono releases—where Julie, dressed in a skintight one-piece black bathing suit, gets the once-over from a mustachioed man in an old-fashioned striped bathing suit.

Julie's relaxed performances of the swinging adaptation of Robert Burns's eighteenth-century poem "Comin' Thru the Rye," the vaudeville hit "How Come You Do Me Like You Do," the cute "Be My Little Baby Bumble Bee" (with Jack Sheldon on a buzzing, muted trumpet), and the classic "Darktown Strutters' Ball" (here retitled "Downtown Strutters' Ball" to remove the dated racial reference in the original) are due, in large part, to her childhood familiarity with the material. Yet it isn't all familiar and cozy: the innocently salacious "Row, Row, Row" (clearly *not* the children's nursery rhyme) goes from Dixieland to modern jazz in two and a half minutes, and Stephen Foster's classic minstrel song "Old Folks at Home" wanders from an unaccompanied, heavily echoed vocal to an eerie chorus, from swinging piano to brass and reeds, before concluding on a hushed instrumental tag.

Her second LP of the year, and the tenth of her career, was a significant departure from the sound of her recent recordings. The jazz combos of *Julie* and *Swing Me an Old Song* and the back-to-basics combination of the second *Julie Is Her Name* album were replaced by the lush arrangements of composer and pianist André Previn for *Your Number Please*. *Cash Box* called the album a "well-conceived session of superior music" and praised the singer's "breathless, languid, sensuous interpretations" of songs associated with popular male vocalists from Nat King Cole ("When I Fall in Love") to the Four Freshmen ("It's a Blue World"). Previn's film-scoring skills, honed through his work at MGM during the decade, are on full display in his confident use of the large string section—particularly on a ghostly "Angel Eyes"—but the slow tempos tend toward the soporific. Only the opening track, a laid-back yet swinging run through "Makin' Whoopee," breaks the spell.*

Another provocative cover designed to catch the eye of record buyers showed Julie posed in bed, one breast nearly tumbling out of her flimsy nightgown, a telephone held to one ear as if she'd been caught in the midst of a bedtime conversation with a lover. Neither the cover nor the release of "Makin' Whoopee" as a single helped to land *Your Number Please* on the album charts, a fate equaled by a pointless, decade-ending remake of "Cry Me a River." Produced by classical violinist Felix Slatkin, who had joined Liberty Records as an A&R executive in 1959, and perhaps released as a reaction to a new recording of the song by Janice Harper on the Capitol label, which reached the lower rungs of the singles charts, Julie's sparse original was drowned out by dramatic strings, tinkling cocktail piano, and a wordless choral accompaniment.

Julie's on-again, off-again relationship with Bobby Troup had been the stuff of gossip columns for years. No resolution seemed visible on the horizon. Not even a telegram sending him forty kisses from Mexico for his fortieth birthday, which had him jumping on an airplane for Mazatlan to spend one night with Julie during the filming of *The Wonderful Country*, could settle the matter in a mutually agreeable manner. Many reasons can be cited for the delay, chief among them Julie's

---

* It was a busy year for Previn. His adaptation of George Gershwin's score for Samuel Goldwyn's movie of *Porgy and Bess* won him his second Academy Award, his soundtrack work for MGM's *Gigi* gave him his first Grammy, and he released three jazz albums for Los Angeles–based Contemporary Records. Perhaps he can be forgiven for his largely by-the-numbers work on *Your Number Please*.

unease over the effect remarriage would have on her finances. Marrying Bobby would mean the end of her alimony payments from Jack Webb, money she had relied on to raise her children, maintain her lifestyle, and complete the construction and furnishing of the costly Encino house.

Personal issues held up the marriage as well. After Julie's divorce from Jack Webb, she had lived with her daughters while Bobby, whose divorce from his first wife became final in August of 1955, rented a series of single man's apartments in Los Angeles. The proprieties of the day meant that the couple spent much of their time apart, and while this allowed them a sense of independence, it kept them from having the concentrated moments they needed to hash out their differences. One of the things that especially angered Julie was Bobby's seeming inability to completely separate himself emotionally from his ex-wife. While she certainly gave him credit for wanting to remain close to his daughters—Jack Webb had a lot to learn from Bobby on that score—she had difficulty comprehending how he could visit Cynthia and the girls on an almost daily basis and really commit himself to a relationship and a family with her. Had Cynthia become the shadow woman of Arthur Hamilton's song, with Julie in the role of the woman asking her to "let all of him belong to me"?

Despite all this, as the end of the 1950s approached and their excitement grew during visits to the construction site in Royal Oaks ("The upstairs master bedroom [is] going to be a knock-out—big enough for a queen which you is!" Bobby wrote on the back of a photograph he took of the half-finished structure) the couple became closer. It was, after all, a house built for a large family.

Invitations went to many of Julie's and Bobby's friends asking them to help celebrate the opening of the house at a lavish, black-tie New Year's Eve party. As Julie dealt with the myriad major and minor details involved in entertaining the first visitors to 16074 Royal Oak Road, she was struck by a severe bout of bronchial pneumonia and the resulting 104-degree fever put her under a doctor's care. The prospect of Julie being able to host such a lavish party seemed increasingly unlikely as the calendar turned to December 31.

After the occupancy permit for the house was delivered, Bobby made a spur-of-the-moment decision. Why not make it a double celebration by finally getting married? Julie complained that she was sick and didn't look her best. Bobby was adamant, as he always had been. She wasn't getting away from him again. "Not this time!"

Late in the day on New Year's Eve, Bobby dragged the weakened Julie—disguised in dark glasses and a plain outfit—out of the house for a quick drive to the Burbank courthouse, where they obtained a marriage license. As they exited the building, they avoided the photographers who had been alerted to the developments. Bobby sidestepped their questions, saying that their "marriage has been postponed so many times we feel like we've almost become a laughing stock." Back at the house, only a few friends and relatives were in attendance when the ceremony was performed by a Los Angeles Superior Court judge, and the groom presented his bride with a crown-shaped, five-carat diamond ring.

The legion of guests began to arrive shortly thereafter. The movie and television industry was represented by the likes of Bob Hope, Gary Cooper, Dick Powell, John Cassavetes, Edmond O'Brien, George Montgomery, and José Ferrer, while Nat King Cole, Russ Garcia, Henry Mancini, Jimmy Rowles, Pete King, André Previn, Rosemary Clooney, and members of the Four Freshmen stood in for the music side of the newlyweds' careers. (Among those who sent regrets was Johnny Mercer, who later wrote Julie to express his congratulations that Bobby had finally gotten her.) It was too much for Julie to take. The stress of the move from Ethel Avenue, preparing for the huge party, the unexpected wedding, and the endless congratulations from each and every guest sent her reeling. Raucous toasts to the new decade rang in her ears as she retreated up the spiral staircase to the second-floor master bedroom, where she spent her first night as Mrs. Bobby Troup in a sickbed.

9

Julie at Home

I'm not one for going out of town too much.

—Julie London, 1962 Liberty Records interview disc

"THE THING THAT MOVED HER SO—that got to her center—was jazz, both instrumental and vocal," recalled songwriter Arthur Hamilton. She'd ask her friends, "'What is everybody doing on Thursday night? Come on by at nine o'clock and we'll start singing at twelve,' and [we'd] sing until five in the morning." The only thing she asked for was the "chance to sing at two or three o'clock in the morning," moments that had their origins in Julie's childhood memories of hearing Jo Peck and her friends singing together around the house.

Members of the jazzy vocal quartet the Four Freshmen were frequent attendees at Julie's parties, where so much alcohol flowed, one of them joked, that her guests wouldn't be sitting *on* the piano, they'd be *under* it. It was Julie's hospitality and warmth—an enticing aura of late-night relaxation and good times that "made everyone feel welcome"—that remained fresh in the memories of the musicians who parked their cars in the broad driveway of her new home on a January afternoon in 1960.

Guitarist Al Viola walked up the broad brick steps, crossed the wide porch, and rang the doorbell. With him was vibraphonist Emil Richards, who had only recently moved to Los Angeles after spending four years on the East Coast as a member of the George Shearing Quintet. Julie opened one of the eight-foot-high double doors and ushered the pair into the huge oblong foyer covered with a black-and-white checkerboard pattern. After she hugged and kissed Viola, he introduced Richards, who was surprised when she hugged and kissed him too. "Welcome!" she smiled. "Have a drink and something to eat before we start!"

Don Bagley was a veteran of Stan Kenton's orchestra during the bandleader's string-laden Innovations in Modern Music period (1950–1954). In an interview with writer Bill Reed, the bassist recalled the warm feeling of immediately being treated like he was part of Julie's family. He soon became an integral part of her musical entourage. The small group of talented musicians was rounded out by pianist Jimmy Rowles and the versatile drummer Earl Palmer, whose discography included early hits by Fats Domino ("The Fat Man") and Little Richard ("Tutti Frutti" and "The Girl Can't Help It").

Julie was ecstatic when Bobby had suggested that the large, acoustically perfect all-purpose room of their new house would be the perfect venue to make her next album. Getting studio-quality sound from a remote recording wasn't an easy task in 1960, however, and Liberty brought in expert engineer John Kraus from Capitol Records to create the proper audio separation for the microphones in the carpeted and draped space. All Julie needed was a little liquid lubrication, the right key, and the proper tempo to set the mood. "We talked a little and played a little," said Don Bagley, "and took a dinner break. There was no time pressure, unlike most studio recording sessions." On some of the takes, Julie sang live; others were laid down instrumentally for her to work with at a later date.

At over sixty-three hundred square feet, the lavish six-bedroom, six-bathroom hilltop dream house stunned everyone. Its Georgian exterior featured stately columns flanking a courtyard entrance. Guests gasped in astonishment at the nineteenth-century marble fireplace mantels that Julie had imported from France. A dramatically curved staircase led upstairs to a French Regency master suite that covered the entire second floor. Julie's collection of designer gowns was housed in a sizable walk-in dressing room, and she relaxed in a large, sunken bathtub finished in terrazzo. Downstairs, the oversized (forty feet by forty feet) family room—familiarly known as "Julie's room"—was paneled in wood, with a vaulted, beamed ceiling, built-in bookcases, a huge used-brick fireplace with a built-in broiler, and an always fully stocked wet bar.

French doors led out to the patio, where everyone relaxed before taking a swim in the king-size, piano-shaped pool. The state-of-the-art sound system in the family room provided music not only in the house but also to the patio and pool through thirty-six-inch-diameter speakers built into the exterior of the building. The breathtaking view encompassed much of the San Fernando Valley. The entire package was a testimony to Julie's wish to make the house something that reflected her personality. Eschewing an interior designer, she and Bobby furnished the house themselves with an eclectic assortment of pieces. Julie's longings for comfort and security were fulfilled. She and her new family could enjoy the good life.

Sympathetic musicians always helped ease Julie's nerves. She was so relaxed during the recordings, released as *Julie at Home*, that at times a smile is audible in her voice, and she surely got a kick out of the irony of singing "Give Me the Simple Life" while gazing around her magnificent new abode. At this moment in her life, Julie was as much the mistress of her musical world as she was the mistress of 16074 Royal Oak Road. The love between Julie and her musician friends was mutual, and the sessions continued, as Jimmy Rowles wrote in his liner notes for the album, until "everyone was happy with the results." From the first piano and vibraphone notes of Cole Porter's "You'd Be So Nice to Come Home To" to the final guitar chord on "Everything Happens to Me," *Julie at Home* showed off the Julie London her friends knew. Even the cover said domesticity. Rather than the familiar sultry outfit, Julie is demurely dressed in a turtleneck sweater while relaxing in front of a roaring fireplace.

Punctuated by the subtle solos of Rowles, Richards, Viola, and Bob Flanigan of the Four Freshmen, who dropped in for a visit on the second night of recording and got his trombone out from its case to join in on a couple of songs, the soft cushion of sound was the ideal setting for swinging sensuality. In addition Julie and Al Viola recalled their *Lonely Girl* duets with two songs taped after most of the other musicians had left. If the "intimate, warm feeling" of the disc wasn't widely noticed by the record-buying public, the men who made *Julie at Home* remembered the experience with pleasure. Emil Richards recalled that Julie "was so excited to have all these fine musicians playing for her. She kept mentioning it over and over. She wished she could take us on the road with her, and said she couldn't wait to do another album with us."

Julie's new house was built for a star. But her career was beginning to show some cracks in its facade. She had spent much of the past two years accepting and completing project after project—records, movies, television—in order to afford building and furnishing the Encino house, but her dual life as singer and actress had reached a plateau. Five years after her unexpectedly successful return to show business, she found herself wondering where to turn next.

While Julie enjoyed working with top jazz musicians to make some very successful records, nearly every movie she had made since her return to acting had been a box office failure; that fact, coupled with the unhappiness of some studio executives regarding her blunt, negative comments about the industry, left her on the outside just when she most needed to be part of the conversation. When her new agents at William Morris could only land her a supporting role in *The 3rd Voice*, a low-budget thriller shot at 20th Century Fox in the fall of 1959, her fears seemed to have been confirmed.

For all her concerns, however, the movie, based on the 1958 novel *All the Way* by the prolific crime novelist Charles Williams, turned out to be a good little picture, and Julie had a juicy part in it. *The 3rd Voice* was the fourth feature from writer/director/coproducer Hubert Cornfield, whose previous efforts included the low-budget film noirs *Sudden Danger* (1955) and *Plunder Road* (1957). Cornfield said his goal as a filmmaker was to "insure the excitement of the spectator every ticking second that goes by," and he was successful in getting many impressive moments into the brief seventy-nine minutes of *The 3rd Voice*. Many of the best moments involved the alternately cocky and nervous performance of leading man Edmond O'Brien as the unnamed protagonist who is hired to kill and impersonate a wealthy businessman in a bold scheme to get hold of his money.

If Julie's role as Corey Scott ("the type of girl who picks up men") didn't give her much screen time, it was critical to the plot and displayed her sexuality to an extent not seen in movies since *The Red House*. It was a glimpse of the potential she had as an actress when offered the right combination of elements. With Julie outfitted in slinky, low-cut dresses, she and O'Brien make the most of their scenes together, and newspapers had a field day with publicity pictures of the moment when his character deliberately dumped a glass of champagne down her cleavage. The writers noted that several takes were "necessary" in order to find the proper angle to show her breasts getting doused.

Julie's recollections of making the movie focused on its poor ending. "The studio was dissatisfied" after a screening, and the female lead, Laraine Day (costar of the Dr. Kildare series for MGM), "had decamped, so I was in that day and I dubbed her scream. I can't see that scene without laughing a bit." *The 3rd Voice* opened in early 1960 and moved sporadically across the country, typically as half of a double bill. Julie merited positive critical responses, with the *Independent Exhibitors Film Bulletin* praising her "strong dramatic ability," while the *Los Angeles*

Times noted that her performance "to a degree justifies the faith in her acting ability held by her supporters in the early days of her career."

Harrison's Reports called the movie "vividly acted, smartly produced and first-rate." The *New York Times* said it was "complex and eerily fascinating," while *Variety* dubbed it "a superior exploitation film." The strong work of the director and actors was complemented by excellent black-and-white CinemaScope photography by Academy Award–winner Ernest Haller (*Gone with the Wind*), who had shot the rich colors of *Man of the West*, and a great jazz score by Johnny Mandel—his second, following the groundbreaking *I Want to Live* for director Robert Wise in 1958. Despite these elements and the generally positive reviews, *The 3rd Voice* garnered little box office success, did nothing to stop the downward spiral of Julie's movie career, and remains largely forgotten.

Although Julie's days as a leading lady in movies had seemingly reached an end, her name still appeared in gossip columns and Hollywood trade paper tidbits about potential big-screen projects. These included *The Virginius Affair*, a drama with Alan Ladd set in nineteenth-century South America; *The End Is Known*, a Hitchcock-style thriller for director Ida Lupino, for which Bobby Troup was to have written the score; and *Don't Come Back Without It*, adapted from Gael Greene's book about the life of a young female reporter dealing with male chauvinism in the newspaper business.

The only movie in which Julie had any personal interest was a proposed biopic of the glamorous nineteenth-century English actress— and early endorser of commercial products—Lillie Langtry. *The Gilded Lily*, with a screenplay by Paul King and Joe Scott (Academy Award nominees for the original story of the 1959 comedy *Operation Petticoat*) was to have been directed by José Ferrer and made by Julie's production company Stalis for release by United Artists. "Both José and I have had performances ruined by poor judgement in the front office or lousy editing. So we just decided that we would be bosses ourselves. If we make lousy pictures, then we have no one to blame but ourselves." Her performance as a dipsomaniac singer in *The Great Man* remained her best on-screen work; no director since Ferrer had been as successful in helping her to translate the alluring yet distant image on her album covers into a solid, believable acting performance. But as with most Hollywood projects, *The Gilded Lily* died in development, and it became increasingly clear to Julie that her future as a performer was not on the big screen. (The idea flickered to life again the following year, when producer David Susskind tried—unsuccessfully—to bring the biopic to television.)

Many actors in Hollywood looked down their noses at television as being the last refuge for a sputtering career. Unable to move beyond the status of a second-level leading lady, and without a profitable movie star image to protect, Julie's decision to pursue small-screen roles was economic rather than artistic. Over the next two years, she would become a familiar face on all three American television networks in lucrative guest appearances that ranged from hit shows like the classic western *Rawhide* to flops like the crime drama *Dan Raven*.

Her initial, tentative step into the waters of series television had taken place in November 1959 with an episode of ABC's *Adventures in Paradise*. Based on ideas by bestselling author James A. Michener (*Tales of the South Pacific*), the show's star was Gardner McKay, whose character finds intrigue and romance while sailing the South Pacific on his schooner *Tiki*. Although "Mission to Manila" was standard television action fare of the period, Julie comes off well as the sultry singer Dalisay Lynch. Her performances of "If I'm Lucky" and "The Show Must Go On," a late-night lament Bobby Troup wrote for the episode, are the show's highlights.

Julie disliked "playing second fiddle to a horse," but it was back to the crinoline petticoats of the Old West for NBC's *Laramie* and CBS's *Rawhide*, which aired ten days apart from one another in September 1960. The hit western *Laramie* starred John Smith and Julie's future *Emergency!* costar Robert Fuller as the operators of a stagecoach stop in

1870s Wyoming Territory. Well directed by veteran western specialist Lesley Selander, Julie appeared as the mysterious June Brown in "Queen of Diamonds," the first episode of the show's second season. She is sympathetic yet determined in her scenes opposite Claude Akins as her former-lawman husband and in her scenes as a tough cookie dealing cards in the local saloon. (Although she once helped another gambler turn $60 into $10,000 at a blackjack table in Las Vegas, Julie was usually a terrible cardplayer who "could eat up her salary in two nights.")

The season premiere of the even more popular *Rawhide*, "Incident at Rojo Canyon," featured Julie as Anne Danvers, a poor relation to her saloon-singer role in *Man of the West*, who joined the cattle drovers, including a young Clint Eastwood, on a search for her father. Eastwood, a devoted jazz fan, said Julie was the sultriest of the many actresses he worked with during his years on the show. "Between rehearsals, we spent most of our time discussing our favorite musicians. . . . I really appreciated the little concerts she gave us." The only notable aspect of the show was that it marked the first joint acting appearance of Julie and her husband. Otherwise the flat script doesn't allow for much of a dramatic arc, which leaves her limited to batting her eyelashes at series lead Eric Fleming. Even her songs—a rendition of the traditional English ballad "Greensleeves" and the forgettable "Perfect Love"—are perfunctory.

The new NBC mystery series *Michael Shayne* starred Richard Denning as the Miami Beach private investigator created by prolific mystery writer Brett Halliday. As the sexy Anita Rogell in the October 1960 episode "Die Like a Dog," Julie got away from the dusty western soundstage and into modern clothes. The plot has Shayne looking into the mysterious deaths of Anita's elderly, wealthy husband and her spinster sister-in-law's dog; both had died after eating creamed chicken Anita had fixed. (Dog-loving Julie probably cringed at this plotline.)

Her final television appearance of 1960 was one of the final episodes of the short-lived NBC show *Dan Raven*. In a poor time slot opposite *Rawhide*, it was already on the cancellation list by the time "Tinge of Red" was broadcast in mid-December. As June Carey, another nightclub singer, Julie was the victim of blackmail by a Hollywood scandal magazine that threatened to reveal her alleged Communist ties. Skip Homeier as the title character, a police lieutenant working the Sunset Strip beat, cleared her name by the time the credits rolled around.

Julie also continued her appearances on popular television variety shows during 1960, hoping that her performances, as uncomfortable as she often found them, would help sell records. Fans of Red Skelton and Steve Allen got an opportunity to see her in January and February, respectively, while Dave Garroway, the host of the early morning *Today* show, featured her in his nighttime November special *Dave's Place*. Julie often bemoaned the fact that she, like many female performers, was frequently judged for her outward appearance rather than her work. Sharp viewers who tuned in to see her on an episode of the *Chevy Show* on May 15, 1960, might have caught the irony of Julie singing the slinky "You'd Be So Nice to Come Home To" as part of a Carl Reiner sketch about the difference between reality and dreams.

Julie's twelfth album was tentatively entitled *Miss-ty London*, an all-too-obvious take on *The Misty Miss [June] Christy*. Fortunately, better heads prevailed; the resulting selection of late-night moods became *Around Midnight* and featured one of her most memorable visual representations. It showed Julie as the hands of a clock, shapely legs clothed in tight-fitting gold capri pants pointing to the hour of twelve. (The concept was the idea of artist Leo Monahan of Pate/Francis & Associates, a graphic design firm that later merged with Garrett-Howard to become Studio Five.) Julie "understood the commercial value of the thought involved" in creating her record covers, said photographer Murray Garrett. Unlike some performers who objected to his more outlandish ideas, Julie was always cooperative.

Arranger Dick Reynolds brought a myriad of stylish elements to *Around Midnight*—swooping strings, blaring trumpets and trombones, trilling flutes, mournful oboes, and the occasional choral vocal background (his best-known work was with the Four Freshmen). From big-band swing ("You and the Night and the Music") to gentle blues ("The Party's Over"), from the bass-driven Bobby Troup number "Lonely Night in Paris" to dramatic renditions of "Black Coffee" and "Don't Smoke in Bed," the album is a fine example of the varied aspects of Julie London's unique performing personality. A nice pairing of the drowsy "In the Wee Small Hours of the Morning" and "Time for Lovers," a nonalbum track by songwriter Harold Rustigian (who became a prominent record company executive under the name Russ Regan) was her only single released during 1960. Its failure to reach the charts was yet another sign that her label had not found a suitable way to promote her records in the changing music scene.

It had been more than three years since Julie had done anything more than a one-off singing engagement. Her only live performances after the 1956 shows at the New Frontier were a 1958 American Cancer Society benefit in Puerto Rico and an impromptu appearance with Bobby Troup's trio at the Sacramento Jazz Festival the following year. So when she accepted a last-minute offer from Harrah's in Lake Tahoe to replace the Mills Brothers as headliner Dennis Day's opening act for a two-week run in April 1960, her fears of performing before audiences began all over again. With little time to prepare a set list or arrangements, she was still greeted with lusty applause from the opening-night crowd in the South Shore Room when she entered the room to a refrain of Bobby's "Julie Is Her Name" before launching into a sultry version of "Sunday Blues."

The high altitude in the Sierra Nevada Mountains started to affect Day's voice in the middle of the first evening's second show, and he bowed out of the engagement with laryngitis the following night. All Julie had hoped to do was get through the run without making a fool of herself; now she had unexpectedly become the headliner. While her fans were happy to hear her sing "Cry Me a River" again and the gig paid well, it was another tough experience. If performing in front of a live audience made her so nervous, why had she accepted the offer in the first place? Julie sighed and said perhaps it was to prove to herself that she could, but equally important was her husband's constant encouragement. "Bobby . . . keeps telling me that if I sing before people often enough I'll learn to relax." Once again she vowed to quit the nightclub circuit.

The newlyweds had been prevented from taking a honeymoon due to Julie's illness at the time of the wedding, so she and Bobby were overjoyed when Brazilian billionaire playboy and jazz fan Jorge Guinle invited them to attend Carnival in Rio de Janeiro in late February of 1960. After gathering their passports and luggage, they boarded a Real Lockheed L-1049 Super Constellation airliner for South America. Greeted by their host amid showers of confetti and serenaded by local musicians as they disembarked, the days in Rio and São Paulo that followed were a welcome relief, and photographers captured the happy couple indulging in the raucous Carnival festivities and soaking up the sun at the hotel pool. Julie's visit went over so well that local entrepreneurs paid her ten million Brazilian cruzeiros ($50,000) to return in September. She attended a dinner in her honor with Brazilian president Juscelino Kubitschek, made television appearances, and did a three-day series of concerts at the Golden Room of the Copacabana Palace. One of her accompanists was the fine guitarist Herb Ellis, formerly of the Oscar Peterson Trio, who had been working with Bobby as a member of his trio at clubs around Los Angeles.

The first signs of desperation from both the singer and her record label became visible in 1961. Even if Liberty was loath to call her new album the dawn of a "new" Julie London in its promotional material, the short hairdo she displayed on the cover of *Send for Me* was the visual equivalent to the stylistic changes in the grooves. Jimmy Rowles returned, but the off-beat, swinging arrangements he had created for *Julie* and *Swing Me an Old Song* were replaced by something akin to a Ray Charles rhythm-and-blues record.

Bones Howe, who recorded the album's backing tracks, recalled the liquor-filled studio atmosphere. "[Julie and Bobby] came in, armed with bottles of Scotch and soda and all kinds of stuff, and drank their way through the session!" Julie and Jimmy Rowles frequently put their heads together before the tapes rolled. "She'd sort of sing along in the booth, and say, 'Yeah, that's gonna be okay. I can reach the low or high notes.'" When everyone was satisfied with a take they moved on.

The few songs done in a comfortable late-night tempo—Mary Lou Williams's "What's Your Story, Morning Glory" and the Jimmy McHugh and Dorothy Fields classic "I Must Have That Man"—are excellent, but little joy can be found from the majority of the album. The raucous horns, honking saxophones, and bluesy guitar might have been fine for another singer, but it's often hard to take here, particularly when a jarring glee club–style vocal chorus is added to cover Julie's lack of vocal power on the hard-sell shouters. (A single of the strange title track—a number-six hit for Nat King Cole in 1957—with an unidentified male voice manically responding to Julie's, snuck onto store shelves at the same time as the album. Unsurprisingly, it never entered the charts.)

Liberty marketed *Send for Me* as an audio version of Elizabeth Taylor's Oscar-winning role as a prostitute in the film version of *BUtterfield 8*, right down to the brass headboard positioned behind a bare-shouldered Julie on the cover. It was the best thing about an album that did nothing for her record sales but, oddly, planted a seed that would soon flower in much-stronger soil.

A pair of singles released during the first half of 1961 showed how effective Julie could be with good material and how easily she slipped into mediocrity. The first was "Sanctuary," an Alex North–composed theme (lyrics by Marilyn Keith and Alan Bergman) from the eponymous 20th Century Fox movie with Lee Remick and Yves Montand. Disc jockeys quickly flipped the record to "Every Chance I Get," another up-tempo tune from songwriter Ray Stanley, whose "Must Be Catchin'" Julie had recorded so effectively two years earlier. Arranged and conducted by Dick Reynolds, "Every Chance I Get" begins as another

"Fever"-like combination of bass and drums before expanding into a swinging blues. The husky, throaty performance of "Sanctuary" is augmented by a moody tenor saxophone that embodies the sticky Southern heat of the William Faulkner works that formed the basis of the movie.

Producer Clyde Otis and arranger/conductor Belford Hendricks had been responsible for hits by vocalists Brook Benton, Dinah Washington, and Sarah Vaughan. Liberty had hired Otis away from Mercury Records, hoping that he could repeat his success with their stable of artists. Julie's disc with the duo—"My Darling, My Darling," from Frank Loesser's hit Broadway musical *Where's Charley?*, and "My Love, My Love," a top-ten hit for Joni James—is the nadir of her career, five minutes of bland and unconvincing pablum. She sounds infinitely bored by the whole thing. (Otis was Liberty's East Coast A&R man, so it's probable that Julie overdubbed her vocals to backing tracks done in New York.) Better results were had from four unreleased tracks: a cute duet with Bobby Troup on the 1944 hit "Candy," a remake of Bobby's "Tell Me You're Home," the Eddie Beal/Joe Greene song "Softly," and "Then I'll Be Tired of You" by Arthur Schwartz and Yip Harburg.

Whatever Julie Wants, released in August 1961, provided a welcome return to more comfortable—and pleasing—territory. Vocally and visually, the record riffs on the now familiar trope of the singer as gold digger. A revised version of Bobby Troup's "Daddy" is an obvious example, with the lyricist adding a San Juan vacation and "charge accounts / at Saks' for large amounts" to the lady's original requests. (Julie gives out an audible "bump and grind" in a version of the song released on the 1991 *Time for Love* compilation.) When she returned to live performances shortly after the release of the album, "Daddy" became a nightly highlight. During every show Julie looked out into the audience for the loudest man she could find—preferably one not accompanied by his wife—and dropped into his lap to purr the song in his ear. To no one's surprise, he would almost immediately grow silent. If she made the mistake of picking out a quiet man, she was certain to feel his hands pawing her.

A knowing humor is audible in renditions of Cole Porter's "My Heart Belongs to Daddy," "Love for Sale," and "Always True to You in My Fashion," all properly detached from a real passion for anything but a good bargain. Relaxed yet swinging versions of "Take Back Your Mink" from *Guys and Dolls* and "Diamonds Are a Girl's Best Friend" from *Gentlemen Prefer Blondes* are paeans to the luxury goods pictured on the album's satirical cover photograph. (*Whatever Julie Wants* lacks any arranger credit, but at least one song—"Do It Again"—was the work of Dick Reynolds.)

Julie was "not only a great talent," recalled Murray Garrett, "she was also a great subject." The cover of *Whatever Julie Wants* is typically sexy yet also reveals her eager willingness to playfully mock her own image. All the little details that mark a prototypical gold digger are evident: a fur coat—artfully slipping down to reveal bare shoulders and cleavage—$750,000 worth of sparkling diamonds, stacks of bank notes, scattered stock certificates, and an as-yet-unopened bottle of sparkling wine. But Julie doesn't show a typical come-hither look; rather it's a blasé stare that matches the weariness embodied in the album's final song, Allan Roberts and Doris Fisher's "Tired."

Records continued to take a backseat to television appearances during 1961, but her simmering anger about being typecast was evident in a *TV Guide* interview. Most television producers, Julie lamented, couldn't see beyond a woman's measurements, and if they "go beyond a certain point, they figure she can't possibly act." "Slight she might be," commented one wag, "but where it counts she's got what Venus had."

This theory was proven once again as she largely went through the motions in episodes of three action-adventure shows. "Suitable for Framing," an early January episode of the ABC series *Hong Kong*, saw Julie lip-synching to her recordings of "If I'm Lucky" and "Blue Moon" in between moments when she helps series star Rod Taylor clear himself from a murder charge. In "Good-bye, Griff," an April episode of *Checkmate* on CBS, she played an ambitious magazine editor saddled with a jealous ex-convict husband (Harry Guardino) who becomes a murder suspect when a death threat is made against her publisher (Simon Oakland). Both shows are routine, although Julie's role in *Checkmate* at least gave her the opportunity to ultimately be revealed as the scheming villain of the piece.

She summed up her work in the November 26 episode of the short-lived ABC series *Follow the Sun* as nothing more than getting knocked "around a little bit. I managed a couple of bruises." In "Night Song," Julie played a "far-out nightingale" who takes refuge as a waitress in a Manila coffee shop to hide from the Chicago gangster, played by veteran tough guy Lawrence Tierney, who had manufactured her career. The teleplay by Harold Jack Bloom was generic, and Julie couldn't understand why writers constantly depicted musicians as "kooks, clowns, and dope fiends. In almost every show about musicians, there's some way-out nut who gets up to bleat, 'I'd just die if I couldn't blow my horn.'" The only happy moments of the otherwise bland hour were—as usual—her musical performances of small-group arrangements of "Comin' Thru the Rye" and "Let There Be Love." The process of acting and the final results were frustrating, and Julie lamented that all she really wanted was "what every other girl in this town wants—a really good script."

These small-screen appearances typically offered little more than a nice paycheck. It was the rare producer who thought about casting Julie London without expecting her to sing. "There just aren't many good scripts for women, and I'm not the one they send them to." Producer Louis F. Edelman, who hired her for a straight acting role in "Night Visitor," a January 1961 episode of Barbara Stanwyck's eponymous NBC anthology series, was an exception. The initially intriguing teleplay is spoiled by an unsatisfactory conclusion, but Julie turns in a fine performance, cast against type as a money-crazed weirdo who schemes with her butler husband (Michael Ansara) to rob a wealthy woman (Stanwyck).

The opportunity to work alongside the older actress was important to Julie, who called the Hollywood legend "one of the finest people" she'd ever met. Now in her early fifties, Stanwyck had watched as her own movie roles diminished during the preceding decade, and like Loretta Young before her, she had moved to television to keep her career afloat. Julie similarly sensed that time was taking away her big-screen opportunities. She hoped to be able to follow the same career path. The pair shared many character traits: mistrustful of compliments, they were leery of adulation, responded bluntly to questions, and were conservative in their feelings about gender roles. Julie was a man's woman in a man's world. She had little time for women who tried to act otherwise. "The way for a woman to detract from her femininity is to do masculine things unattractively."

Julie received $10,000 for appearing on the January 1961 broadcast of the splashy *Gershwin Years* special on CBS (approximately $80,000 today) but joked that "NOTHING is too much when you consider how shaky and nervous I get over doing these shows!" If two of her numbers (including the silly "Tum on and Tiss Me" from one of Gershwin's early revues) are throwaways, a simple and affecting "The Man I Love" and a sultry "How Long Has This Been Going On" struck the right note with critics who had previously given her variety show appearances a thumbs down. "She manages to achieve some very sound and striking effects, while maintaining that husky, languid air that seems to say, 'Move your pillow closer, honey.'"

She traveled to New York in April for her third and final mystery guest appearance on *What's My Line?* and once again stumped the panel, disguising her familiar voice with a series of grunts. Dual appearances on the *Garry Moore Show* were bookended by a return to Bob Hope's NBC variety show in May, which gave Julie a rare opportunity to display her lighthearted side. A sweet, relaxed duet with Hope and two playful cocker spaniel puppies on "Two Sleepy People" showed that she was also capable of conquering her fear of television.

There was nothing Julie liked more than to be home, basking in the Southern California sunshine, particularly now that she had an ultra-luxurious place in which to lie by the pool and watch the kids swim. But following the success of her September 1960 performances in Brazil and the lack of any solid footing as an actress, she was finding it harder to resist the offers from promoters around the country looking to book her into their nightclubs. It was particularly hard to say no when she was offered good sums of money for relatively brief engagements.

After sharing the bill with Dave Brubeck, the Four Freshmen, and Wes Montgomery at the Detroit Jazz Festival on August 5, 1961, Julie's name was at the top of the marquee two days later when she opened at Mister Kelly's, the noted jazz venue on Chicago's North Side. Backed by a local rhythm section led by pianist Dick Marx—who worked with Julie again when he became an arranger on the Marlboro advertising account—and bassist Johnny Frigo, Julie and Bobby brought two musicians with them from California, each of whom added his own individual brand of musical and personal enjoyment to the successful three weeks.

The distinctive sound of twenty-nine-year-old Jack Sheldon had been audible on a number of Julie's records, and the native Floridian had earned a reputation as one of the top trumpeters on the West Coast. His alternately lyrical and fiery playing had graced many late 1950s recordings by alto saxophonist Art Pepper, pianist/arranger Marty Paich, and the short-lived hard-bop outfit led by bassist Curtis Counce. As part of a group of wits who surrounded the controversial comedian Lenny Bruce, he had developed a similarly outrageous sense of humor, and his wicked, frequently off-color stories were catnip to the like-minded Julie, who was more than willing to cede the spotlight to him. "During her show," Sheldon recalled, "she'd take a break and we'd talk back and forth and I'd get laughs."

Guitarist John Gray (born 1924) was raised in Oklahoma and arrived in California from Chicago in the late 1950s. Brought to Julie and Bobby's attention by Herb Ellis, the guitarist had a unique style of simultaneously using a pick and three fingers to produce distinctive block chords. Bobby Troup called John Gray "the best accompanist Julie ever had."

Sheldon and Gray were also ideal off-stage companions for the couple. They joined Julie and Bobby to form a hard-drinking quartet that kept the party going long after audiences had experienced what a critic from *Variety* called Julie's "room-hushing sense of intimacy."

The performances that followed the run at Mister Kelly's weren't as notable. Although Julie pleased the males in an audience of fifteen thousand at the Hollywood Bowl in late September, when she appeared as the special guest star at the third annual Stereo at the Bowl concert, her style wasn't suited for such a large venue. Frequently overwhelmed by the sound of Dick Reynolds's orchestra, she was also criticized for being "not always as accurate in pitch as [she] might have been." A nine-day run at the five-hundred-seat Club Russo in Middletown, Connecticut, and a two-week engagement at the plush Cabaret Riviera in Kansas City, Missouri, were filled with breezy performances "wrapped up in glamor," yet the singer didn't find the venues to be so glamorous. "Some of the people running those places scare me . . . . I get the feeling sometimes that if the show doesn't start right at 8:30 I'll get machine-gunned."

⊶∞∞⊷

The December 1961 release of *The George Raft Story* marked Julie's return to the big screen after an absence of more than a year. The highly fictionalized biopic of the tough-guy actor of the 1930s, directed by Joseph M. Newman (*This Island Earth*, 1955), was—by coincidence— made for Allied Artists, the direct successor to the Poverty Row studio Monogram. She had come full circle to where she had begun her acting career eighteen years earlier.

Filmed during the preceding summer, producer Ben Schwalb arranged to bring George Raft himself to the set during production in the hopes that some of the actor's Hollywood star power would rub off on his cast, yet everyone—particularly the notoriously lead-footed

Julie—seemed ill at ease when the aging hoofer tried to teach them a few rudimentary steps.

Ray Danton, coming off his successful portrayal of the title role in director Budd Boetticher's *The Rise and Fall of Legs Diamond* for Warner Bros., was cast as Raft. Although Julie couldn't match her leading man in their dance sequence—choreographer Alex Romero was reduced to having her remain largely stationary while the smoothly handsome actor circled around her—her singing is radiant in a fine performance of the standard "What Can I Say After I Say I'm Sorry?" (Studio publicity indicated that she was to sing several other songs in the film, including a Jeff Alexander original titled "Lonesome Guy, Lonesome Gal.") She's far too curvy to accurately portray a torch-queen flapper of the 1920s, yet she sparkles physically—certainly in comparison to Jayne Mansfield, who played another of the many women who came into Raft's orbit. Mansfield was seven years younger than Julie yet looked at least a decade older.

The bland picture was poorly received and Julie's brief role in it ignored, as most of the critics harped on the clichéd screenplay. The *Los Angeles Times* characterized the movie's actresses as "more-or-less shadowy figures." *Variety* agreed, calling each of the five women's segments "a shallow . . . inconclusive interlude." Decades later, *The George Raft Story* had become so forgettable to Julie London that she couldn't even recall its name.

10

There'll Be
Some Changes Made

You are talking to the original Miss Type-casting.

—Julie London to journalist Donald Freeman, 1963

T HE GEORGE RAFT STORY was Julie London's swan song as a movie actress. (Her appearance in 1968's *The Helicopter Spies*, one of a number of theatrical features that combined episodes of the popular television series *The Man from U.N.C.L.E.*, was only released overseas.) In less than two decades, she had gone from small roles as a studio contract player to leading-lady roles opposite some of Hollywood's greatest stars; from seeing her name above a movie's title to secondary parts that gave her little time to make an impression.

The unlikely success of "Cry Me a River" and *Julie Is Her Name* had led some people to think that Julie could duplicate it on the screen. While she *was* one of the few women who had simultaneous extended success as a singer and an actress, she couldn't sustain the two careers the way, for example, Doris Day had. There were many factors—and many of them of Julie's own making—why this was so.

It's obvious from the barest glimpse at her movie performances that the confidence she projected in the safety of the studio for her three-minute recorded dramas and the pure sexual effect she had on audiences who saw her in person were sorely missing from the majority of her dramatic roles. A clearly visible, palpable sense of unease prevented her from holding an audience's attention, and her inability to create a distinct image on-screen—whether as femme fatale or serious actress—dealt a series of fatal blows to her acting career.

Money and power played their parts as well. None of the movies in which she had a significant role was a notable box office success, a fact that influenced any producer who might have considered her for his movie. Her complaints about the types of roles she received and her helplessness at the hands of producers and studio executives were not uncommon. Most actors during Julie's time had little say over the final cut of a movie, and since she never found a film project that she could control, she remained at the mercy of others who had little compunction about treating her as just another cookie-cutter actress.

Finally, excluding the early period of her career when she had no option but to accept the roles offered to her under her contracts with Universal and Warner Bros., the movies she chose to make in the years following her return to show business were often bland, repetitive, and forgettable. All actors take roles for the money; Julie rarely seemed able to take a role for any other reason.

Even with all these factors, however, there *are* moments when— amid the longueurs—she was able to express the unfulfilled longings of her characters, longings that had their equal in the quiet yearning frequently heard in her recordings. These moments of searching for something ultimately unreachable can be found in her performances as the saloon singer torn between rival brothers in *Saddle the Wind*; as another saloon singer, looking for a good man's love, in *Man of the West*; as the forlorn wife of an army major in *The Wonderful Country*; as the unrepentant Southern belle in *Drango*; and as the sympathetic wife of an alcoholic in *Voice in the Mirror*. Her ten minutes on-screen as the drunken band singer in José Ferrer's *The Great Man* was the best glimpse of what she was capable of as an actress. To the end of her life, it remained the only big-screen work of which she was ever truly proud.

The movie business during the early 1960s slowly began to mirror changes in contemporary society. New, more daring films touched on controversial subjects and featured risqué dialogue and scenes. Julie was having none of it. She still wanted "good, wholesome scripts"; instead, she insisted, "everything they send me is pornographic." She was particularly appalled by a script that was presented to her by actor and comedian Tommy Noonan (*Gentlemen Prefer Blondes*), who opened for her during a February 1962 engagement at the sophisticated Chi Chi supper club in Palm Springs. Noonan was searching for an actress to star opposite him in a low-budget comedy he was also producing. Julie's fear of finding herself in another exploitation picture that would further tarnish her reputation led her to turn down the offer. Had she made *The Baby Maker*, as the script was then called, it might have been the end of her entire career; as it was, the retitled *Promises! Promises!* became a dire episode in the fading career of another sex symbol of the 1950s, Jayne Mansfield, whose nude scenes were the first by a mainstream actress in an American movie.

Instead Julie concentrated on home and family. The announcement that she and Bobby Troup were expecting their first child together in the spring of 1962 meant the cancellation of a welcome return to Mister Kelly's in Chicago. The Palm Springs performances went on as planned, although some critics asked why a woman in her condition was still onstage. There was nothing to worry about. The *Variety* critic who attended opening night at the Chi Chi reported that Julie was "in consummate good taste," with a "fluffy white ostrich boa" draped over her arms, so "that even an obstetrician couldn't tell, is she or isn't she?"

Sophisticated Lady, an album of weary reminiscence, was released in February 1962. It was a logical successor to *Whatever Julie Wants*, which had concluded with an exclamation of weariness with the gold-digger facade. The new record was one of the few of her own that Julie ever praised, albeit in typically faint fashion: "Yeah, that's okay. That'll do." Her positive response may have been due to her close relationship with Si

Waronker, who is credited for the last time as Julie's producer on this LP. The lush, soaring strings on *Sophisticated Lady* might be a reflection of his belief that this type of large-scale recording was soon going to be very rare at the label he had founded.

The results are mixed. Julie's sighing rendition of Duke Ellington's title song, Cole Porter's witty "Make It Another Old Fashioned Please," and the *très sophistiqué* "When the World Was Young" are reminders that the soul of the hard-hearted gal of *Whatever Julie Wants* remained within the aging body of the *Sophisticated Lady.* "Spring Can Really Hang You Up the Most," by the talented team of composer Tommy Wolf and lyricist Fran Landesman, stands out for Julie's laid-back hipness, while the mournful "If I Should Lose You" benefits from a gentle Latin flavor.

Unfortunately, the balance of the tracks lack character, which even affected the album's cover design. The photograph of Julie in a blue strapless floor-length gown is as attractive as ever, yet the overall design is bland and appears to have been cobbled together without much thought. It was a precursor of things to come.

Like the movies, popular music in the first years of the 1960s was undergoing cataclysmic changes, although a broad spectrum of artists and styles—from the new sounds of Motown and Bob Dylan to the Grammy Award–winning records of Henry Mancini and Judy Garland—remained. It appeared there was still room for a myriad of musical tastes, including buyers of records by the now thirty-five-year-old Julie London, whose discs were still selling at a respectable rate, albeit without the impact they had once had. It was time for something new.

"My father," recalled Lenny Waronker, "felt [Julie] needed a change, and Snuff was interested." So when Julie entered the studios at United Recording on Sunset Boulevard in March of 1962 to begin work on her sixteenth album, a new face looked out at her through the glass of the control room window: Thomas "Snuff" Garrett, a twenty-two-year-old wunderkind from the outskirts of Dallas, Texas. Waronker called Snuff "an astute listener [who] may have had—for pure pop stuff (and other things too)—a sharper ear than Phil Spector." Garrett was hired as a member of Liberty's promotional team, yet Si Waronker "would always call him when he was working on projects, and say 'You have any song ideas?' What [Waronker] found out was that, every time he would send him a song, whether he used it or not, it was something that was valid and good, and after awhile, he just said 'Come sit in my office for six months, come to every session, keep your mouth shut, and I'm going to make you into a producer.' And that's what happened!"

Snuff's ability to hear a song and find exactly the right singer to record it quickly turned into numerous successful records for Liberty in the first two years of the 1960s, including hits like "Dreamin'" and "You're Sixteen" by rockabilly singer Johnny Burnette and "Devil or Angel" and "Take Good Care of My Baby" by Bobby Vee. Garrett was sure he could replicate that success with the woman who was still synonymous with the label. When Si Waronker brought him over to Julie and Bobby's house, the trio "instantly liked each other." Snuff remembered that "Si handed the baton over to me before he left [Liberty]. Julie and Bobby were special to him. He put us together, and Julie and Bobby and I always got along great."

Snuff Garrett's philosophy of hit making was total artistic control. "Give me a good melody and set of lyrics and I'll do the rest." His musical knowledge and instincts ran deep. From his teenage days listening to the thousands of 78-rpm records he rescued from a dumpster at a radio station in Dallas ("I listened to both sides of every record") to his friendship with fellow Texan Buddy Holly, with whom he shared a passion for Ray Charles ("I remember when 'Swanee River Rock' came out. . . . We must have played it a thousand times over the next two or three days."), he knew what sounded good—both on vinyl and coming out of a small portable AM radio.

Although they came from vastly different musical worlds, Julie and Snuff quickly developed an easy, humor-filled working relationship. "We both liked late-night sessions. We didn't know what daytime [was]. Julie was quick. We always had a good time." She also "knew her way around [the studio]. I'd have her there with me when I was doing the backing tracks, just in case she wanted it a little higher, a little lower, or whatever. I always wanted to make sure we didn't come out with a track that we couldn't use. That gave us a lot of time to joke and kid around, and get serious for a few minutes about the songs."

Snuff appeared at just the right time in Julie's career. She was in need of a hit; he was a hit maker. The process of making records in the Snuff Garrett way was relatively simple. Julie took the acetates of the backing tracks home with her and lived with them for a week or two, wearing out the grooves, until she was ready to return to the studio to lay down her vocals. At that point, "our time was our own," said Garrett. Buzz Cason, Garrett's assistant at Liberty from 1962 to 1964, remembered Julie as being the most impressive of all the singers he worked with when it came to recording her overdubs. She was a real perfectionist, had a terrific ear and near-perfect recall of what had previously been taped, down to the specific reel that had the best takes or words that could be cut into the master tape.

Love Letters, the first result of the Julie London / Snuff Garrett partnership, came out in April 1962. Each track on the disc had been a hit for another artist, but unfortunately *Love Letters* wasn't any sort of hit for Julie. In fact from the choice of songs to the cover design, it was a distinct disappointment. The only standout tracks are a moving rendition of the Gershwins' "I Loves You, Porgy," featuring Barney Kessel on guitar—an arrangement Julie admitted she stole from Nina Simone's 1959 hit recording (right down to phrasing the title as "I Love [*sic*] You, Porgy")—and a cute version of "Never on Sunday." The bulk of the album is made up of largely uninspired attempts at good songs ("All the Way," "Hey There," and "The Second Time Around") or outright failures ("And That Reminds Me," "Fascination," and "Broken Hearted Melody").

The appearance on *Love Letters* of Julie's finger-snapping rendition of "Come on-a My House" was, remembered Snuff Garrett, probably the idea of his friend and the song's cowriter, Ross Bagdasarian. "I'm sure [Ross] told me, 'Julie recorded that a couple years ago,' and I said, 'Well, fuck, that'll kind of save [some time in putting the album together].'" (The version included on the album was slightly extended from the original single by delaying the entrance of the bass.)

The blandness of the record was matched by the utter failure of the cover. The usual sexy or glamorous photograph was replaced by a simple line drawing on the front and a decidedly plain black-and-white image on the reverse. Snuff Garrett admitted he "didn't like that [drawing] worth a shit, but I was just starting with her, so I didn't interfere. Later, I would have said, 'Give me a fuckin' picture of Jules!'" (This nickname was often used by Julie's close friends.)

Some of these changes in Julie's recordings and image were likely due to the changes that had occurred at Liberty. In seven years the company had grown from a small-time independent label grossing less than $200,000 annually to a significant player in the industry. This was initially due, in no small part, to Julie's records, particularly *Julie Is Her Name* and "Cry Me a River." She remained a major figure on the roster, yet by the end of 1961, the majority of Liberty's income was derived from records that appealed to the growing audience of teenagers: hit novelty songs by Alvin and the Chipmunks and Patience and Prudence, rock 'n' roll smashes by Eddie Cochran and Johnny Burnette, and a myriad of pop successes by Bobby Vee, Timi Yuro, and Gene McDaniels.

Yet even with this success, trouble was looming on the horizon. A year earlier Liberty had gone public, and when the first stockholders' report was issued, the numbers revealed that the company's gross income of nearly $5.9 million represented a measly 2 percent increase over the prior year (it had been a whopping 69 percent in the prior year), while net income had declined 35 percent. The stress of managing the expanding company, which had opened satellite offices in New York and Nashville, had taken its toll on Si Waronker, and the day-to-day management of the label had been left in the hands of the more commercially minded Al Bennett.

A solution to the financial problems appeared in the form of an unlikely merger with Avnet, a New York–based electronics corporation. In April 1962 an exchange of stock, with Liberty's shares equal to approximately 60 percent of Avnet's, was agreed upon. The deal seemed like a good one for all concerned: Avnet could expand its business and Liberty, which had previously relied on other companies to release its product in Europe, now had the financial resources to issue records under its own imprint via an agreement with EMI.

For Julie business matters were happily ignored in favor of joyous family pleasures. On April 30, 1962, she gave birth to a five-pound, four-ounce daughter named Kelly—whose name commemorated her conception in Chicago during the engagement at Mister Kelly's the previous year—at Valley Presbyterian Hospital in Van Nuys, California. Julie doted on the new addition, and the time she spent with Kelly was so precious that when she returned to concert engagements that summer, the baby and her nanny became a regular part of Julie's entourage.

Bobby, Jack Sheldon, John Gray, former Patti Page drummer Kenny Hume, and twenty-five-year-old bass player Chuck Berghofer rehearsed for the upcoming tour in the living room of the Encino house. The bassist had been part of Bobby Troup's rhythm section for some time, but this was Chuck Berghofer's first musical encounter with Julie London. He laughingly recalled the vivid impression she made. She "was about the most beautiful woman I saw in my life, with big eyes and a beautiful face. Then she'd open her mouth and the foulest stuff would come out of it! It was amazing!"

Rehearsals were informal. "It was mainly just her getting it right herself, that was the big thing," Berghofer said. "The band, we didn't have to do much; it was straight ahead." But the singer never seemed comfortable with her own performance. She "always figured she was awful and shouldn't be doing this."

An appearance at the sort of venue she despised—the Vapors Club, a front for a notorious gambling den in Hot Springs, Arkansas—was relieved by a second engagement at Mister Kelly's in Chicago. The entire family, including her older daughters Stacy and Lisa, enjoyed the luxuries of the largest apartment at the recently opened Carriage House. Julie's performances of songs about a "wistful, pleading kind of love" went over well, and audiences were attentive. "They loved her because she was so beautiful," Berghofer remembered. "She'd sit up there and there was a glow around her. She had a great appearance and a very soft kind of voice, very laid back; there was nothing tense about her." Julie and Jack Sheldon were always good for a laugh that often broke up the band more than it did the audience. "He'd do his little bit and she'd kind of follow it up. Jack could be pretty risqué too all the time, so they got into some of that stuff. They bounced off each other for sure."

Liberty Records' Chicago branch office opened during Julie's run at Mister Kelly's, and with Snuff Garrett in town, it seemed like a good opportunity to book some studio time and lay down the basic tracks for a new album. Taking a cue from a lachrymose new ballad that examined a crumbling relationship through the blurry lens of the bottom of a pebbled drink glass, the group gathered at Universal Recording after finishing their night's work at the club for three early morning sessions. (Additional tracks were recorded back in Los Angeles, where Pete King—hired specifically by Snuff Garrett because of his work with Jackie Gleason—added a luscious string section to the mix.)

The result was *Love on the Rocks*, a top-notch record that, in its emphasis on the sorrows and the heartaches of love, echoes Frank Sinatra's striking trilogy of melancholy, late-1950s Capitol concept albums arranged by Gordon Jenkins and Nelson Riddle: *Only the Lonely, No One Cares*, and *Where Are You?* As Sinatra's interpretations of lyrics had deepened as he aged, so too had Julie's, with the years giving her breathless sadness an additional depth that allowed her to reach the "spine and [the] soul" of a song. Even the album's cover photo riffs on elements of the Sinatra sleeves: cigarette in hand, Julie stares blankly into space (*Where Are You?*), one elbow leaning on a white piano (Sinatra leans on the bar on the cover of *No One Cares*) while behind her is a pastel-colored painting of clown masks (*Only the Lonely*).

The album's twelve tracks run the gamut of emotions, from the heartbreak of "How Did He Look?" and "Guess Who I Saw Today," the mournfulness of "A Cottage for Sale" and "Willow Weep for Me," the bitterness of Bobby Troup's "Where Did the Gentleman Go," and finally to the poignant "End of a Love Affair" set to a gentle Latin beat. *Love on the Rocks* concludes with two of the most memorable recordings of Julie's career. Her interpretation of "The Man That Got Away," the Harold Arlen / Ira Gershwin late-night lament from the 1954 film musical *A Star Is Born*, was the last song recorded during the Chicago sessions. She hadn't gotten much sleep as the tape machine rolled. "I was so tired . . . that I did the whole thing with my eyes closed," she said a few years later. Rather than bullying the song into submission, as Judy Garland had, Julie stays in a minor mood throughout, and her enunciation conjures new shades of meaning in Gershwin's lyrics, a point confirmed by songwriter Hugh Martin, who worked on the film. "The Man That Got Away" was *intended* to be performed the way Julie did it, but Garland insisted on her own, typically brash, interpretation.

Julie was well versed in the tonic effects of alcohol, and the end of the day signaled the beginning of what author Bernard DeVoto referred to as "The Hour." According to the dark title song by Francine Forest and Bob Hughes, love was a heady cocktail:

> *A dash of lost dreams,*
> *Then stir with regret.*
> *Shake well and pour,*
> *Then drink and forget.*

Rarely had the depth of the singer's understanding of lyrics been so exquisitely realized, and Pete King's sympathetic string arrangements provide the perfect cushion for her voice, while trumpeter Jack Sheldon interjects a complementary lyrical tone on his horn. Snuff Garrett admitted he was still "trying to feel [his] way" with Julie, yet he expected *Love on the Rocks* to be an important addition to her catalog. "Really excited" about trying to create another "Cry Me a River" with the title song, Snuff and Julie easily erase memories of the negligible *Love Letters*, even if *Love on the Rocks* failed to make an impression in the marketplace.

Snuff's hopes for commercial success with Julie London would be realized with a song saved from the Chicago sessions, which became the A-side of her only 1962 single. Two years earlier, during the visit with Bobby to Brazil during Carnival, Julie had been introduced to the languid melodies of the bossa nova. She counted herself among the many fans of the Brazilian torch singer Maysa, whose albums she had carried home with her. The bossa nova had exploded across the world in the wake of the hit instrumental version of Antonio Carlos Jobim's "Desafinado" by tenor saxophonist Stan Getz and guitarist Charlie Byrd. Now vocalist Jon Hendricks had added English-language lyrics to the song, and Snuff was certain that "Slightly Out of Tune," if he could persuade Julie to record it, would also be a chart-making single.

Julie never showed much patience when asked to learn new material, and exhausted after finishing her nightly gig at Mister Kelly's, it took hours to get just the last verse down successfully and dozens of takes to complete the entire recording. Yet Snuff was right: "Slightly Out of Tune" became Julie's first song to make the singles charts since "Cry Me a River." Although it didn't crack the top one hundred, the success of the record encouraged his belief that he was taking Julie in the right direction, one that Liberty president Al Bennett likened to following the whims of the average record buyer, who "doesn't know a round note from a flat note [but] just knows he likes something or doesn't."

The personal success of *Love on the Rocks* and her recent concert appearances had raised Julie's profile as a singer at the same time as her television work began to suffer. The long-running series of Marlboro commercials that had brought her equal measures of money, recognition, and derision cost her three lucrative guest shots on the variety shows of Ed Sullivan, Garry Moore, and Andy Williams because their sponsors associated her with a rival product. It was ridiculous, Julie laughed, that people would switch "from one brand to another just because I was using it." Her 1962 variety show appearances were limited to a March episode of Jack Benny's show on CBS and a December segment of ABC's *Voice of Firestone*, where she performed in front of an eight-member vocal group and a sixty-piece orchestra.

As the calendar turned to 1963, the joyous news that Julie was going to have twins was coupled with the obvious fact that she and Bobby needed another source of income to replenish their bank accounts. Although Julie's LP sales were reported to still be in the neighborhood of two million copies annually, her movie career had collapsed and her television bookings had sharply declined. Bobby's songwriting and recording career had stagnated; his last album, *Bobby Troup and His Stars of Jazz* (RCA Victor), had come out four years earlier and flopped. He was bitter about the way his style of song had disappeared in the flood of the "just dreadful" sounds of rock 'n' roll. (Although he saw financial rewards from the Rolling Stones' cover of "Route 66," the first track on their smash-hit debut album, Bobby never ceased to disparage the new sounds. By contrast Julie was more forgiving; as her recordings through the remainder of the decade indicate, she was able to find qualities in contemporary songs that suited her style.)

They needed to get back on the road. Bobby welcomed the opportunity; Julie was, as always, more reluctant, and according to one critic, her stage facade was badly in need of repair. A concert in San Francisco's cavernous, acoustically poor Masonic Auditorium was plagued by technical difficulties, and the noticeably pregnant singer was taken to task by prickly *San Francisco Chronicle* critic Ralph Gleason, who had clearly changed his opinion of her since his approving remarks about *Julie Is Her Name* eight years earlier. Gleason now thought that one had to "listen to Julie London with your eyes open. It's not too important to have your ears open." She was an unconvincing live performer; a "[product] of the Hollywood electronic world," whose lack of stage presence was only rivaled by her inability to get any "expression at all into the lyrics." Julie was rarely affected by what unsatisfied pundits or unhappy promoters had to say about her performances, bluntly telling them that if what she was doing wasn't good enough, they could hire someone else.

Julie's rusty stage act may have required some lubrication, but her television work picked up steam with an appearance on the NBC medical-mystery series *The Eleventh Hour*. She desperately wanted a part she could feel good about having done and was convinced by the strength of Alfred Brenner's teleplay that this could be the one. Yet even after she accepted the role of the much-loved sex symbol Joan Ashmond in "Like a Diamond in the Sky," Julie wondered whether playing another "terribly neurotic singer" was just another bit of typecasting.

As the episode opens, the beautiful and troubled Joan Ashmond sprawls across a bed in her Hollywood mansion, whispering into a tape recorder. The next morning, her dead body is found in the same location. To determine whether her death was an accident or suicide, the coroner's office orders a postmortem psychiatric examination. As part of the investigation, those who knew the fragile star, including her manager (Herschel Bernardi) and sound engineer (Everett Sloane), are interviewed by psychiatrist Theodore Bassett (Wendell Corey) and clinical psychologist Paul Graham (Jack Ging). Via flashback, the story of a lonely woman and her inability to handle her manufactured fame is unspooled.

Julie received praise for her performances of "I've Got You Under My Skin," "Saddle the Wind," and "Should I?," as well as the show's newly lyricized theme song and for her "sincere acting" under director Jack Arnold (*Creature from the Black Lagoon* and *The Incredible Shrinking Man*). Yet most critics spent their column space noting the similarity of the plot to the August 1962 death of Marilyn Monroe. Producer Sam Rolfe scrambled to issue denials that the show had any parallel to the movie star's demise, and Julie was quick to point out that she and Monroe had little in common. "Marilyn was the sexpot—a sex symbol. I never think of myself that way. I'm strictly the housewife-mother type. I played Joan Ashmond as she was written—a sick gal, lost and afraid."

Her other acting role during the year came via the comedy-mystery "Charlie's Duet," an episode of NBC's *Dick Powell Theatre*, where she played yet *another* nightclub singer as part of an eclectic cast that included Cesar Romero, Zsa Zsa Gabor, Jim Backus, and Jules Munchin. Julie's character is the former flame of a swanky Los Angeles nightclub owner played by Anthony Franciosa; Romero plays the gambler who schemes to take over the club. (If the well-trodden elements of the plot sound like Julie's failed *Maggie Malone* pilot, blame writer Richard Carr, who penned both.*)

Interviewed on the set during production, Julie had no problem expressing her continued frustration with television, lamenting, "If the script says, 'sultry singer who slinks around the set and sometimes sings,' they send out a call for me." This is painfully evident in "Charlie's Duet": *all* she is asked to do is slink around and sing, yet the program is so poorly structured that her three numbers are largely buried under dialogue. (Producer Snuff Garrett liked one of the songs so much that he had Julie rerecord it, and her version of "Guilty Heart," written for a 1961 episode of the NBC television series *The Detectives*, was issued in 1964 as the B-side of "I Want to Find Out for Myself.")

Julie London may not have been the sex symbol that Marilyn Monroe was, but the cover of the smoothly sensuous *Latin in a Satin Mood*, released shortly after *The Eleventh Hour* aired, certainly had a Marilyn-like look to it. While the music is solidly entertaining, the glorious cover photograph—perhaps the most memorable of her career—is what lodges in the mind. If Julie held "the record for posing in disappearing necklines," this one took the top prize. Neck, arms, and cleavage bare, the rest of Julie's curvy figure is wrapped from bosom to toe in red, blue, and purple swathes of satin.

Latin in a Satin Mood was the first of Julie's albums to credit the work of Snuff Garrett's favorite arranger, Ernie Freeman. (His name

---

* The episode had originally been intended for Dick Powell, who died of cancer in January 1961, in his character of Willie Dante, a swank restaurateur the actor had played numerous times on *Four Star Playhouse* in the 1950s.

was on the label of the "Slightly Out of Tune" single.) The Cleveland native had been on the Los Angeles scene since the late 1940s and had worked with everyone from the Platters to guitarist Duane Eddy to multi-instrumentalist Buddy Collette. According to drummer Earl Palmer, who played on countless sessions for the Garrett/Freeman combination, Freeman was "an undersung genius. It didn't matter if he was drunk or not; he could hear a wrong note in the last row of the orchestra." At the peak of Freeman's work with Garrett, the producer recalled, they "used to go into [the studio] on Monday and not come out until Friday."

The concept for the laid-back *Latin in a Satin Mood* may have come from Snuff Garrett's two *50 Guitars Go South of the Border* albums, part of a popular decade-long series of Liberty recordings. (Ten of the twelve songs Julie sings on this album appear as instrumentals on those records.) *Latin in a Satin Mood* benefits from some tasty trumpet-section work, along with guitars, percussion, and a (hardly Latin-sounding) male vocal chorus. Two big-band hits of the 1940s—"Frenesi" and "Perfidia"—are among the best performances on the disc: the former a lively cha-cha and the latter a relaxed, nuanced number in which Julie sings *perfidious* just like she sang *plebeian* in "Cry Me a River." But the only standout track is the mambo "Sway," an unlikely result since swaying was about the limit of Julie's dancing ability.

Snuff Garrett's first set of "modern-day songs" with Julie, *The End of the World*, followed *Latin in a Satin Mood* onto the market a few months later. It was a "big album," he proudly recalled, and it "really came out well." Ernie Freeman's straightforward arrangements gave Julie room to interpret the material with what *Variety* called her "ballad caress . . . still one of the warmest vocal pitches on disks today." That vocal warmth is most evident as she dived into the despairing heart at the center of Sasha Distel and Jack Reardon's "The Good Life," one of her most moving—yet unheralded—interpretations. (Some pressings of the album are titled *The Good Life*.) The bluesy, loping performance of "I Wanna Be Around," a piano-centered rendition of "I Left My Heart in San Francisco," and a whispered take on the Henry Mancini/Johnny

Mercer Academy Award–winning "Days of Wine and Roses" were also well suited to her understated style, which remained in focus even on the more contemporary-sounding tunes, such as "Our Day Will Come," and the Latin-flavored remake of an oldie, "I Remember You," which featured the sound of the popular Hammond organ.

It was also apparent that Julie had become increasingly comfortable with up-tempo material. Memories of the awkward *Send for Me* three years before disappeared as she glided over the pizzicato strings and pop/jazz piano interjections of the high-energy bossa nova of Bart Howard's "Fly Me to the Moon," an arrangement Ernie Freeman borrowed from a hit version by pianist Joe Parnell. Thanks to the recent chart successes of Tony Bennett's recording of "I Left My Heart in San Francisco," country singer Skeeter Davis's crossover title track, and the number-one hit "Our Day Will Come" for the rhythm-and-blues group Ruby and the Romantics, *The End of the World* returned Julie to the album charts—number 77 at *Cash Box* and number 127 at *Billboard*—for the first time in five years.

✸

Julie and Bobby were hoping for boys when she returned to the maternity ward of Valley Presbyterian Hospital. That wish came true in the early morning hours of May 28, 1963, when she gave birth to Reese and Jody Troup. The names honored their grandmothers: Reese was the maiden name of their paternal grandmother; Jody was the nickname of Julie's mother as a child.

Their half-sister Cynnie Troup retains a vivid recollection of the events:

> The cutest thing about this—the boys were born long before ultra-sounds—was that they didn't know whether they were going to be boys or girls. They didn't need twin girls! I remember being in the labor room, and Julie smoking, of course. When she went into delivery, my dad was in the waiting room. This was exactly where [he] had been the year before, when Kelly was born, and my

dad—who was cutely superstitious—wanted boys, so we thought that if he was in the same place, it wouldn't be a boy, so he went downstairs to wait by himself. Later, the doctors came out, and I know before he does that they're boys, so as a group, we all march on down the stairs, and I remember the look on my dad's face when Dr. Forbes told him "Bobby, congratulations, you have identical twin boys!"

With five children ranging in age from thirteen-year-old Stacy to the babies, as well as the frequent appearances of Bobby's eighteen- and twenty-year-old daughters, Julie now had a significant extended family that filled her large house. This meant finding an equally significant amount of ready income as quickly and simply as possible. Snuff Garrett's assembly-line method of recording made perfect sense at this point in her life and career, and it certainly alleviated some of her studio nerves. But invention quickly began to flag, and blandness—what Garrett referred to as an "Andy Williams approach" to her records—clearly shone through in the results.

The quality of her material steadily deteriorated. While *The End of the World* was a well-selected, nicely arranged, and expertly performed set of songs that have remained popular over the decades, Julie's next LP, *The Wonderful World of Julie London*, was its polar opposite. The songs were largely lesser ones, the arrangements equally so, and the performances inconsistent at best. Even the covers had been struck dumb, marked by poor photographs and dull graphics, with little of what Lenny Waronker called his father's ethic of "the importance of the whole package" when selling records. "There was an aesthetic concern there. What made [Liberty] work was his understanding and concern about things that really counted in music and the way that music was presented."

The only track on *Wonderful World* worth more than a cursory listen is an engaging performance of the Bobby Scott / Ric Marlow waltz "A Taste of Honey." Otherwise the tone of the album is set by a version of the Andy Williams hit "Can't Get Used to Losing You." A pale imitation of Julie's "Fly Me to the Moon," complete with nearly identical pizzicato strings, the bland song is more suited to the princess of 1960s teenage angst Lesley Gore than the self-determined Julie London. Yet the album somehow appealed to the record-buying public of 1963, and their purchases helped *Wonderful World* reach number 136 on the *Billboard* album charts. Even the accompanying single, the simpleminded "I'm Coming Back to You," made an impact and peaked at number 118. Yet it was all a far cry from the intimacy and sensuality typically associated with Julie London.

Four months after giving birth to the boys, Julie was back on the road. She jokingly refused to return to Mister Kelly's, telling a friend she was never going to work in Chicago again since Kelly, Reese, and Jody had all been conceived there! (When she played the city in the fall of 1966, she moved from the smoky nightclub scene to the elegant Empire Room of the opulent Palmer House.) The first indication of the type of venues into which she was now making inroads was a performance on the campus of San Diego State University in October.

Julie had been scheduled to appear there the year before, but the show was canceled after it was revealed that she was seven months pregnant and expecting twins, which caused a campus activities adviser to admit that Julie wouldn't have "that old sock appeal." Now back to her prechildbirth looks, she performed before an audience of two thousand at an outdoor theater on a chilly night, an unfortunate locale for a singer whose efforts to project her voice frequently failed. Julie was "always wary of personal appearances," Cynnie Troup—a student at the university at the time—told the school newspaper. "She's very self-conscious about her singing."

Julie's decisions about what to record were increasingly motivated by ever-present concerns about financial security. While she rapidly laid down tracks with Snuff Garrett, Liberty Records was suffering under the frequent demands of its new owner. Label founder Si Waronker was frustrated by the continued interference in what he thought was his prerogative to decide the direction of Liberty's recordings. "I thought I was working in a business that I knew so well, the music business," he said in 1993. "But with Avnet, suddenly I was working for a company that made steel and electronics. And they are telling me what they would like to hear."

Waronker also argued with company president Al Bennett over musical direction, as well as staffing and royalties, which only made a difficult situation worse. "Al could sell anything, but he knew nothing about music [and still] tried to say what was good. . . . I was brought up as a musician . . . and some of the other guys [at Liberty] knew nothing about music. In many things we had a different perception of what the music should be."

Lenny Waronker confirmed his father's disenchantment. "It got to a point where he just didn't want to do it anymore. Everybody in a record company has an opinion, and my father wasn't good in having people—outside of music people—having opinions, and I think that bothered him. I think he could feel the company sort of drifting away and it wasn't his cup of tea anymore." After starting Liberty Records on a wing and a prayer—and the subtle sounds of "Cry Me a River"—Si Waronker departed from the label in the summer of 1963.

In the first year after the sale to Avnet, Liberty lost $1 million. "No decent merchandise was coming out, and Al was spending dough so it was flowing out of that place," Si Waronker later told Liberty Records historian Michael "Doc Rock" Kelly. Avnet executives wanted nothing more to do with a business they never understood, and Al Bennett, who had negotiated the earlier record-breaking sale, was now in a position to take advantage of the situation he had helped create. In October 1963 Julie London signed a new five-year deal with Liberty at the same time as Bennett purchased the label from Avnet at a fire-sale price, thus ending the difficult sixteen-month marriage of the two companies.

11

$\mathcal{L}ive \ldots in \ \mathcal{P}erson!$

She never took crap from anybody.

—Robert Fuller, 2016

J ULIE PREFERRED AUDIENCES who were there to listen to her, not the ambience of the raucous nightclubs where "people are drinking and often have very little interest in the performer." The changing music scene, however, had left her with few obvious venue choices beyond clubs. One new option had cropped up in 1960, when she had been approached to perform at a North Carolina college, but her price was too steep for a deal to be reached. Three years later, a group of like-minded schools had devised a solution to the problem of high-priced entertainment: block booking, which allowed the costs to be shared among an entire group.

Presented with this novel concept—and the guarantee of $3,500 to $5,000 per night—in the fall of 1963 Julie eagerly accepted the offer and followed a path that had been trodden for many years by her friends in the Four Freshmen. In early November she headed out with Bobby and a quartet of musicians on a three-week tour through the midwestern and southern United States. Bassist Don Bagley and drummer Kenny Hume were joined by two newcomers. Joe Pass was the latest in Julie's line of virtuoso guitarists. A largely self-taught musician, Pass, under the spell of bebop, had made his way to New York in the late 1940s, where he developed his technique and a serious heroin habit. He was in California by 1960, where he cleaned himself up through participation in the controversial Synanon drug rehabilitation program. Pass was a well-known player among the jazz cognoscenti of Southern California and had made his first album for Pacific Jazz Records when he joined up with Julie. Joe Burnett, on trumpet and flugelhorn, was married to singer Irene Kral and had played with Woody Herman and Maynard Ferguson before joining Stan Kenton's trumpet section in 1959, switching to the mellophonium when the orchestra leader added the difficult instrument to his band.

Julie and the quartet worked up a combination of numbers she had been performing for the last couple of years—"Cry Me a River," "'Deed I Do," "I Love Paris," and "Lonesome Road"—with new material, including "Bye Bye Blackbird," "Send for Me," "Something Cool," "How About Me," and a nightly duet with Bobby on his slightly risqué "Hot Chocolate," one of the few songs he had written in the last few years that saw the light of day.

The tour took the group from a standing-room-only performance in downtown Lincoln, Nebraska, through dates at student unions and campus gymnasiums in Iowa, Missouri, North and South Carolina, Ohio, Michigan, Alabama, Mississippi, and Louisiana. The novelty quickly wore off. "The kids are down with colds," the tired singer told a journalist while she waited for a taxi at the Lincoln airport after the first night's show. "Right now I'm just a worried mother who wishes she were home."

Worried or not, her performances were well received. The audiences were largely made up of adults who lustily applauded her "sulky, haunting style [and] lively up-beat manner." Audible sighs could be heard from the "red-blooded American males" during the "modified twist" she tried out during an instrumental break. Following each performance Julie retreated to her dressing room to down a drink or two and smoke a few cigarettes while answering the generally innocuous questions of college newspaper reporters. A Marlboro always at the ready—her ties to the brand were still strong, particularly in the southern tobacco regions—she would sign autographs for the eager groups of white male students whose conservative suits, ties, and flattop hairdos would soon be replaced by jeans, long hair, and beards.

November 22, 1963. The entire world was plunged into a state of stunned disbelief by the assassination of President John F. Kennedy in Dallas, Texas. A dumbstruck Julie could only sit and recall one of her favorite moments of her career. On February 25, 1961, she had performed for the handsome, smiling Kennedy and fifteen hundred guests as the headliner of the annual White House Correspondents' Dinner at the Sheraton-Park Hotel in Washington, DC. The newly inaugurated chief executive had personally chosen her for the program, and the evening was a huge success. Kennedy's delight in the singer's performance with guitarist Al Viola was only equaled by her pleasure at being introduced to him backstage.

It was with a heavy heart that Julie gathered her strength to complete the last shows of the tour at the Outrigger Inn in St. Petersburg, Florida, where her looks and her way with a song impressed a local critic. She had "the sleek, don't-give-a-damn class of a Jaguar XKE roadster" yet could caress "a whole new character into old standard songs—then [convince] you her way may be right."

Julie returned to California from her first series of one-nighters exhausted but pleased, knowing that the shows had been well received and well attended. They proved that she remained a popular singing attraction with a diverse audience of fans. Yet she still harbored dreams of quitting this life of singing for her supper. She was quickly given a reason to think that wasn't going to happen soon.

Philip Morris had been reassessing her value to the company, and after making her next two spots for the Leo Burnett Agency, which introduced the "Julie London in Marlboro Country" slogan, she was told that her lucrative, seven-year run of commercials was at an end. Although she continued to receive income from the advertisements through the remainder of the decade, as Philip Morris profited from increased sales to overseas markets, they *had* become a liability to her career. "I got a beautiful script from 'Breaking Point,' a real dinger to tear your insides out," she told a journalist. (The show was a short-lived spin-off from the successful ABC medical drama *Ben Casey*.) "Couldn't do it, because their cigarette sponsor said I was too identified with Marlboro."

She had little choice but to move forward, and when an offer came from the Associated Booking Corporation, a large theatrical agency that wanted to book her in larger venues, which would require a big band to back her rather than a small group, she and Bobby started to think about suitable songs and how the show would work. These discussions began during the November tour, Don Bagley remembered. Julie's existing arrangements were largely those "she had done for records, by Russ Garcia and various people, but she needed a new book and a new one-hour act."

"We started out picking tunes," Bagley said. "Early on there was a meeting in the same family room where we recorded [*Julie at Home*]. I loved going to the house; the first thing they did was put a drink in your hand! All the planning sessions and rehearsals were in that family room. I was up there a lot, and we'd get together, talk about tunes, and talk about music, sometimes it was just a cocktail hour of whoever she invited." Progress was made between the raising of glasses. "Julie knew a lot about music—good music—and had very definite tastes. She insisted on good songs."

Bagley, who had recently performed with Barbra Streisand, suggested the up-tempo Peter Matz tune "Gotta Move" as a signal of new intentions, and the singer "encouraged arrangers and musicians, especially her guitar accompanists, to go as far out as possible. 'I want you to play as far out as you can,' she'd say, as far as you want to go with the harmonies. She wanted everything to be unusual—the very best.""

Some months later Julie said that she "just decided it would be kind of interesting to do something different." In reality it took six weeks and $30,000 (almost $250,000 today) to put the show together. Bagley wrote arrangements that would help transform her casual quartet performances into a full-blown production, with a quartet of male backup singers, several costume changes, and choreography. "Once in a while, her mom would be at the house, in a wheelchair," the arranger continued. "They had a good musical relationship. Julie would get her to sing duets." Ken Albers of the Four Freshmen was hired to write arrangements for the vocal quartet. Julie "wanted the same kind of close harmony that the Freshmen were known for—even closer. Ken's vocal arrangements were quite complicated."

The singers struggled with the harmonies, a situation further exacerbated by choreographer Jonathan Lucas and director Barry Shear when they began to work on the elaborate staging of the new act. (Lucas began his career as a Broadway dancer in the late 1940s and then moved to television; Shear was a prolific television director.) "Julie hired [Lucas] from New York. The first thing he did was have the singers run around the stage, and whoever passed the microphone, that's the part you heard. It was totally impossible to have them singing and still running around." When the quartet who had worked many of the rehearsals announced they wouldn't be able to make the tour, substitute singers had to be located quickly in order to make opening night on January 10, 1964.

The Deauville Hotel, the site of Julie's expensive new act, was billed at the time of its opening in 1957 as the largest and most luxurious hotel on Miami Beach. Its owners were taking a gamble that Julie's name alone would help them recoup the $15,000 she was being paid. The Deauville, remembered Don Bagley, "was one of those big hotels run by the mob but with an ostensible front man posing as the owner." (Prominent hotelier Morris Lansburgh fronted the Deauville and Julie's next port-of-call, the Flamingo in Las Vegas, for the mob.) "This guy sent word to the dressing room, 'Mister so and so would like to have dinner with Julie after the show.' And she said, 'What about my musicians?' And they said, 'It's principals only.' And she said, 'You tell Mister so and so, I will have dinner with the musicians instead.'"

Julie was more concerned about why she had "to keep proving [herself] over and over again." She told reporters that it took "a long time for a performer to build up a feeling of being able to communicate with an audience." She hoped for a good reaction to every night's first few numbers. "If they respond favorably, their communication will inspire me." Julie struggled to make contact with the crowd in the swanky Casanova Room as she concentrated on the complicated choreography and stage patter, including a satirical comedy routine, based on the Marlboro commercials, that she had worked on during shows with trumpeter Jack Sheldon the previous year. Significantly, with the exception of two songs from *The End of the World*, Julie didn't perform anything from her recent pop-oriented albums or singles.

Her show was still a work in progress. The blending of Julie's voice with the quartet of "solid songsters" dubbed the Casuals struck a harmonious note with *Variety*; with a little tightening to eliminate lulls, success was predicted. Instead she failed to draw much of an audience during her ten days of performances, and her time at the Deauville would quickly be forgotten in the wake of the hotel's role, less than a month later, as the site of the Beatles' second performance on *The Ed Sullivan Show*.

While Julie tinkered with the new act, her twenty-first album, *You Don't Have to Be a Baby to Cry*, was released with little fanfare. Another effort from the Snuff Garrett–Ernie Freeman combination, the LP was another collection of songs that had (largely) been recent hits for others. A few tracks stand out from the dross. Willie Nelson's bluesy "Night Life" featured some fine, muscular tenor saxophone work by Plas Johnson, while Lenny Welch's recent number-four hit "Since I Fell for You" finds Julie's voice breaking at times in a quite moving way.* The Burt Bacharach and Hal David hit "Wives and Lovers" is done with verve and

---

* Nelson released two albums for Liberty in the early 1960s, part of the label's efforts in the country and western market.

élan, and it's a shame that Julie never recorded any more of the duo's material. There was so much in their catalog of adult-oriented songs that would have been far more suitable to her high standards than "I Want to Find Out for Myself," another flaccid attempt at success on the singles charts. For someone like Julie, whose credo was to concentrate on "the lyric more than anything," the words of these juvenile pop songs—as potentially lucrative as she may have hoped the recordings would be—were far beneath her. Her boredom was clearly audible.

You Don't Have to Be a Baby to Cry was symptomatic of the negative changes at Liberty after Al Bennett's return to the helm. (The album is often referred to as *Julie London*, which is how the label copy reads; the accompanying single of "I Want to Find Out for Myself" uses this title.) Bennett, said photographer Murray Garrett, only cared about the money he could make, which meant cutting costs wherever possible. This was reflected in yet another cheap cover design, sadly bereft of the glamour and stimulation of Julie's earlier eye-popping photos. In fact the cover photograph had already been used for the "In the Wee Small Hours of the Morning" sleeve four years earlier.

It wasn't until Julie and her group reached Las Vegas for a four-week run at the Flamingo Hotel on the Strip, where the entire act could be performed for the first time, that things really began to gel. "The Vegas show was about fifty to sixty minutes, because they didn't want people out of the casino for any longer," Don Bagley remembered. "So with the opening, [comedian] Jack Carter would do twenty minutes, and then Julie would do forty."

Snuff Garrett and Buzz Cason flew up from Los Angeles to catch the opening night performance. "Fly Me to the Moon," the first number of the evening, got the audience buzzing. As the sixteen-piece house orchestra launched into the tune, Julie—dressed in a tight, white strapless gown—soared over the heads of the crowd on a polar bear rug that circled around the showroom on a tramline. Don Bagley laughed that choreographer Jonathan Lucas "would have flown her on a piano maybe, if they could have managed it, but she was supposed to be lying back, and there were problems, as always, with the mechanics of it. It was just dangerous! Julie had to get up high to be launched." The choreographer "was always coming up with things like that, which were either dangerous or not musically feasible, stuff that just didn't work. Julie had to find some way of not offending him, since she was paying big money for him, and having to throw out everything he did." The gimmick was abandoned after just a few shows.

Still, Julie was "laid-back and cool," Buzz Cason recalled. After the show was over, he and Garrett accompanied her to the hotel casino, where they gambled and drank until the wee hours of the morning. Julie disliked pretension "more than anything else in the world," so everyone in the band was invited up to her hotel room after the gig to relax with a drink and a smoke. She "didn't treat us like employees," said her first (lead) tenor Cal Sexton, who accompanied Julie from January through March 1964 with singers Ron Parry, Bob Anson, and Don McLeod.

During the Flamingo engagement, Julie flew down to Los Angeles to tape a Bob Hope special that aired in mid-February. The performance of "Night Life" was her only television appearance in 1964. After a little downtime at home, she headed east for a major engagement in New York—her first in eight years. On March 30 radio station WNEW broadcast Julie's opening night at the 350-seat Royal Box supper club located in the fifty-story Americana Hotel. Once again it was a rough start. Distracted by having to entertain both the club and the radio audience, she failed "to make the most of her opportunities," wrote the *Variety* critic on hand. Her act, he continued, "appeared to be thrown askew," and though her duet with Don Bagley on "Bye Bye Blackbird" indicated a potential breakthrough, "it never seemed to come off." (For the song, the bassist moved down to the front of the stage while Julie wrapped herself around him in a palpably erotic duet. "The physical rubbing asses, that was Julie's great idea of choreography! I loved it! The whole attitude was Julie's!")

But the show—two performances a night except Sundays—quickly improved, abetted by the quality of pianist Lee Evans's ten-piece house orchestra. It wasn't just any regular hotel band, Evans recalled, since it was "often augmented" to meet the needs of specific performers. "The people that were in that house band were the top New York people," agreed Don Bagley. "Quincy Jones was recording the score for *The Pawnbroker* [at that time], and all of our guys were working for Quincy."

Among the choice musicians who accompanied Julie at the Royal Box was Jerome Richardson, the versatile reedman who added his dexterous playing to the bands of Lionel Hampton, Jimmie Lunceford, and Earl Hines. His skills as a practiced jazz musician meant there was always a good sound that could break out amid the highly polished hotel band. Yet there was always time during the evening for the show to slow down, for temperatures to cool, and for Julie to delve deeper into the music, to still the laughter and the clinking glasses, as she was accompanied solely by the signature musical element of her sound: the guitar. "When we got to New York," remembered Don Bagley, "the Americana guitarist was a disappointment, and it just didn't work for her." Bagley knew that Sal Salvador, whom he worked with in Stan Kenton's band, was in town. "I called him and asked him if he would do the job. He agreed, but [on the last night of the run] he had a band and had to send a substitute."

That fill-in was Bucky Pizzarelli, who arrived at Julie's busy hotel room in the afternoon before that evening's show and, to the singer's amazement, proceeded to play a note-for-note version of "Cry Me a River." "Who is this guy?" she asked. "I fell right in with her," recalled Pizzarelli, who called Julie the best singer he ever worked with. "When she got going, when she got hot—she was great. There was nobody like her." She loved his playing so much that the guitarist was always her top choice to accompany her in subsequent New York engagements.

The New York audiences welcomed Julie with enthusiasm. She entered from the wings to a chorus of "Julie Is Her Name" from the vocal quartet and proceeded through a set that combined brassiness and subtlety in equal measure. Julie didn't like belting out a song, and it wasn't something that she excelled at, but as a friend said about the likes of "Send for Me," "Kansas City," and "Gotta Move," "The guys would help her so much—they could really add to that, because they could sing the high parts and fill in, and she'd just kind of be part of the group, which she loved."

The concerts, even if they were often a grind, were financially and artistically successful and proved that she could do more than whisper "Cry Me a River." To toast her success, Liberty Records hosted a cocktail party in her honor at the Americana, attended by more than 250 disc jockeys and radio and newspaper personnel. Julie's month in New York coincided with the opening of the 1964 World's Fair, and the influx of out-of-town journalists and business executives helped the Royal Box do some of its best business of the year.

The idea of making a live record had been tossed around during the November 1963 college tour, but enthusiasm at Liberty only took off after the good reviews started coming in from New York. Snuff Garrett flew out from California to oversee the recording of a few nights of performances and brought RCA's Dave Hassinger along with him to work with local engineer Tom Dowd in capturing the sounds on tape. The album, released in August as *In Person—Julie London at the Americana*, is a good representation of the big-band act and covers the varied range of styles Julie had incorporated into her performances. It garnered little notice, but *Variety* called the disc "a superb change of pace . . . all done with firm control of the material."

"Did I play on that?" Don Bagley joked when asked about the recording of "The Boy from Ipanema," a song Liberty rush released as a single, hoping to take advantage of the continued popularity of the bossa nova. Bagley joined familiar faces John Gray, Jimmy Rowles, and Emil Richards, plus Shelly Manne on drums and Plas Johnson on reeds, for what was nothing more than "a pick-up session" at RCA on April 30, 1964. Even with the benefit of Johnson's Stan Getz–like tenor, this version doesn't measure up to the record by saxophonist Getz, singer and guitarist João Gilberto, and Gilberto's wife, Astrud (whose whispery vocal had a Julie-like quality to it), which topped the charts in July.

The "slow, haunting idea" of the B-side, "My Lover Is a Stranger," by Jack Segal and Marvin Fisher, with Johnson switching to flute and some tasty guitar chords by Gray, hint at a change in musical direction that Julie would soon pursue. "She appreciated the good jazz players, as Johnny Gray was," Don Bagley remembered. "For substitute changes, he was the best, and along with that, the best accompanist. He knew how to put in the good changes and not throw the singer. But nothing threw Julie; she would sing the song no matter what was going on."

While Julie's popularity was dimming at home, her records continued to sell well overseas. To capitalize on this new opportunity, Sol Shapiro, the head of the Foreign Department at the William Morris Agency, and Tatsuji "Tats" Nagashima, the most successful concert promoter in Tokyo, reached a deal to book Julie for a series of concerts, nightclub performances, and the filming of a television special for the Japanese market. It was a good choice: her latest album stayed at number one on the record charts in Japan for more than two months, and her single of "I Left My Heart in San Francisco" was a top-ten hit. Educated in England, Tats was tall, handsome, and well liked by everyone. Ross Barbour, who had played in Japan earlier that year with the Four Freshmen, recalled that Tats was a "gentle and clever man . . . who knew not only the meaning of English words but also understood Western slang and humor."

The costs associated with bringing the vocal quartet—"her boys" in Julie's phrase—to Japan were deemed prohibitive, so they were left at home when she arrived in Tokyo on May 19. "They used them for a while," said Don Bagley, who continued to act as Julie's musical director for the Japanese tour. "They had put in a lot of time rehearsing. They were, more or less, hired for whatever Julie wanted to do, until I guess it just didn't pay off anymore, at that point. Four extra people on the road, and paying their transportation and hotels and all that. Julie always had a hairdresser and a nurse for Kelly, and Troup of course, so they had a pretty big entourage."

Trumpeter Joe Burnett returned as the other familiar name backing Julie and Bobby during their separate sets. Two newcomers made up the rest of the quartet. Guitarist Dennis Budimir had played in drummer Chico Hamilton's outfit and had backed Peggy Lee prior to being drafted into the army; the gig with Julie and Bobby was one of his first after completing his military service. He would soon concentrate on a career as a studio musician, becoming one of the most in-demand guitarists in Los Angeles. Dewells "Dee" Barton was only four years removed from the University of North Texas and had just come off a stint as the drummer/arranger for the Stan Kenton orchestra, which he had joined as a trombonist.

The concerts got underway at Tokyo's Sankei Hall on May 21–23 and concluded with a performance at Osaka Festival Hall on June 2.* The main venue of the tour, however, was the three-hundred-seat New Latin Quarter nightclub, located in the basement of the luxurious Hotel New Japan, where the group stayed for much of their time in the country. The diverse clientele at the New Latin Quarter, which on any given night might include members of the Japanese *yakuza* (the local mafia), American and Japanese businessmen making deals, and suspected spies and intriguers of all nationalities, was tended to by one hundred beautiful hostesses and a staff of forty. Tickets for Julie's shows commanded a cover price of nearly fourteen dollars, equal to a hundred dollars today, and in some cases the cost of tickets to her other performances in Japan were the highest on record at that time.

A week of enthusiastically received performances gave Julie, Bobby, and the group the chance to gel as a unit. (Bobby's nightly set of five or six songs afforded Julie a break to head backstage to change outfits

---

* Other shows were held at the Grand Banquet Hall of the Hotel Okura in Tokyo (May 27), the Officers Club and Civilian Club at the US Air Force base at Tachikawa (May 29), the Kyoto Kaikan (May 31), and the CBC Hall in Nagoya (June 1).

and have a smoke and down a drink or two.) It also gave the Lobsters, the New Latin Quarter's house band ("the best band in Tokyo as far as nightclub backing acts"), time to become familiar with Don Bagley's charts before they were scheduled to convene in Studio G of the Tokyo Broadcasting System on May 28 to tape the *Julie London in Japan* television special. The show, and the *Live at New Latin Quarter* recording, unearthed and released in 2013, reveals a relaxed, confident singer at the height of her beauty and abilities.

The eighteen songs Julie performed on the two recordings showcased the visual and aural facets of a singer now nearly a decade into her musical career. The mixture of smoky ballads, up-tempo numbers with the big band, and a jazzy set backed by the trio of Bagley, Budimir, and Barton kept the focus on the music. Even the television show had a sense of single-minded focus, with little set decoration to distract viewers from the ample distraction provided by Julie herself.

Without the assistance of the vocal quartet, Julie had to rely on her ability as a performer to get across the swinging arrangements on "Kansas City" and "Send for Me." If she wasn't totally convincing as a belter, the effort did accomplish its goal of varying the tone of her act enough so that the quieter numbers became notably more effective. In the small-group numbers like "'Deed I Do," "Let There Be Love," and "You'd Be So Nice to Come Home To," she showed off her love of interplay with good musicians. Yet as ever in an evening with Julie London, it was her performance of "Cry Me a River" and the duets with her guitarist that stood out and silenced even the noisiest of crowds. "Everything Happens to Me" came true one night when Dennis Budimir joined Julie at the front of the stage. After he received an electric shock from an ungrounded cable, the guitarist laughed that she made it all better by giving him a restorative kiss. While working with other singers was sometimes a "big production," Budimir said Julie London had "no attitude."

It was a high time for all concerned, even Julie and Bobby's two-year-old daughter, Kelly, who enjoyed stealing the spotlight from her parents during their many press conferences and interviews. "Some of the people we know seemed surprised that we'd want to bother taking Kelly," Julie told a United Press International reporter. "I guess they thought she'd cramp our style or something. Every time we were asked why we were taking her with us, Bobby would very matter-of-factly reply: 'Why, because Kelly's never been to Japan!'"

After concluding the Japanese shows, Julie, Bobby, and Kelly joined the other members of the family in Honolulu, where they spent an extended vacation in a lavish eight-bedroom house owned by Julie's manager. She was content to lay back, enjoy the sunshine, and do nothing at all.

It didn't take long for Julie to move to advertising a new—complimentary—product following the loss of the lucrative Marlboro contract. A pair of sexy print advertisements for Smirnoff vodka appeared in magazines and newspapers throughout the United States in the spring and summer of 1964. The promotion for screwdrivers (vodka and orange juice) worked on lot of Americans, including Julie, who made it her new drink of choice.

The rest of the year saw Julie and Bobby hopping back and forth from California through Texas, Indiana, Illinois, and Canada for a series of short dates, usually billed as the New Julie London Show, which took them through early December. "We mostly just worked with a quartet [on] those college tours," remembered Don Bagley. "We just used what we had: a trumpet and rhythm section, because [for] Julie, the guitar was her main thing. As long as she had Johnny Gray or somebody equally as good an accompanist, that was her style, and we could do a whole show with that."

Like many American parents in the early 1960s, Julie and Bobby found themselves frustrated by the music their children loved. Stacy and Lisa Webb, now fourteen and eleven years old, respectively, hounded them for money to buy records by the Beatles and plastered their bedroom walls with pictures of the Fab Four. Yet while Bobby recoiled from the music that was relegating his songs to the oldies, Julie was more sanguine. "As long as there are good things like '[I Left My Heart in] San Francisco' and people like Tony Bennett, Sinatra, and Peggy Lee to sing them," there was still good music to be found.

Few people could push Julie London around. As the recording industry turned away from the Great American Songbook, she fought to keep her standards high—chart success be damned. Yet the demands of the market were not easy to ignore, and the battle was not always winnable. In December 1964 Liberty released "You're Free to Go," Julie's remake of a 1955 hit by country singer Carl Smith, as her newest single. It was the first example of the label's A&R men trying to fit Julie into the increasingly mainstream country music genre. Taken from a session done at RCA Studios in Hollywood two months earlier with arranger Richard Wess, best known for his work with vocalist Bobby Darin, Julie sounds bored, as she does on the B-side, "We Proved Them Wrong," another bland Brill Building pop tune, probably a leftover from one of her many sessions with Snuff Garrett and Ernie Freeman. The pairing flopped.

Country music, unless it was done by Ray Charles, held no interest for Julie. This didn't prevent a second attempt. A year after the release of "You're Free to Go," Don Bagley and the Nashville-based rock'n'roll and country producer/arranger Bill Justis ("Raunchy") were hired to put together an entire album of country songs for Julie. On the evening of December 16, 1965, Julie London arrived at RCA Studios on Sunset Boulevard to hear the playback of the tracks Bill Justis had already laid down. Don Bagley, more familiar with the singer's style (she "knew what she wanted and she knew how to do it"), had written charts with "better harmonies, a little more jazz harmonies." Julie made it through one vocal take during the second session, quickly realized this was not for her, and stomped out the door, yelling, "We're not going to do it; we're not going to release it and forget it!"*

---

* The Bagley and Justis–arranged backing tracks became the basis of an album by country and western guitarists Jimmy Bryant and Glenn Keener, released on Liberty's budget Sunset label in 1967.

According to Snuff Garrett, the album *Our Fair Lady*, which reached record stores in January 1965, was probably "something put together with some shit that I did!" It collected a set of previously released material with four tracks from the Richard Wess session that may have been intended for a full album of songs from movies. (The album's title was clearly intended to play on the popularity of the contemporaneous film version of *My Fair Lady* but nonsensically contains no songs from it.) Versatile reedman Gene Cipriano, who played oboe during the session, remembered that Julie "sang beautifully" that evening as she floated effortlessly over Wess's interplay of strings, cocktail piano, Paul Horn's flute, and the vibes of former Martin Denny sideman Julius Wechter. Julie's rendition of "More" followed Wess's arrangement of the same song for Bobby Darin by just a month. Her version is as perfect for her as Darin's was for him: his brashness echoed by horns and saxophones, her subtlety accented by a more exotic combination of instruments. (The final song from the RCA session, "House Where Love Is," presumably remains in the vaults.)

On January 4, 1965, as Julie and her family celebrated the holidays on the ski slopes of Aspen, Colorado, NBC broadcast an episode of the final season of the long-running *Alfred Hitchcock* anthology series. In "Crimson Witness," which marked her return to the small screen after a nearly two-year absence, Julie found a good supporting role as the secretary and mistress to an industrial engineer played by Peter Lawford. Over the course of the hour, he loses his mistress, his job, and his wife to his walrus-like brother (the witty Roger C. Carmel). Although the focus of "Crimson Witness" is on Lawford and Carmel, Julie gets the best line of dialogue as she explains Lawford's lack of appeal to women: "You're very sweet, Ernie, and most pleasant to look at, but your problems are pretty uncomplicated and kinda stupid!" (A more negligible role came in "Three Hours on a Sunday Night," a December episode of the NBC action-adventure/comedy series *I Spy* in which Julie played a rich woman who falls for the series' tennis pro / secret agent, played by Robert Culp.)

The winter and spring of 1965 saw Julie shuttling from California to concert venues domestic and foreign. In February she spent two weeks on the road, traveling from the snow-covered campus of Michigan Technical University, where she packed the house yet must have wished she was home by the pool, to a covered ice rink at the Mid-South Coliseum in Memphis, Tennessee. By far the oddest of the gigs was in North Carolina, where she played three sets at the Cotswold Shopping Center in Charlotte before an all-male audience of fourteen hundred students from Davidson College.

But she returned home with $24,000 (approximately $180,000 today) in her bank account and memories of the good time that was had by all concerned. The short tour was a career highlight for Chicago-based drummer Harry Hawthorne, who along with guitarist Joe Diorio accompanied Julie, Bobby, Don Bagley, and Joe Burnett. "She was exquisite, jazzy, and very sexy. The charts were good, the band was good, the whiskey and the hash were good."

The successful Japan tour led to more offers for Julie to perform outside of the United States. Don Bagley continued as her musical director for a series of lucrative shows at the Americana Hotel in San Juan, Puerto Rico, and in Melbourne, Australia, during April and May 1965. Drummer Dee Barton returned, but John Gray, Julie's first-call guitarist, was unavailable. His replacement was John Abate, a little-known Florida-based musician who had played with Andy Williams in the Miami hotel band of Jackie Gleason. Abate, according to Don Bagley, was "the nearest thing we ever had" to Gray.

The visit to Melbourne provided a new signature song for Julie's repertoire. During backstage rehearsals before an evening performance, precocious three-year-old Kelly Troup, who had joined her mother on the trip, became restless. The only thing Julie could do to get her attention was sing. John Abate began to accompany Julie and Kelly settled down. Singer and guitarist thought they had something and "ended up doing the song in the show that night. And it went over well." That typically understated statement belies the significance of her off-the-cuff performance of the melancholy yet ultimately cheerful farewell theme from television's *Mickey Mouse Club*. It soon would influence a new direction in Julie's recorded output.

Julie may have needed some cheering up herself in Melbourne. She performed once nightly at each of two hotels owned by the same firm, but the atmosphere and audiences at the Savoy Plaza and the Menzies Hotel varied wildly, and the conservative crowd in the latter responded tepidly to Julie's sometimes earthy stage act. (Her image overseas was still firmly tied to her cigarette commercials, so when a filmed performance at the Menzies was broadcast on Australian television, it was titled *The Julie London Marlboro Show*.) Fortunately, her little "night owl" Kelly was always able to provide the singer with a spirit-rejuvenating smile. "She is a great leveler. When I am upset or depressed, I can always rely on her to pull me out of it."

12

For the Night People

Mainly I'm a lyric reader.

—Julie London, 1968 radio interview

T HE MARKETING BUDGET for Julie London's records had been on
the decline for years, but label executives were aware that they still
needed a diverse collection of artists to fill a broad catalog of musical
styles. She was a safe, reasonably inexpensive bet, and she continued
to turn out product that brought in a steady, if unspectacular, rate of
return. The arrangement also had advantages for her; singers of higher
reputation than Julie had been axed from the rosters of large record
companies like Capitol and Columbia in recent years, so it was more
likely that she could fly under the radar and ride out the turbulence
roiling the music business if she remained with a lesser label like Liberty.

Fortunately, there was still a profitable niche for jazz recordings in
the mid-1960s—at least for those with a good melody. (Vince Guaraldi's
"Cast Your Fate to the Wind" and Ramsey Lewis's "The In-Crowd"
were both hits.) Dick Bock's Pacific Jazz/World Pacific label had successfully mined the sounds of West Coast jazz for more than a decade
with many solid recordings by the likes of Gerry Mulligan and Chet
Baker, bandleader Gerald Wilson, and the Mastersounds. In the spring
of 1965, Bock sold his master tapes and the Pacific Jazz studios in Los

Angeles to Liberty Records and joined the label as a vice president and general manager.

Dick Bock's arrival at Liberty had an immediate impact on Julie London's career. When Snuff Garrett resigned to go into independent production, Bock became the conduit through which the singer returned to more familiar, comfortable sonic settings. The decision to record the types of songs *she wanted to record*—and less of the material picked by A&R men looking for hits—gave Julie the opportunity to create a series of albums over the next three years that were produced *by adults for adults*. The two discs she made with Bock—the big-band bash *Feeling Good* and the cool, nocturnal Cole Porter tribute *All Through the Night*—became the templates for an unlikely resurgence in what had become a moribund recording career.

Feeling Good, which paired Julie with the explosive sound of Gerald Wilson's big band, was released—somewhat ironically—as tensions ran high in August 1965 following the devastating riots in the black Los Angeles neighborhood of Watts. It was her most energetic studio work in years. A raucous rendition of Herbie Hancock's funky "Watermelon Man" and the title track, from the Anthony Newley and Leslie Bricusse Broadway hit *The Roar of the Greasepaint—the Smell of the Crowd* (a UK hit in 1964 that was about to open on Broadway), signaled her confident attitude. The driving "My Kind of Town" was personalized with lyrical references—likely penned by Bobby Troup—to Chicago's Loop, O'Hare Airport, Rush Street, and "the stadium at fight time," the last a reference to Julie and Bobby's having attended the September 25, 1962, heavyweight boxing championship fight at Comiskey Park between Sonny Liston and Floyd Patterson. Her more intimate style was brilliantly represented by the obscure "I Bruise Easily," while Julie's teenage daughter Stacy was the catalyst for a recording of "Summertime" that turned the classic Gershwin lullaby into a suggestive come-on.*

---

* The version of "Summertime" Stacy suggested may have been the recording by the British band the Zombies, which had been released in early 1965.

One notable reason for the success of *Feeling Good* was the welcome inclusion of two new songs by Bobby Troup, whose name had been conspicuously absent from all but one of his wife's records during the Snuff Garrett years. Troup's lack of musical output during the early 1960s was mirrored by many other songwriters of his and earlier generations who had been left in the commercial dust when, rather than rely on outside writers, Bob Dylan and the musical teams of Lennon and McCartney and Jagger and Richards opted to write and record material that reflected the thoughts and opinions of their own generation.

The minor-key swinger "Won't Someone Please Belong to Me" was composed during the spring of 1964 when Julie was performing at the Americana Hotel in Manhattan. Julie enjoyably stays behind the beat of the Basie-style arrangement of a song Bobby reluctantly admitted was the first he had written in years. "Girl Talk" was his witty lyrical companion to composer Neal Hefti's melody for the recent film biopic of Hollywood siren Jean Harlow. It was paired with the other Troup song as the album's sole single; although it never reached the charts, "Girl Talk" quickly became an audience favorite and stayed in his wife's act for years.

A satire on the daily lifestyle of the prototypical suburban housewife, "Girl Talk" also appears to hold clues to Julie's feelings about women. She "adored very few people," particularly other women, said a friend. But "if she loved you, then she wanted you to be around a lot." She had little time for anyone who fawned over her. The women who made up her circle of close friends "had a sense of humor, and would laugh at her jokes." San Bernardino schoolmate Caroline Woods, Dorothy Gurnee, Theda Golden (her doctor's wife), and Linda Wheeler (the wife of Jim Wheeler, one of Julie's backup singers during the last few years of her career), were among the women Julie called her "buddies." As traveling companions for Julie and babysitters for her children, it could be tremendous fun: top-flight lodgings, great food and drink, and the bonus of hobnobbing with celebrities. Yet if Julie felt that a woman had done her wrong, there was "no forgiving."

"Girl Talk" also comments on the relationship between Julie and Bobby Troup. Their drawn-out years of dating and the on-again, off-again engagement had by 1965 settled into a comfortable marriage. They were an "engaging pair," devoted to each other, to their large family, their dogs, and their shared love of good music.

Yet they were very different people, each marked by personality traits that set them apart from each other. Bobby was essentially upbeat, a gregarious entertainer who was always ready to perform; "generous, funny, kind, witty," in the words of his younger daughter Ronne. Julie was, to a large degree, "inside of herself." She didn't always need—or welcome—Bobby's so obvious adoration and worship. While she was "forever grateful" for his willingness to step up and be so clearly devoted to Stacy and Lisa, one friend was certain that Julie's "insecurities and lack of self-esteem went over into everything," including her relationship with Bobby. "She liked to yell at him. She got a lot of stuff out just yelling at Bobby, because he could take it, and it didn't bother him. He wanted to please her, no matter what it took, and she knew that, she took advantage of it."

On April 29, 1965, while Julie was at home between engagements in Puerto Rico and Australia, she did another one-off session at the studios of RCA Victor for what may have been intended as a new single. A septet of largely familiar faces (Don Bagley, Jimmy Rowles, guitarists Dennis Budimir and John Gray, vibraphonist Victor Feldman, and multi-instrumentalist Leon Russell) plus drummer Hal Blaine laid down tracks for two songs taken from hit musicals. "Soon It's Gonna Rain" from the 1960 off-Broadway success *The Fantasticks* and Anthony Newley and Leslie Bricusse's "Who Can I Turn To?" from *The Roar of the Greasepaint—the Smell of the Crowd* remain unreleased, as does an unusual item from a second session that evening. This produced the backing tracks for "I'll Love You for a While" by pop songwriters Carole King and Gerry Goffin. A Liberty audition record of the song was issued in the summer of 1965, credited to a singer named Josie

Taylor with Snuff Garrett as producer. Yet if one listens very carefully, is that Julie's voice sunk in the mix? We may never know.

All Through the Night followed a few months after *Feeling Good*. The idea for a tribute to the late Cole Porter came from the album's producer, and the record's featured soloist, alto saxophonist Bud Shank, was "doing whatever Dick Bock could think up." While the album is credited to the Bud Shank Quintet, the arrangements on *All Through the Night* are by pianist Russ Freeman, best known for his stellar work with trumpeter Chet Baker and his years as a member of the long-running jazz combo Shelly Manne and His Men. Freeman's time with the similarly understated Baker gave him a keen comprehension of Julie London's vocal strengths and limitations.

The Porter collection remains one of her strongest, most jazz-oriented recordings (a "sultry and sophisticated" romp through the songwriter's catalog, according to *Billboard*). Her floating, slurring, sensual voice is complemented by the expert musicianship of Shank, Freeman, guitarist Joe Pass, bassist Monty Budwig, and drummer Colin Bailey, who said that Julie "could [have been] a jazz singer, if she wanted to." Bailey recalled that the sessions went smoothly for the most part, although the singer had "a few nips from her flask, and by the end of the second date, she was a little juiced." When the producer tried to give her some advice from the control booth, she quickly told him to "fuck off!"

Pure sexuality was evoked by the glacial pace and whispered ecstasy of the title song. "Projecting sex" was a significant component of Julie's image. "When she got in a low-cut gown and started singing that breathy-quality kind of sound, it was just sex in a bottle." Joe Pass's introduction to "At Long Last Love" invoked memories of the duets on *Lonely Girl*, but this slow, sensual version turns into a fine collaborative, highlighted by Shank's alto solo. Beautiful piano chording by Freeman and Budwig's solid bass work support a heartbreaking rendition of "Ev'ry Time We Say Goodbye." A decade later, Colin Bailey ran into Julie when he was performing at a club. She told him that the Porter album was one of the most enjoyable dates she'd ever done. Years of substandard songs had not affected her ability to dig into the soul of a great lyric.

———⚬⚬⚬———

Supporting Julie's good work on records was a pair of syndicated television specials that aired during the summer and fall of 1965. *An Evening with Julie London* was a half-hour black-and-white program taped at Chicago television station WGN in February, which presented Julie in an intimate faux nightclub setting. Having gone through a phase when she had grown tired of singing her career-making hit, Julie's venomous performance of "Cry Me a River" was striking in its intensity.

Show number two lived up to its title. The full-color *Something Special*, directed by John Bradford (*The Judy Garland Show*), featured Julie in twelve songs and eight different costumes and made no pretense that it was anything but a series of staged sequences. Ten years into her singing career, she had fully entered the ranks of those who could be identified by first name only, joining the exalted company of Ella (Fitzgerald), Lena (Horne), and Peggy (Lee).

Something Special opened with a fanfare of "Julie Is Her Name," and she made her first appearance descending a spiral staircase, dressed in an off-the-shoulder yellow gown, singing "Lonesome Road." (A photograph from this sequence was used for the cover of the *All Through the Night* LP.) Her sensuous performance of "Am I Blue" takes place while horizontal on a large brass bed, and she wanders among a series of stained-glass panels for the poignant Billy Barnes song "(Have I Stayed) Too Long at the Fair." A medley of "Soon It's Gonna Rain" and "Here's That Rainy Day" showed Julie "getting out on a plane by herself where no one can reach her."

The highlights of the show were the closing sequence—"Mickey Mouse," done in an extreme close-up, which ends with Julie planting a wet kiss on the camera lens, leaving an impression of her red lipstick that remains as she turns and the final credits roll—and the intensely emotional eye contact between Julie and Bobby during his three-song sequence of the humorous "Lemon Twist," the poignant "It Happened Once Before," and the heartfelt "Won't Someone Please Belong to Me." Even Julie's free commercial for the tobacco industry, as she lights *two* cigarettes in her mouth (part of a gag she shared onstage with trumpeter Jack Sheldon), takes a luxurious puff, and places *both* of them in Bobby's mouth, can't distract from the clearly deep feeling they held for each other.

The year 1965 had been a lucrative one. Julie earned more than $125,000 from performances and royalties (more than $1 million today). That income included $17,500 from Liberty Records, which—if Julie's contract was, at the very minimum, similar to those of other artists on the label—reflected sales of around 350,000 copies of her records. It was a good number for a singer celebrating more than a decade in the music business. Yet as she neared forty, bookings for aging female singers with declining record sales were becoming harder to find, and the stark reality of the disappearance of venues suitable to her subtle style was hard to ignore. In the months before she returned to New York in February 1966 for a return engagement at the Americana Hotel, her calendar was largely restricted to two choices: big-city hotel nightclubs and smaller, off-the-beaten-track halls. The map of North America was crossed east to west, north to south. Her journeys covered historic hotels like the Shoreham in Washington, DC, and the Royal York in Toronto, a small town in Indiana for an appearance on a bill with Woody Herman, and a warehouse in Venice, California, where she performed at a benefit for Synanon, the controversial self-help group for recovering addicts. She also returned to the college campus circuit with performances at the University of Cincinnati and the University of New Mexico's campus in Albuquerque, where she sang before crowning the homecoming queen, a task far removed from entertaining President Kennedy four years earlier.

Before every performance during the three-week run at the Americana, guitarist Bucky Pizzarelli would go up to Julie's forty-second-floor suite for a little relaxation. Even ten years after her nightclub debut, it still took at least a few shots of Jack Daniel's for her to get the nerve to face an audience. Other changes to the act kept her on edge, at least temporarily. With Don Bagley too busy with other projects to make the trip, she had to quickly find a new and, more important, compatible musical director. Pianist Hal Serra, who had studied with the influential arranger and pianist Lennie Tristano, became the first musician to lead Julie's band from behind the keyboard. Even with the unfamiliar backing, the pianist quickly gained Julie's confidence, and when she came through the curtain at the Americana with a come-hither rendition of Hank Williams's country classic "Hey Good Lookin'," she was simply spectacular.

So much was new about the act that Julie needed someone nearby she could count on for onstage support and asked a friend to help her out in lieu of her singing quartet. She and Bobby had met Tom Williams four years earlier in Chicago. The actor came to see them perform at Mister Kelly's, and when he arrived in California, Julie invited him to their Christmas party with the offer of a chance to meet Jack Webb. The chilly relationship between Julie and her ex-husband had gradually warmed over the years, and Jack never stinted in showing his gratitude that his daughters had the steady Bobby Troup as their father.

Tom Williams was living with Julie and Bobby during the sessions for the *Feeling Good* album, and he came in the door one day to find Julie "lying on the living room floor listening to a recording of some music that was spread out in front of her on the floor." She looked over at him and said, "Get your ass over here and sing this with me!" The song was Roger Miller's recent smash success "King of the Road." For more than an hour, they worked on harmonies and made sure that he followed her pronunciations exactly. "When we started 'cookin','" he recalled, Julie said, "I'll take the bridge by myself and you come back on the last chorus." He stayed with her "on every note except the last," when Julie told him to "hold on to your note and I'll rooooooaaddd all over the place." When she returned to the studio to overdub her vocal on the track, she asked him to come with her, where they would make one take just for them. It wound up on the album, and they sang the duet through the balance of the shows they did together in 1966.*

Overall she received mixed reviews. Popular music critic John S. Wilson said Julie's best moments were "when the lights are dimmed and she murmurs a torch song to the gentle accompaniment of Bucky Pizzarelli's guitar." He was not so complimentary about how she performed when she had to push her voice. *Variety* concurred, acknowledging that the visual glory of Julie's "natural endowments" was not equaled by the uneven and shallow design of the act. Nevertheless, she brought in the customers, one of whom remarked, after she murmured her way through "Mickey Mouse," "Jesus Christ, she can even make that sexy!"

After the shows it was a party, and you were lucky if you got out of her room by five in the morning. "Every time I looked around," remembered Bucky Pizzarelli, "there was a big star!" From pianist Erroll Garner to bandleader Woody Herman, everyone loved to be around Julie. She rarely left the hotel during the New York engagement, although she managed to spend an afternoon in New Jersey at a Pizzarelli family barbecue. Julie also made an appearance before a governmental committee to testify about deceptive record industry practices and was asked to discuss *Tenderly Yours*, an LP that used her 1955 demos—and her photograph on the cover—as a come-on to buyers who otherwise wound up with a set of bland instrumentals. (This wasn't the first time those four recordings had been exploited. After the success of "Cry Me a River," executives at Bethlehem Records, no doubt regretting their decision not to sign Julie when they had the opportunity, capitalized on what little they had by releasing the songs as singles and on various compilation albums.)

---

* Williams later worked as Jack Webb's personal assistant and as a producer on *Dragnet* (1967–1970) and *Adam-12* (1968–1975). He also acted, most memorably in an episode of *Emergency!* in which he played a maniacal soap opera producer who told Julie's character, Nurse Dixie McCall, that he could put her in his show because "she's got a fabulous bod!"

Julie's appearance on the popular *Dean Martin Show* was broadcast by NBC during her time in New York. Since its debut in September 1965, television audiences had come to love the ever-casual and cool Martin, a man who never seemed anything less than perfectly at ease in his own skin. After performances of "Never on Sunday" and "Girl Talk," Julie joined the host for a probably well-in-their-cups duet of "Two Sleepy People," as she lazed on a bed of pillows and a white bearskin rug. (The duo paired up again—posthumously—in a 2009 Chrysler television commercial that mashed-up her 1963 recording of "Sway" with his 1954 version.)

/ Her return to the Shoreham Hotel in Washington, DC, in March featured Julie sipping an audience member's martini during "Daddy" and adding "Walk Right In," the 1963 folk hit for the Rooftop Singers, and the medley of "Here's That Rainy Day" and "Soon It's Gonna Rain" to her concert repertoire. Yet the venue worked against her intimate style, which left a critic wondering "why a booking agent who knows the size of the place would send her there to die." But again, business was great, although Julie agreed with the critics who panned her performances. "Nothing seemed to go right; it happens sometimes and the only thing to do is to forget it, like a bad dream." The dream became a nightmare a few weeks later when Julie opened at Caesar's Monticello Inn in Framingham, Massachusetts. Advertised as "New England's finest supper club," it was more low-end motel than high-class nightclub, and the audience was largely made up of drunken conventioneers.

When she got home, Julie was content to be lazy and let her husband pick up the kids from school and attend the meetings of the local parent-teacher association. Home also meant nights on the town. "We would go nightclubbing," recalled Tom Williams, "and end up at the house with some of the musicians that we had met. You couldn't get out of there!" Even as the sun was coming up, Julie would be calling that there was always "one more Ray Charles tune you've *gotta* listen to!"

The summer of 1966 was filled with good times. Bobby was working more again, and Julie was part of the audience for his opening night at the China Trader restaurant in Toluca Lake. Bobby's group became a regular feature at the spot, which was located near the Warner Bros. studio lot where Jack Webb had his office. Jack was also the owner of the China Trader, and Bobby later had a financial share in the restaurant for a number of years. Julie said "it helped enormously" when the two men "became such great friends." (Jack also hired Bobby to act in a couple of *Dragnet* episodes.) There were even nights when Julie could be persuaded to sing.

For shows at the Tudor Inn in the Los Angeles suburb of Norwalk, she was accompanied by former Nat King Cole guitarist John Collins, who had been playing regularly with Bobby. "In today's show business world of raucous, extroverted singers," wrote a critic, "one yearns now and then for the smoky, soft-sell feminine voice that delivers the 'message' with an apparent minimum of effort but maximum result." Other gigs that summer saw Julie spending a week at the Celebrity Room of the Cal-Neva Lodge in Lake Tahoe and sharing a bill with pianist Ramsey Lewis and folk singer Chad Mitchell at the Royal Tahitian's New Concert Gardens in Ontario, California.

Few singers were more aware of their limitations than Julie London. After grinding out product for the first half of the 1960s, the personal success of *Feeling Good* and *All Through the Night* had convinced her that she needed to be in control of the ambience and the material when making records. "I go in first with a small group and do the phrasing MY way," she told a journalist about her new routine. "The orchestra cuts their tape after listening to mine, and that means we don't have to follow any of those stiff arrangements anymore."

The results of this new style of recording became clear in the fall of 1966 with the release of the evocative, after-sundown mood that is *For the Night People*. At first glance producer Calvin Carter was an unlikely choice to work with Julie London, "the one class act that Liberty had." Carter had worked A&R and made records for Vee-Jay in Chicago. Under his guidance, it had developed into one of the great soul labels and, prior to Berry Gordy's Motown, was the largest black-owned record label in the nation. Carter's arrival at Liberty happened at exactly the right moment for Julie, because he "was wise enough to let Julie pick the material."

For the Night People was recorded by United/Western engineer Joe Sidore. When he arrived at the studio to discover he'd been assigned to work with an artist he'd been "head over heels" with since his teenage years, he vowed to make Julie's record sound like nothing she'd ever done before. "I kind of felt responsible for Julie." Convinced that she wasn't getting the respect from Liberty that she deserved, he "went the extra mile to make sure the set-up [of the studio] was right." His suspicions about how the singer was being treated by her label were confirmed when he later complained about the mixing job—done by another hand—on his recordings. A Liberty staffer insisted that no more time or money was going to be spent on her material.

In the studio, however, Julie was firmly in charge. The musicians "listened to her," he said. They "always followed her." Don Bagley confirmed this sea change. "We had done 'Bill Bailey' on some of the college jobs [years before]. To do it in that relaxed way, she was good at that. Especially if we were recording, she would say, 'Let's try this.' She'd have a tune in mind, and we knew her style. John Gray and I were intuitive; Julie liked us for that, because she could go anyplace she wanted to go."

Bagley's deceptively simple string arrangements heightened Gray's sympathetic guitar chording, which weaved around Julie's voice. The sparse sound of four violins, two violas, vibraphone, and piano was enlarged by the engineer bouncing the result between the left and right channels, with the application of the studio echo chamber to lend further ethereal ambience to an already high, palpable sense of romantic loss.

Julie's performances on *For the Night People* ache with the pain of late nights and solitary drinking. "Saturday Night (Is the Loneliest Night in the Week)" and Duke Ellington's "I Got It Bad (and That Ain't Good)" are slowed to a crawl, the former emphasizing the tormented loneliness in Sammy Cahn's lyrics. Having sung "God Bless the Child" as a child with her mother, Julie had a special feeling for this

Billie Holiday classic. Her interpretation—ragged and rough in voice, much like the latter-day recordings of Lady Day herself—is filled with memories of the Peck family's hard times during the Great Depression. Julie's voice on Johnny Mercer's ghostly "Dream" harkens back to her translucent performance of "Laura" a decade earlier. "Here's That Rainy Day" and "I'll Never Smile Again" plunge into the depths of despair, yet with hope of finding a renewed vision of her lover as she swoops down to a very low and atonal *you.*

Sales of the album couldn't have been helped by the unattractive cover, which showed the boozy-looking singer holding a champagne glass while posing by a fake Grecian urn. (The image came from a short film of "Daddy" that was made at Paramount Studios in Hollywood for the Color-Sonics sixteen-millimeter jukebox series.*) Record buyers paid little heed to *For the Night People,* although Julie retained a strong fan base in Asia and returned there in November 1966 for a tour that took her to Japan, Thailand, and the Philippines. Backed by Hal Serra, whose piano became the featured solo instrument, she traveled from Tokyo to Bangkok for concerts at the Café de Paris, followed by three shows in the Philippines, including a benefit performance for an Imelda Marcos–sponsored charity at a supper club in Manila. At her best on slow tunes like "Bill Bailey" and "How Long Has This Been Going On," where she could unearth the songs' often-hidden treasure of emotions, the upbeat numbers were tossed off as just so much noise.

Las Vegas had lost much of its glamorous image by the middle of the 1960s. The lounges and showrooms on the Strip, the swinging night-life capital of the Rat Pack days of Frank Sinatra, Dean Martin, and Sammy Davis Jr. had become the home for aging singers and musicians

---

* A film of "Watermelon Man" was supposedly made yet remains unseen. A humorously mod Bobby Troup appeared in his own version of "Girl Talk," directed by Robert Altman, who later famously gave him the last line ("Goddamn Army!") in his Oscar-winning film *M*A*S*H.*

who could find few options elsewhere in a musical world dominated by rock 'n' roll. Julie London turned forty in September 1966. She joined the procession to the desert.

The Tropicana Hotel was nicknamed the "Tiffany of the Strip," yet eight years after its opening, the polish had worn off its jewels. The risqué Folies Bergère had been a popular attraction since 1959 and regularly sold out the eight-hundred-seat showroom; now higher-quality musical entertainment was needed to keep the coffers filled with gambling money. Maynard Sloate—a veteran booker from the Los Angeles jazz and comedy scene—was hired as the hotel's new entertainment director and was tasked to fill the Blue Room, an elegant "second showroom" that had been added on to the property.

Still-popular entertainers like Mel Tormé, Benny Goodman, Dave Brubeck, Anita O'Day, Pete Fountain, Gene Krupa, and George Shearing had all played the five-hundred-seat lounge before Julie made her debut. She joined the room's self-proclaimed "galaxy of stars" on December 2, 1966, as part of a bill with Woody Herman, whose New Thundering Herd was led by pianist Hal Serra for Julie's three nightly performances. Her sensuous act was an immediate hit with the gamblers and conventioneers who patronized the hotel, and the Blue Room became Julie's steadiest, if not happiest, gig into the next decade.

Sophisticated Lady: Julie London in the early 1960s.
Troup-London estate

Julie's father, Jack Peck.
Troup-London estate

Julie's mother, Jo Peck.
Troup-London estate

Age four, posing for her parents' camera.
Troup-London estate

Childhood fun on horseback, early 1930s.
Lynn Todd

With her parents in Laguna Beach,
California, 1930s. *Lynn Todd*

Already aware of her good looks at age fifteen, 1942.
Troup-London estate

Jack Webb saw this pinup on his barracks wall: Julie as the "Golden Mould" in *Esquire* magazine, November 1943. Photo by Henry Waxman. *Author's collection*

At nineteen: a budding star poses by the family car. *Author's collection*

A gorgeous publicity photograph taken during Julie's days as a starlet at Universal, 1945. Photo by Ray Jones.
Author's collection

Not "a bad comeback for a kid of 21": as a high school temptress in the 1946 psychological thriller *The Red House*.
Troup-London estate

"I want to clear out of these hills when I get married!" Dreaming with costar Lon McCallister in *The Red House*, 1946.
Author's collection

All she had to show after seven years as an actress were a few good memories and a stack of eight-by-ten glossies: with Rock Hudson in *The Fat Man*, 1951.
Author's collection

The happy couple celebrates the success of *Dragnet*: Julie and her first husband, Jack Webb, New York City, April 1951.
Author's collection

A place in the sun: Julie soaks up the California rays.
Troup-London estate

The cover that launched a million dreams a[nd] helped to sell a million records. From a 19[ ] EP release.
Author's collection

posites attract: Julie and her new boyfriend, gwriter Bobby Troup, ca. 1955.
up-London estate

She knew the Meaning of the Blues: with José Ferrer in *The Great Man*, 1956.
Author's collection

Headliner on the Sunset Strip: Interlude, Hollywood, February 1956.
Troup-London estate

Sheet music cover for Bobby Troup's "Meaning of the Blues," promoting Julie's performance of the song in *The Great Man*, 1956.
Author's collection

Julie London and Spike Jones? Marquee of the New Frontier, Las Vegas, October 1956.
Troup-London estate

"The Thirteenth Month": the eye-openi surprise that awaited buyers of the elabora packaged *Calendar Girl* album, 1956.
Author's collection

With daughters Lisa and Stacy exiting from Julie's dressing room during the filming of *Saddle the Wind* at MGM, June 1957.
Troup-London estate

Alcohol only deadened the pain: as a Southern belle caught between two worlds in *Drango*, 1957.
Troup-London estate

Little Girl Blue: thinking about building a "dream house" of her own, ca. 1957.
Troup-London estate

Behind the bar on Ethel Avenue with her beloved
dachshund, Patsy, late 1950s.
Troup-London estate

1958: Julie swings gently through a set of jazzy standards
The singer's only Grammy-nominated record, the cover
design lost to Frank Sinatra's iconic *Only the Lonely*.
Troup-London estate

"Anything you do for me—do it gently": a tender moment with leading man Robert Taylor in *Saddle the Wind*, 1958.
Author's collection

Adoration: Bobby often gazed at Julie this way.
Troup-London estate

Menaced by Jack Lord in director Anthony Mann's violent western *Man of the West*, 1958.
Troup-London estate

A late 1950s example of why Julie London h "the record for posing in disappearing neckline
Troup-London estate

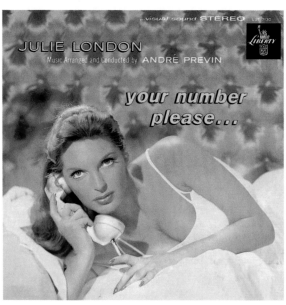

More décolletage for the cover of *Your Number Please*, 1959.
Author's collection

Miss Julie London

requests the pleasure of your company

New Year's Eve

Thursday, the thirty-first of December

from eight o'clock

Sixteen thousand seventy-four Royal Oaks Road

Encino, California

Late Supper

R. s. v. p.
CRestview 4-1417   Black tie

Invitation to the housewarming party that became a
wedding celebration, New Year's Eve, 1959.
Troup-London Estate

nstruction of the house that Julie built,
:ino, California, 1958.
hor's collection

The front door was almost always open, so Jack Webb
called it the "orphanage on the hill."
Author's collection

The front room of the Encino house, looking toward the circular foyer and the spiral staircase that leads to the second floor (left) and the swimming pool (right). *Author's collection*

The music room includes one of the numerous fireplace mantels Julie brought back from Europe; the clown painting is featured on the cover of *Love on the Rocks* (1962). *Author's collection*

delayed honeymoon: Julie and Bobby arrive in [Rio] de Janeiro, Brazil, to enjoy the festivities at [Car]nival, February 1960.

[Fitz]up-London estate

Julie meets JFK after her performance at the White House Correspondents' Dinner, Sheraton-Park Hotel, Washington, DC, February 25, 1961.

Abbie Rowe. White House Photographs. John F. Kennedy Presidential Library and Museum, Boston

"The Real Julie": Liberty Records offered these booklets to anyone who bought the 1961 album *Send for Me*.

Author's collection

"What Can I Say After I Say I'm Sorry": her final big-screen role in *The George Raft Story*, 1961. *Author's collection*

Performing "Black Coffee" on the NBC television variety show *The Lively Ones*, September 1963.
Troup-London estate

Julie and Bobby pose with the five children they raised in Encino: Stacy, Lisa, Kelly, Jody, and Reese, 1963. Photo by Lewis Rhodes.
Troup-London estate

A relaxed, confident singer performing in Japan, 1964.
Troup-London estate

"The whole attitude was Julie's": the sexy duet with bassist Don Bagley on "Bye Bye Blackbird," Japan 1964.
Troup-London estate

Doing it for the money: Bobby Troup's "Daddy" as interpreted for the short-lived Color-Sonics video jukebox, 1966.
Troup-London estate

"Two Sleepy People": the *Dean Martin Show*, NBC, February 1966.
Author's collection

With daughter Kelly, April 1966: "When I am upset or depressed, I can always rely on her to pull me out of it." *Troup-London estate*

Entertaining the "nocturnal swingers" the Century Plaza Hotel, Los Ange March 1967. *Troup-London estate*

Another airplane . . . another gig . . . another town, May 1966. *Troup-London estate*

orming in London on an episode of the *Show-* television variety series, CBS, July 1968. *'or's collection*

"Didn't We" in the Blue Room at the Tropicana in Las Vegas with guitarist Don Overberg, late 1970. *Troup-London estate*

Early 1970s, after trading in those glamorous gowns for a steady gig on *Emergency!* *Troup-London estate*

Never happier than at home, Julie enjoys the good life with longtime friend and guitarist Al Viola, 1970s.
Troup-London estate

"Their hearts were full of spring": Julie London and Bobby Troup, October 1977.
Troup-London estate

13

Lonesome Road

What the fuck key are we in!?

—Julie London, recording outtake ca. 1966

MANY SINGERS ARE EAGER to feed off the energy and conviviality of a studio filled with musicians, friends, and assorted hangers-on. Not Julie London. She desperately wanted and needed the protective shell of solitude in late-night sessions where she could be left alone to hone her one-on-one connection with a song. Her acute sensitivity to other people being witness to her "failures" had little basis in the reality of her often-wonderful performances.

"Julie was always a pleasure to work with," said engineer Joe Sidore. "She was very professional and had a very laid back and mellow personality. There was never any pressure. She was sure of herself. She knew what she wanted out of a song and she knew how to get it. She would pick a song and if for any reason she wasn't happy with the way it was turning out, she would stop and go on to another."

The artistic certainty of *Nice Girls Don't Stay for Breakfast* is aptly described by writer Arnold Shaw as an example of Julie's "art of nuance," her natural ability to hold back her emotions while simultaneously drawing listeners in. It's a typically intimate yet jazzy collection, enhanced by augmenting the sympathetic combination of guitar, bass, and drums

173

with instrumental overdubs from Jack Sheldon on trumpet and singer June Christy's husband Bob Cooper on tenor saxophone.

Don Bagley recalled the recording of the sly title song: "I had suggested to Julie that she do it as a slow ballad. She liked the idea and we rehearsed it with Troup. We showed up at the session and did a few bars, and [composer] Jerry Leshay came racing out of the booth and said, 'That's not the way that song goes!' It was his first exposure [to the new tempo]. When he quieted down and let us do the whole thing through with the strings, he agreed it was a good idea." Hearing Julie's interpretation of Bobby Troup's teasing lyrics about a barfly who is not quite the nice girl she pretends to be, it is hard to imagine the song as anything *but* a ballad. Julie tempts her companion into thinking she would never do anything like that while simultaneously admitting that maybe she did after all, so why not have a good time!

"When I Grow Too Old to Dream" begins in the familiar style of Julie's vocal/double bass duets, although it takes an unexpectedly funky turn toward the end. "I've Got a Crush on You" benefits from textures provided by a subtle piano backing and the romantic tenor saxophone, while the deliberate pacing of "Everything I Have Is Yours" lets her dig deep into Harold Adamson's tortured lyrics of a woman who relinquishes her personality for the sake of her lover. She turns the simple message of "You Made Me Love You," with its lyrical description of total helplessness in the face of love, into a precursor to "Cry Me a River." The classic blues of "Baby, Won't You Please Come Home" had been captured by everyone from Bessie Smith to Louis Armstrong, but Julie makes a case for her own style of blues, and Jack Sheldon solos with some high-end trumpet licks that push the tune to another realm.

A clock-chiming piano opens "I Didn't Know What Time It Was," and to quote the lyrics, it's a "sublime" performance. "Give a Little Whistle," from the 1940 Disney classic *Pinocchio*, is the first of the album's two Disney ditties, and as with "Mickey Mouse," Julie transformed a simple song, with its simple message of friendship, into a burning blue flame. Bing Crosby had made "I Surrender, Dear" a hit in 1931, but Julie combines an unerring grasp of her own technical limitations and a deep understanding of the emotional depth of the lyrics to make this one of her greatest performances. "You Go to My Head" would have been a perfect fit within the alcohol-as-love concept of *Love on the Rocks*, as Julie fluctuates between a whispery delivery that floats to the brain like the song's bubbles of champagne and the more brittle, evocative vocal edge she had developed in recent years.

The simplicity and unexpected sexuality of Julie's unlikely interpretation of "Mickey Mouse," aided by John Gray's elegant chording—a combination of pick and fingering—brings the album to an unexpected conclusion. Her signature whisper imparts a somber yet soothing tone to Jimmie Dodd's minor-key melody, particularly during the final "M-I-C . . . K . . . E-Y / M . . . O . . . U . . . S . . . E," yet without a trace of irony or the sense that this material was beneath her. The two Disney songs were a fitting tribute to the recently deceased Walt Disney, who had responded positively to Julie's interpretation of the mouse song during her act and had thanked her for doing it. "That was a big deal," recalled Don Bagley, "since it was rare to get any recognition from him." Another tribute came from actor Buddy Ebsen, who congratulated Julie after hearing her sing "Mickey Mouse" on the radio.

At the end of 1966, Liberty Records announced that they were turning away from the singles market to focus on revitalizing some of its established acts. Based on the lack of promotion that *Nice Girls* received, Julie was no longer counted among those stars. The album was a major highlight of her late-career renaissance and received critical acclaim. Praised as a "throaty commentary of brittle songs about unrequited love" by one writer who was particularly enamored with the "steamed, marinated, smoked and highly seasoned" mouse number, another raved that Julie's style continued to be "soft, sentimental and gripping." Yet *Nice Girls*—and the two singles pulled from it, the title song and "Mickey Mouse"—passed with little notice in the marketplace. Even the provocative cover image of the singer half reclining on a bed, cigarette in hand and cleavage exposed in a man's raincoat, was old—a reversed drawing from the back cover of 1961's *Send for Me*.

Valentine's Day 1967: Julie makes her debut at the plush, Vegas-style Westside Room in the Century Plaza Hotel in Century City. The opening-night review acknowledged that her "low-keyed, sultry voice isn't everyone's cup of Lipton's, but her fans were numerous . . . and she gave them what they came to hear." For the gig Julie introduced a new quartet of male singers, who had been brought to her attention by Arthur Hamilton. "She was a blast to work with," recalled vocalist John Bähler. Julie had a "great naughty sense of humor. She was a consummate professional; we adored every minute of it!"

"If some of her numbers were mumbled," *Variety* noted, "it mattered not to the cash customers, who liked the way she [did] things." Her act included a number of recent ballads, including "Nice Girls Don't Stay for Breakfast," "Saturday Night (Is the Loneliest Night of the Week)," and Henry Mancini's "Slow Hot Wind," a song based on "Lujon," an instrumental number from the composer's *Mr. Lucky Goes Latin* album to which Norman Gimbel added lyrics. (Julie never recorded the song, which had been popularized by Sarah Vaughan on her 1965 Mancini songbook LP for Mercury.) A wild version of "Accentuate the Positive," arranged in Hi-Lo's style by Earl Brown, had John Bähler and his brother Tom adding trumpets to the sound.*

Julie London rarely professed any strong political beliefs, yet there were occasions when she could be persuaded to use her glamorous appeal for a particular purpose. On April 11, 1967, while in Washington, DC, for another engagement at the Shoreham Hotel, she made the most unusual, and well publicized, personal appearance of her career.

Clothed in "a blue woolly shifty thing that touched all the bases like a grand slam home run," she sat before a microphone in a second-floor

---

* The Bähler brothers recorded three albums as the psychedelic pop band the Love Generation for the Liberty subsidiary Imperial Records.

hearing room on Capitol Hill to testify before a Senate subcommittee in support of an amendment to the nation's copyright laws. Sponsored by Senator Harrison Williams Jr. (D-NJ), the amendment proposed the extension of royalty payments to performers when their records were broadcast on radio and television. Existing copyright law only allowed payments to songwriters and publishers. Under the auspices of the newly organized National Committee for the Recording Arts, bandleader Stan Kenton, Mitch Miller, and the assistant concertmaster of the Boston Symphony Orchestra took turns pledging their support, but it was Julie who packed the room and entertained the senators and their staff.

Her carefully crafted and prepared statement is a unique glimpse into the relationship between the song and the singer:

> Whatever creative talent I have lies in my ability to "reach" an audience with the way I interpret a song. . . . The success we achieve with our audiences is dependent upon the degree of our creative skill, the original manner in which we are able to take the printed note and bring it to life. . . . The interpretive performance of a skilled professional performer is by definition a creative act. . . . I study a song and ask myself what I can do with it that will give it individuality. What sort of mood do I want to create, and how shall I create it. This is discussed with my arranger. We talk about the kind of instrumentation that will be required, the musical introduction, the tempo or beat. Before I record a song, I may have spent dozens of hours working it out in different ways, making many changes, listening each time on a tape recorder, and then making still further changes in an effort to put in my own feelings and emotions. Finally, when all of those with whom I work—my arranger, my conductor, my manager, my producer—are all convinced that we have created a unique and highly individualistic product which expresses my style, we are ready to make our record.

What followed was Julie's inspired method of making her case. A battery-operated portable phonograph was on a nearby table, and Julie asked a young man to play the record currently on the turntable: the original cheerful ditty of the *Mickey Mouse Club* theme. After listening to a few bars, Julie's sensual recording of the same song was heard. The Senate employees who packed the normally sparsely populated hearing room rocked with laughter, and Senator Quentin Burdick (D-ND) told Julie she had made her point. "I never thought I would enjoy that Mickey Mouse song," quipped Democratic senator Philip Hart of Michigan. A reporter covering the hearing noted the "bemused look" on the faces of the subcommittee members, who seemed to be "thinking of running away and joining the Mouseketeers." Most of the men who had come in expressly to see Julie left in one large group after she finished her statement. Bobby Troup, who spoke next, joked that anything he might say would be anticlimactic. Although the publicity may have helped sell a few additional copies of Julie's latest single, the amendment failed to pass.

Other than a week of performances at the Ilikai Hotel in Honolulu during May, the spring of 1967 was spent quietly at home. Julie returned to the Tropicana in Las Vegas for a three-week run in August with the sixteen-piece house orchestra of the popular big-band trombonist Si Zentner who, like Julie, was in his second decade of making records for Liberty. The engagement launched her new show, and she brought on board an elegant-looking pianist named Kirk Stuart to lead the band. Born in West Virginia in 1934, Stuart had backed Billie Holiday and Della Reese and had been Sarah Vaughan's regular accompanist in the early 1960s. (His Nat King Cole–style singing can be heard on Vaughan's Mercury album *Sassy Swings the Tivoli*, recorded live in Copenhagen, Denmark.)

"Miss Julie's provocative song stylings are well suited to the plush lounge's atmosphere," wrote one critic. Although her opening night "drew an overflow crowd and many had to wait in line for [the] second show," Julie's more "expressive" up-tempo mode wasn't to everyone's taste, particularly a new number, John Phillips's "Straight Shooter," in which she needed the aid of her vocal quartet to get the message across.

She tried to add some hipness to her act by moving around the stage, but she "let the boys do most of it with her, and she'd lean on them, or walk around them, or they'd lift her up." Still, her sultry performances were well received by the "nocturnal swingers" who now made up the majority of her fans.

The pattern of Julie's career had stabilized, although its long-term viability remained in question. She did a few weeks at the Tropicana, found an increasingly limited number of hotel engagements elsewhere, and searched for the isolated one-nighter to keep the money coming in. She admitted she could work much more, but staying at home to "goof off" with the kids was more fun.

Acting roles had all but dried up. Casting directors weren't hiring many women over the age of forty—particularly those without a successful track record—when there were so many younger, less expensive actresses around town. Julie remained willing to face the cameras again when the odd television part came up, yet she remained ambivalent about acting and disappointed in the quality of the scripts. She must have really hated "The Prince of Darkness Affair, Part Two," an October 1967 episode of *The Man from U.N.C.L.E.*, since she sleepwalks through the measly role and clearly reads most of her lines from cue cards. The producers of the successful NBC television espionage series were so eager to have her that they chartered an airplane to fly her back and forth from Las Vegas to the MGM studios in Culver City for an entire week so she could work on the show during the day and return to the Tropicana for her evening performances. Julie's two brief scenes as the mysterious Laura Sebastian opposite series star Robert Vaughn as U.N.C.L.E. agent Napoleon Solo are both silly and a waste of time. (When the two episodes were combined into *The Helicopter Spies* for theatrical release, Julie's second scene became more risqué and showed her in bed with a bare-chested young man.) The paycheck presumably compensated for such a negligible piece of work.

Liberty released *With Body and Soul* in the midst of the epochal Summer of Love in 1967, with Julie billed as "Miss Julie London" (à la "Miss Peggy Lee"). It was her fifth consecutive fine late-career LP. Cal Carter again occupied the producer's chair for sessions that took place in the summer at United/Western. Don Bagley, increasingly occupied with movie and television commitments, was succeeded as musical director by Kirk Stuart. *For the Night People* and *Nice Girls Don't Stay for Breakfast* featured limited instrumentation; *With Body and Soul* had a big-band sound that made it a worthy companion to *Feeling Good*, the singer's superb 1965 recording with Gerald Wilson. (The album's cover photograph, with Julie sporting a set of oversized pearl earrings, was shot by well-known Hollywood lensman Gene Trindl.)

The album is an assortment of straightforward rhythm-and-blues-style numbers, with a slurry take on Irving Berlin's "Alexander's Ragtime Band" thrown into the mix. Rather than relying on vintage tunes, five of the eleven songs are new. Though Julie was, by this point in her career, able to tackle the material with an assurance not audible on the similarly styled *Send for Me*, *With Body and Soul* didn't register with a record-buying public that was more in tune with the sounds of *Sgt. Pepper's Lonely Hearts Club Band*.

Highlights include "Come on By," an early songwriting effort by composer Angelo Badalamenti (under his pseudonym Andy Badale), who rose to fame twenty years later with his eerie scores for director David Lynch. Julie grooves on this one, audibly snapping her fingers and reaching into an unfamiliar upper register toward the end. Her insinuating vocal purr is all over a rendition of Lil Green's "Romance in the Dark," while the slinky, boozy version of "Alexander's Ragtime Band" begins as the antithesis of typical flag-waving renditions before rousing itself into that good-old martial beat. Singer/songwriter Sonny Knight, who had recorded for Aura, a small Liberty-distributed label, supplied the obscure "If You Want This Love," the title song of his equally obscure 1964 album. Nat King Cole hit the top five on the pop charts in 1958 with "Looking Back," but his weak, plodding rendition of the Brook

Benton/Clyde Otis/Belford Hendricks song pales in comparison with Julie's poignant, gospel-tinged reading.

"I sing low and sexy because I can't sing any higher," Julie admitted, and the low and sexy "Treat Me Good" by the obscure soul singers/songwriters Buddy Scott and Jimmy Radcliffe is a perfect fit. An increasing hoarseness was now audible in her voice, the result of the continual abuse she gave her body with copious amounts of tobacco and alcohol. "It was always fortunate that she was a sultry singer," said a friend, "because she had that edge on it anyway . . . that kind of raspy sound. In the first years of her singing, it was higher, it was clearer; she got away with what it turned into."

"Straight Shooter," a song from *If You Can Believe Your Eyes and Ears*, the 1966 debut album by the popular folk-rock quartet the Mamas and the Papas, is a testament to Julie's willingness to explore new musical avenues. She may not have been aware of the drug connotations in the lyrics (a "straight shooter" injects drugs directly into his veins), but she gets into a fine groove on the song, which is the only recorded example of how Julie's latter-day backing singers circled around her voice as she wailed away in front of them.

With a $25,000 wardrobe of new Travilla gowns hanging in her dressing room, Julie returned to the Royal Box in New York City on her forty-first birthday, September 26, 1967. Pianist Hal Serra conducted the band, Bucky Pizzarelli accompanied her on guitar, and her vocals were boosted by her current quartet of singers, known as the Dappers. "Miss London's major failure," wrote a *Variety* critic, "stems from the fact that she shows only one, albeit mighty, facet of herself. . . . The audience would like to know more of her." He missed the point: it was that very unknowable quality that set Julie London apart from other singers. She wasn't going to change her act for the sake of critics.

There were always good times to be had when Julie was in town. Liberty's East Coast sales manager Mel Fuhrman recalled one evening when she came to sit as his table after a performance and cussed like a sailor in front of his guest, Father Norman O'Connor. Known as "the jazz priest" for his longtime support of music and musicians, O'Connor didn't seem to be offended. Pianist Lee Evans, whose band performed behind Julie, remembered that she was "understandably tense" when she learned that both Sarah Vaughan and Carmen McRae—two of Julie's favorite vocalists, to whom she would never compare her own singing abilities in anything but disparaging terms—were in the audience.

These 1967 dates would be Julie's last shows at the club that had played host to her career-changing big-band performances three years earlier. Shortly after her run at the Tropicana had ended in August, she signed a deal with the renowned Ashley-Famous Agency, a firm born out of the merger of Ted Ashley's company with Famous Artists, which had represented Julie in the late 1950s. The most significant move that her new representatives would make on her behalf was to upgrade her Manhattan performance venue to the higher-end Empire Room of the Waldorf-Astoria Hotel on Park Avenue.

The run at the Americana was cut short by news from home that Julie's father had died on October 9, 1967, in Encino Hospital at the age of sixty-seven. Returning to California for the funeral, Julie joined her family as Jack Peck was buried three days later in a private ceremony at Forest Lawn Memorial Park in Glendale. A series of strokes—exacerbated by bouts of heavy drinking—had left the once "extremely handsome" man without his good looks and his voice, bitter that his final years were spent confined to a wheelchair.

Julie remained close to her father over the years, and after the success of "Cry Me a River," she had purchased a small house for her parents in Sherman Oaks, California, and became the source of much of their income after Jack Peck's retirement. She adored her mother, but Jo's own troubles with alcohol made it increasingly difficult for Julie, who had her own similar issues, to spend much time around her. Julie's relationship with Jo Peck was, according to Julie's daughter Lisa, "very strange." Jo was a "pistol," so it's easy to see where Julie got some of her personality traits. Unfortunately, that similarity, when drinking got the best of both of them, could lead to embarrassing incidents, particularly on the occasions when Julie would bring her mother along for one of her out-of-town shows. The love remained, however, and Julie never forgot or took lightly the trust her parents had in her when she was a teenager. Even in her later years, when Jo was bound to a wheelchair, she and her daughter still connected through music, and the pair would casually sing duets around the house. Josephine Peck died nearly nine years after her husband, on February 15, 1976, as a result of a fall in the bathtub of her house. She was seventy years old.

Mourning for her father had to take a backseat to contractual obligations. October saw Julie doing one-night stands at Idaho State University, the University of Montana, and at Chico State College in Northern California, where she was backed by Kirk Stuart's trio, including the stalwart Don Bagley on bass, as well as a stint as part of an eclectic bill at the 1967 Arizona State Fair in Phoenix in November.

She returned to the Deep South for the first time in four years when she opened at the plush Blue Room of the Roosevelt Hotel in New Orleans in January 1968. Musical director Kirk Stuart conducted the house band for her nightly shows. In a flowing red chiffon gown with dangling diamond-shaped earrings, she opened with "Hey Good Lookin'" in a voice that required "absolute attention." Julie was "in a class by herself. . . . No one can do to a song what she does. No one, probably, can even come close." As always her appearances attracted celebrities, including trumpeter and New Orleans native Al Hirt, and coincided with Mardi Gras, where she appeared as the guest of the mayor at the *Wizard of Oz*–themed Caliphs of Cairo Ball at the city's Municipal Auditorium.

During her stay in New Orleans, her newest syndicated television special, *The Julie London Show*, made its broadcast debut. The show was filmed on November 21, 1967, at NBC in Burbank, California, where Julie cracked up the audience after one unsuccessful take by sarcastically joking that the director would "never get that same marvelous reading" from her again. The success of the show was in no small measure due to Julie's "cool projection [which] tends to disguise the extent of her vocal gifts and versatility." The program, the first of a series of syndicated Screen Gems Presents specials, ranked at the top of its time period when it was broadcast in New York, beating out Johnny Carson and ABC's *Movie of the Week*.

The Julie London Show included a wealth of songs she never recorded elsewhere: renditions of "Accentuate the Positive," "Never Will I Marry" from Frank Loesser's Broadway musical, *Greenwillow*, the Antonio Carlos Jobim bossa nova, "Meditation," the frothy Sammy Cahn and Jimmy Van Heusen title song from *Thoroughly Modern Millie*, and a show-closing performance of "Cabaret" with the entire cast. The show's highlight, though, was something familiar: a heart-stopping performance of "Nice Girls Don't Stay for Breakfast" in which Julie's breathtaking physical beauty only accentuated her knowing attitude.

By the late 1960s, executives at Liberty Records were diversifying the label by signing popular young acts like the Nitty Gritty Dirt Band and Canned Heat as quickly as they could draw up the contracts. The company's marketing staff greeted the January 1968 release of *Easy Does It* by disparaging Julie London's work as unworthy of their time and effort. Her deal, said Al Stoffel, the writer of the album's liner notes, "called for delivery of a certain amount of 'product,' and she was obligated to record albums, so they could go into the release schedule. I sure got the impression that nobody was getting rich from her efforts at that point." Stoffel, who had joined Liberty in the fall of 1967 straight out of the University of California, Los Angeles (UCLA), recalled the singer as "rather abrupt in her interaction [with people]. Not *bored* with singing as much as jaded and feeling the effects of having gone through the wars."

His most vivid memory of Julie London took place during the photo session for the album cover. John Engstead was hired "because he was an old time glamour photographer to the stars." The singer told Engstead to "watch the angles"—she was an old broad. "It was a clear snapshot of someone who was tired of the process, had done it all at various levels of success and was over it." The photographer did his job well, and the final image was all soft-focus glamour. (Another photo from the session was used for Julie's final album, *Yummy, Yummy, Yummy*, and an alternate shot appeared on the cover of an early 1980s Liberty/Capitol abridged reissue of *Julie Is Her Name*.)

She was always her own worst critic. "I get bugged when I can't sing," she admitted in a 1964 interview. "I'm frustrated when I want to do something and because I'm not a singer, I'm incapable or unable to do it." This self-criticism—and Julie's often-blunt manner of expressing her displeasure—was on full display during the recording sessions for *Easy Does It*. She always knew when what she was doing was absolutely right for the song. The expletives were quick and loud when she wasn't happy with the way things were going.

A widely circulated excerpt from an unsuccessful attempt to lay down George and Ira Gershwin's "The Man I Love" has often been ridiculed for its profanity-filled outbursts and salty humor ("I sound like Carol Channing—in drag!"). The ridicule misses the point; what the outtake truly reveals is Julie London's single-minded focus on finding the precise feel and tempo that suited how she felt about a song. Her repeated emphasis on slowing the pace ("That's too Goddamn fast!")—to the point of verbally disagreeing with producer Cal Carter and having guitarist John Gray accompany her solo until everyone else picked up on her tempo ("No, it's not slow enough!")—emphasizes just how certain she was of just what was needed to show off her ability to hold a lyric and draw from it the last ounce of meaning.

Years later she told jazz critic Leonard Feather that *Easy Does It* was the best album she ever made. Recorded in a series of November 1967 sessions at United Recording with the usual familiar faces (Don Bagley, John Gray, Earl Palmer on drums, and Kirk Stuart on piano and Hammond organ), Julie was at the top of her game, in full control of the repertoire and the mood. Bagley, Stuart, and Allyn Ferguson shared the credit for the minimal string arrangements that make the album sound like outtakes from *Nice Girls Don't Stay for Breakfast* and *For the Night People.* This was no surprise to engineer Joe Sidore. "I think that [*Easy Does It* engineer Lanky Linstrot] was inspired the same as I was when he heard the arrangements and wound up giving it the same treatment with echo and the like."

"Show Me the Way to Go Home" is boozy and bluesy, and Bagley acts as the singer's silhouette on "Me and My Shadow," recalling their work on "Bye Bye Blackbird." She gets behind the beat on "This Can't Be Love," a performance "pulsating as flickering candlelight." The inno-cent joy of "Soon It's Gonna Rain"—finally heard on record—is tem-pered by her knowledge of life's fragility. The laid-back mood continues with "April in Paris," the instrumental break riffing on the classic Count Basie rendition, while the Gershwins' "Bidin' My Time" becomes an uncanny characterization of the lazy performer Julie professed to be. (She also managed to finally get "The Man I Love" in shape for the record.) The glacial pace of her second recording of "It Had to Be You" poi-gnantly recalls her parents' meeting decades earlier—the song was taped shortly after Jack Peck's death—and this makes it a significantly more moving one than her perfunctory 1957 version. A second rerecording—"The One I Love Belongs to Somebody Else"—is, happily, opened up from the short, rhythmic version heard on the second volume of *Julie Is Her Name* and concludes the first of her albums to be released only in stereo. *Easy Does It* would turn out to be Julie London's final collection of the standards from the Great American Songbook, which had made up the bulk of her repertoire.*

Nearly two dozen songs were taped during the sessions, enough to fill two complete albums, yet only one track, Irving Berlin's "I've Got My Love to Keep Me Warm"—released in 2004 on a Christmas-themed volume in Capitol's popular Ultra-Lounge series—has seen the

---

* It was also the last work she did with guitarist John Gray. Often unhappy with the Los Angeles music scene, Gray moved away from California and years later suffered a stroke that deprived him of his ability to play the guitar. He died in Oklahoma in 1983 at the age of fifty-nine, a largely forgotten talent. His two recordings for Capitol, *The New Wave* (1962) and *Togetherness* (1963, with trombonist Bob Flanigan) are worth seeking out.

light of day. It shows Julie in the type of warm, intimate session that was always her forte.

Fortunately, most—if not all—of the other tracks Julie laid down were located on a set of acetates during the writing of this book. Like the Berlin song, these didn't make the final cut of the LP, so they never received the distracting string overdubs; the bare-bones nature of these cuts leaves Julie's voice and her interplay with the guitar and bass as the focal point. Characteristically, almost all the outtakes are ballads: "This Love of Mine," "In Love in Vain," "I'm Always Chasing Rainbows," Bobby Troup's "Hot Chocolate," "Oh! Look at Me Now," Duke Ellington's "I'm Beginning to See the Light," "Exactly Like You," and "Love Is a Simple Thing," which, like the failed attempt at "The Man I Love," breaks down into expletives. The sole up-tempo number is a driving version of Rodgers and Hammerstein's "The Gentleman Is a Dope" in which the singer does an impromptu pseudoscat when she flubs the lyric. Of particular note is "You Don't Know What Love Is," Julie having expressed her fondness for the 1941 song by Don Raye and Gene de Paul in a blindfold test conducted by Leonard Feather in 1956: "It's a very good record to listen to when you are relaxed and stretched out on the floor with a drink in your hand."

—⸎—

Julie London clearly had had her fill of the music business by the late 1960s. The success of her early years had been followed by a gradual, if steady, decline in record sales, rescued only by the Snuff Garrett period of pop recordings in 1962–1964 and a brief return to the charts. Her albums since that time, while artistically significant, sold modestly at best and had largely been ignored by the music press, which had moved on to cover more popular acts. Her nightclub work had shrunk to an ever-smaller circle of venues and had become an endless cycle of getting to the hotel, doing the gig, partying in her room or gambling in the casino, sleeping late, and starting the process all over again. It wasn't the ideal atmosphere in which to rejuvenate a career or raise a family.

Yet she continued to land *just* enough engagements to fill her date-book, with a loyal cadre of fans who still showed up to fill the seats at lounges and supper clubs. In February 1968 she debuted at the Venetian Room of San Francisco's Fairmont Hotel, backed by pianist Kirk Stuart and the house orchestra of society bandleader Ernie Heckscher. A three-week stint at the Westside Room during March and April with Stuart and the backing vocalists introduced a few new numbers, including the 5th Dimension's smash hit "Up, Up and Away," and a surprising up-tempo version of "Once Upon a Time," the beautiful Charles Strouse / Lee Adams ballad from their Broadway musical *All American*, which was added to the act after she heard Tony Bennett's recording. "He's the best in the world," she enthused. She was back at the Tropicana again in the middle of April for a "very effective" two-week run, with the backing of Si Zentner's band under Kirk Stuart's baton in a repertoire of "sultry, sensuous" numbers. The occasional loud, swinging tune had fans complaining about the noise, but Julie insisted that the contrast made the ballads a more enjoyable listening experience. She remained "every inch a headliner."

As Julie's audiences narrowed to the middle-aged crowds that frequented the Las Vegas casinos or stayed at the Waldorf-Astoria and other high-end hotels, her record company was struggling to maintain its relevance in a changing marketplace. Sales had tripled since Al Bennett bought Liberty back from the Avnet Corporation in 1963, but its roster of artists was graying and lacked the hip vibe that sold records. In the midst of the singer's gig at the Westside Room, Bennett announced the sale of the label, in a deal worth a reported $24 million, to the San Francisco–based Transamerica Corporation, owners of United Artists Records (UA).

Everything seemed fine at the beginning. "Liberty was the larger of the two record companies, so we were told that the UA record division would be folded into Liberty and that we would manage the combined companies," said Al Stoffel. But UA's "cooler, hipper" executives considered Liberty's artists ripe for pruning. One of the first acts to be subjected to the financial scrutiny of the new owners was Julie London. If her contract was to be renewed, a change in style was necessary. But what direction could she realistically take and, more important, how would she react when pushed into a corner?

14

Wild, Smooth, and Sultry

I love the new music.

—Julie London, 1968 radio interview

F OR ALL OF JULIE'S contrariness in other areas, she had been willing—
to some extent—to experiment with her material, and her attitude
that "there's room for all kinds of music" helped her to get out ahead
of many other singers. In the early 1960s, when her contemporaries—
Frank Sinatra, Mel Tormé, and Peggy Lee among them—were largely
avoiding the songs of Brill Building writing teams like Burt Bacharach
and Hal David or Gerry Goffin and Carole King, Julie was ahead of
the field with her Snuff Garrett–produced pop records.

Now as the decade was coming to an end, she needed another new
producer to once again turn around her career with a change of sound
and songs. The job of providing her with a more contemporary, soft-rock
style was assigned to thirty-six-year-old Tommy Oliver, who had moved
up the ranks at Liberty within months of his arrival as an A&R man in
1966. He had given singer Vikki Carr her first chart success with *It Must
Be Him* the following year and worked with acts as diverse as balladeer
Mel Carter, the studio instrumental combo Trombones Unlimited, and
the pop-rock band the Love Generation. Lyle Ritz—a bassist who began
his career playing jazz but became a member of the so-called Wrecking

Crew of Hollywood studio musicians during the 1960s—called Oliver a "creative orchestrator and arranger, and a Never-Say-No guy with a fearless confidence and a wonderful smile and stage presence."

The material Oliver chose for the recording sessions was all of recent vintage, and many of the songs had been hits. Not only were the songs—by acts as diverse as the Beatles, Bob Dylan, the Doors, the 5th Dimension, and the garage band the Kingsmen—different from anything she had recorded before, so were many of the musicians. This reflected the changing nature of the Hollywood recording studio scene. The jazz players who used to be called to back singers were rapidly being replaced by musicians such as reedman Jim Horn or drummers John Guerin and Hal Blaine, whose rock 'n' roll and pop sensibilities were better suited to the new musical styles. These tunes weren't necessarily in Julie's familiar style or among her favorites, "but she enjoyed doing them," said a friend, since they gave her a chance to do her version of "rock[ing] out."

The results were encouraging, but as had happened during Julie's movie career, they were overshadowed by events beyond her control. Transamerica Corporation had purchased Liberty Records to solidify its music division, but according to the label's general manager Bud Dain, president Al Bennett "sold them a bill of goods." Liberty's real financial value was less than half of what Transamerica paid for it, and it didn't take long for questions to be asked about the numbers behind the paper.

"Many of the promises [made] to the Liberty staff were broken," Al Stoffel said. "UA was based in New York . . . so communication and coordination during transition was difficult. It didn't take long for UA to begin influencing Liberty and its people to finally take over our operation." Ultimately, Al Bennett himself fell. In his wake United Artists president Mike Stewart decimated nearly the entire staff of Liberty's West Coast office.

Good sales figures were vital to Julie's future at Liberty, so ignoring what was happening to the company, she pushed on with whatever gigs—large or small—she could get, hoping that some of the people who saw her in person would subsequently look for her records at their local stores. The "old" Julie still received sporadic offers of varying quality for club dates and television performances. In April 1968 the ABC variety show *Operation: Entertainment* featured her return to her childhood home of San Bernardino to perform "Daddy" and "Show Me the Way to Go Home" in front of vibraphonist Terry Gibbs and his swinging big band in an episode filmed at Norton Air Force Base.

Another engagement at the Century Plaza Hotel in Los Angeles was followed by a summer trip to Elstree Studios in London to film an episode of the British variety spectacular *The Big Show*. Renamed *Showtime* for its American broadcast on CBS as a summer replacement for Red Skelton, Julie's episode aired in July and featured huskily effective performances of "Straight Shooter," "The Man That Got Away," and "Cry Me a River."

In the fall she did a series of shows at the El Dorado club in Mexico's Hotel Camino Real, and for a tidy $10,000, appeared at the September grand opening of the Gold Room, a four-hundred-seat club in the Los Angeles suburb of Norwalk. Her show, wrote the *Los Angeles Times* critic, was "geared to persons of voting age and older. While Miss London's repertoire follows a familiar path, it's easy listening for mature people who aren't forced to nudge each other and ask, 'What's the title of that one?'" Insight into Julie London, vintage 1968, came from Tedd Thomey, a columnist for the *Long Beach Press-Telegram*, who caught one of her Gold Room performances:

> She mesmerized the audience. . . . As she sang and quipped, her mouth offered a wide range of expressions. One moment it was a little girl's mouth, happy then pouting; next it was a chanteuse's mouth, sad and sensual, smoking a cigarette borrowed from someone in the audience.

It seemed only appropriate that Julie London's final acting appearance of the 1960s was in the western genre for which she had long expressed mixed feelings. Two days after closing in Norwalk, ABC broadcast "They Called Her Delilah," a good episode of *The Big Valley*, which gave Julie her first real dramatic television performance in years. It was a rare opportunity to develop a character rather than float through yet another meaningless cameo. It's April 1878; the Civil War has been over for more than a decade, but when popular singer Julia Saxon arrives in Stockton, California, it's clear that old wounds haven't healed. Suspected of having been a Confederate spy, Julia is arrested for the murder of a local hotel manager. The Barkley brothers (Richard Long, Peter Breck, and Lee Majors) spend the rest of the hour saving Julia from being lynched.

Bobby Troup, who played an uncredited role as Julia Saxon's piano player, composed the lullaby "The Happy Road" for the episode. His poignant lyrics of a woman's search for comfort and home "where sunshine warmed each day" fit well with Julie's solidly structured performance. The one-time relationship between Julia Saxon and the Barkley brother played by Richard Long is well delineated, and Julie's scene with Linda Evans (the Barkley sister), in which the singer's ambivalence about trading "bits and pieces of information" during the war for help in becoming a star, parallels Julie's own feelings about her career.

The first sign of the new album was the release of her "sexy spoof" of the Ohio Express' bubble-gum-pop hit "Yummy, Yummy, Yummy" as a single in October 1968. It turned out to be a savvy move: the company's promotion of the song as Julie's stab at contemporary hipness, and the use of phrases like "And How!" and "A Happening Thing!" in the advertising, had an immediate, if short-lived, impact. The record may have only reached number 125 on the *Billboard* charts, but it was Julie's first appearance there in five years, and she was praised for giving the tune "a whole new feel and flavor," which transformed the sugary confection into a honey-dripping boudoir ballad as sensual as anything in Julie's repertoire, albeit with a rock beat propelled by a solid rhythm section and some dramatically swooping strings.

In the nightclubs it was business as usual. On November 8, just days after the election of Richard Nixon as the country's thirty-seventh president, Julie opened a two-week run at the plush Empire Room of the Waldorf-Astoria Hotel in New York City, with Kirk Stuart again at the piano and leading the band. Her "sleek, sophisticated song styling glistened luminously against the background of the club's opulence," noted *Cash Box*, whose critic spotlighted "the highly inventive" closing number: Julie's rendition of "Mickey Mouse" with a "funky, soul accompaniment." *Billboard* critic Robert Sobel pithily described her act as having "the organized abandon of a top stripper." Sultry play was her thing. "What she lacks in vocal power she amply makes up in provocativeness, permissiveness and persuasiveness. . . . Miss London stresses make love, not song. There's not much wrong with that."

Publicity was good. Restaurateur Toots Shor and comedian Bob Hope were among those who caught the singer's act, with the lecherous Hope gazing at her low neckline and commenting, "I've known you for 15 years and you haven't changed an inch." Attendance was helped by an appearance on Jonathan Winters's CBS variety show, where she performed "You Do Something to Me" in a skit with the popular comedian playing his octogenarian character, Maynard Tetlinger, and sang "Me and My Shadow" alongside the Andre Tayir Dancers and the orchestra of Paul Weston. (During the run, Julie resumed her role of product promoter when she filmed a television commercial for Arrid deodorant in which she sang Bobby Troup's song "Let Me Baby You" accompanied by guitarist Bucky Pizzarelli.)

From New York she headed south to Washington, DC, for a brief return engagement at the Shoreham Hotel. Billed once again as "Miss Julie London," it was a "low key evening" according to the *Washington Post*. "Her noted figure is admirably displayed and she shows a nice sense of phrasing and timing," but her voice was overwhelmed by the roaring sound of the large band, and even the quartet of harmony singers couldn't help. From DC it was north for a two-week run at the penthouse of the thousand-acre Playboy Club hotel near Lake Geneva, Wisconsin. The lavish resort, complete with an eighteen-hole championship golf course, twenty-five-acre "Bunny Lake," two-hundred-foot vertical-drop ski run, and horse-riding stables with twenty miles of bridle paths, had opened earlier that year. "Julie purrs like a kitten," wrote Will Leonard of the *Chicago Tribune*, "[and] snuggles up to one ringsider while slapping down a heckler across the room. With that big, lovely, 12-man orchestra behind her, she puts on the kind of show a lot of songstresses don't know to put on." Despite the critical plaudits and the appreciative audiences, Julie still found herself searching for a way to expand her audience without totally abandoning the musical style she was known for.

Julie and Bobby celebrated their ninth wedding anniversary in Las Vegas during the middle of her second 1968 engagement at the Tropicana. She returned to the Strip a few weeks later, opening on Valentine's Day 1969 for another three-week run. Away from the spotlights, there wasn't much else to do except hit the blackjack tables, where she lost a good deal of money to the house. "It was pretty addictive," recalled a friend. Once Julie got into the game, it was hard to get her to leave the table, even if she continued to lose hand after hand. "She could eat up her salary in two nights." Julie was all business when she played cards. There was no small talk with her fellow players, and she could be cruelly cutting to fans or hangers-on who didn't respect her privacy.

Julie brought in a new musical director in 1969, one who was more comfortable with the louder numbers she had been adding to her act yet could also provide a subtle accompaniment for the hushed ballads. Guitarist Don Overberg had gigged and recorded in Los Angeles during the 1950s but had been a Las Vegas resident for a number of years and often played in the house bands at the Strip hotels, backing many of the singers who came through town.

She was "in great voice" despite fighting the effects of a bout with the flu, and Overberg's tasty guitar work was notable on a new addition to her repertoire, the strikingly beautiful Jimmy Webb ballad "Didn't We," a contemporary song with a strong melody and bittersweet lyricism that fit right into her vocal wheelhouse. After closing at the Tropicana, Julie boarded a McDonnell Douglas DC-9 jet for a flight to Reno, where she played two nights at the five-hundred-seat Headliner Room at Harrah's as the special guest star of actor/comedian Jerry Van Dyke. Life on the road wasn't what she wanted to do forever—she later confessed that she got through the years of working in nightclubs by throwing up a lot before she went onstage—but what other choice did she have?

The singer's thirty-second album for Liberty Records—only Martin Denny released more albums for the label—originally scheduled for release as *Julie's Back*, was issued in the winter of 1969 under the cringe-inducing title *Yummy, Yummy, Yummy*. More than a decade earlier as rock 'n' roll was surging to the top of the charts, Julie was adamant that she wouldn't sing in the new style, but times—and economic necessity—had forced her hand. For all her earlier protestations, the album was surprisingly successful. Whether this was due to Tommy Oliver's inventive arrangements, which disguise some of the weaker material, or because Julie could sing the phone book sensually, the album just *works*. At least that's how it appears more than forty years after its release. In 1969 it was judged to be yet another pathetic record company scheme to keep a fading artist relevant.

The disc was a logical move for Julie and her record company. It was no different from the many attempts by singers with much higher reputations than Julie's who had modified their repertoire to include songs in an effort to get hip or that label executives insisted be recorded to fulfill contractual obligations. The most significant example of this trend was Frank Sinatra, who recorded entire albums of contemporary material—*Cycles* (1968) and *A Man Alone* (1969), as well as numerous individual songs starting in 1966—and did them for his *own* label, Reprise. With rare exceptions, these recordings are the nadir of Sinatra's career, and his "what is this shit?" attitude clearly defines the final product. Nothing Julie London did during this period of her career, including *Yummy, Yummy, Yummy,* was ever as cringe inducing as Frank Sinatra's embarrassing attempt to turn Paul Simon's "Mrs. Robinson" into a swinger.*

Bobby Troup had nothing but scorn for the whole project, calling the result "terrible" and an embarrassment to his wife, yet perhaps it's really only the album's title that consigned it to the bargain bins during Julie's lifetime. Once past the initial shock of finding the sexy, sensuous Julie and rock 'n' roll in the same musical zip code, her ability to make songs her own by digging down to their core becomes evident, and the end result seems almost strangely natural.

The songs cover most of the popular musical genres of the late 1960s: folk rock ("Like to Get to Know You," "Hushabye Mountain," and "It's Nice to Be with You"), introspective singer-songwriters (Laura Nyro's "Stoned Soul Picnic" and Margo Guryan's "Come to Me Slowly" and "Sunday Mornin'"), and garage-band rock (the Kingsmen's anthem "Louie Louie," which was released as a second single). The masterpiece of the record, filled with undulating strings and a trilling flute, is a trippy version of the Doors' hit "Light My Fire." It seems like an impossible song for a forty-three-year-old self-professed "stylist" to interpret, yet once again Julie makes something her own by tempting listeners with an enticing attention to the lyrics.

Sales were subpar and reviews mixed, but a few perceptive writers caught on to the idea. "A most tasty treat," said *Cash Box,* featuring Julie's "special brand of sophistication." A second critic wrote that Julie's "sensitive approach" to contemporary songs should have been thought of much sooner. Another suggested that it would have been better if

---

* Other singers got on the bandwagon too, including Mel Tormé (the Turtles' "Happy Together" and Donovan's "Sunshine Superman"), Ella Fitzgerald (the Beatles' "Hey Jude," Cream's "Sunshine of Your Love," and Marvin Gaye's "I Heard It Through the Grapevine"), Peggy Lee (Tim Hardin's "Reason to Believe" and the Lovin' Spoonful's "Didn't Want to Have to Do It"), and Tony Bennett (the Beatles' "Something," Harry Nilsson's "Everybody's Talkin'," and O. C. Smith's "Little Green Apples"). The results were generally poor.

she had recorded the songs before the original artists, since much of the material sounded as though it was "written for her in the first place."

The realignment of Liberty Records to the popular music scene proved problematic, and the size of the label's staff, many of whom had worked with Julie for years, was drastically reduced. As the company signed "younger, bigger, potential artists," Liberty's Al Stoffel remembered, "many of the Liberty artists were dropped quickly." The radical transition was more sourly described by Julie's label mate, singer-songwriter Jackie DeShannon: "When Canned Heat [the successful blues/boogie band signed to the label in 1967 by DeShannon's husband, Bud Dain] hit Liberty, the world changed. Otherwise we'd still be putting out Julie London records."

Julie's career as a recording artist effectively ended with the commercial failure of *Yummy, Yummy, Yummy*. Her final recordings for the Liberty label were made with Tommy Oliver in early April 1969 at the former World Pacific studio in Los Angeles. Two of the songs— "Sittin' Pretty" and "Too Much of a Man"—were pressed for a single, which was abruptly pulled before it hit the market. (It would have been her twenty-ninth single, placing her third among Liberty artists in that category between 1955 and 1969.) Bobbie Gentry's "Sittin' Pretty" has an intriguingly off-beat arrangement, but the self-abasing lyrics of Larry Kingston's "Too Much of a Man" are worlds away from the determined voice of "Cry Me a River." It's unclear whether this material was intended for an album, but if this unpromising, pseudopop/country mélange was the direction Liberty intended Julie London to take as the 1960s were coming to an end, the subsequent termination of her contract was probably a blessing in disguise. (The two songs intended for the single were released on compact disc in Japan in 2003, while the remaining items from the sessions—"Come Back When You Grow Up," a 1967 number-three hit for Bobby Vee, and "Memories," recorded by Elvis Presley in 1968—if completed, presumably remain in the vaults.)

—⊶⊶⊶—

Simultaneous to the termination of her recording contract was Julie's last gasp at hosting a television variety program. Filmed in late 1968 and syndicated nationally the following spring, the one-woman show *Yummy, Yummy, Yummy* included four jazzy renditions of songs from the new album with an excellent musical quartet of guitarist Don Overberg, the lyrical trombonist Carl Fontana, double bassist Milt "the Judge" Hinton, and drummer Mousey Alexander. *Variety* called Julie—dressed in a mod paisley jacket over a turtleneck sweater—"sultry and somehow, affectingly sad," even in the modern numbers.

As she pondered her future, Julie alternated between club dates and isolated television appearances for the remainder of 1969. It was a pattern that quickly grew old, even when Bobby and her kids tried to cheer her up when she arrived in Montreal for a gig in the cabaret showroom of the Playboy Club there. A sweet telegram was waiting for her at the front desk: "You're our favorite bunny." A sign that life on the road had to end came as she was leaving Toronto's Royal York Hotel after an engagement at the elegant, five-hundred-seat Imperial Room nightclub. "They were lugging in the oxygen canisters to be positioned right behind the curtain. For Peggy Lee, who felt some night she might need it. And I figured I gotta quit this racket before I'm in that condition."

Still, the Tropicana gig was sure money, and Julie returned to Las Vegas for a successful three-week run at the Blue Room in August, backed by Don Overberg and her now standard vocal quartet. It was a venue that the *Los Angeles Times* called Julie's "own personal showcase." Her sets now opened with "Take Me for a Little While," a strong, rock-oriented number that she picked up from a 1967 album by Dusty Springfield. *Variety*'s critic was ambivalent about the new style, calling it an "experimental diffusion" that saw Julie straying from her usual "mournful murmurings" into "rock and sock," shouting above the roaring band and the singers.

A few weeks later, Julie returned to the East Coast as a last-minute replacement for Lainie Kazan and did a two-week return engagement at the Waldorf-Astoria's Empire Room. "When it comes to working," wrote *Variety*, Julie "gets the message across with a minimum of exertion." Lots of cleavage was visible to leave the men agog as she whispered her way through "Nice Girls Don't Stay for Breakfast" and a sexy duet with Don Overberg. Performing with "the jaded, 'worn woman' quality that has always given her renditions such pathos," the gig turned out to be her final one before New York audiences.

The four hundred people—"tops"—Julie London drew to her night-club performances didn't constitute much of an audience, and life on the road had become a deadly bore. "There was nothing romantic about it." Yet a cadre of loyal—albeit aging—fans remained, and a capacity audience greeted her return to the Blue Room of New Orleans's Roosevelt Hotel in January 1970. It was Super Bowl time in the Big Easy (Julie waved from a convertible to a crowd of more than eighty thousand at Tulane Stadium during the game's halftime festivities on the eleventh), and friends and celebrities appeared in the singer's hotel room every night to party and play bridge. "To get the wallop" of her performance, wrote a local critic, "one must sit back and listen, preferably with an antenna that receives those way-out sounds that ordinary channels don't carry." He remained under Julie's spell yet noticed how she struggled at times to retain control of her voice. The years of smoking and drinking were finally taking their toll, and the remainder of the three-week engagement was canceled after the January 8 performance. Julie returned to California for a medical examination, which revealed signs of an underactive thyroid. Exhausted and weary of the constant travel and life in hotels—however fancy—she welcomed the doctor's recommendation that she stay at home and rest her throat.

This period of inactivity coincided with a blow that affected Julie and Bobby's personal and financial lives. While the changes in the trajectory of their professional careers could perhaps have been predicted, the discovery that much of the money they had worked so hard to obtain had been lost in bad financial deals was a surprise that struck close to home. Julie hired Sam Lutz—whose clients included bandleader Law-rence Welk—as her personal manager on the recommendation of Snuff Garrett, and Meyer Sack was brought on as the couple's new business adviser. By the time they understood what had happened to them, the situation had become so precarious that only a drastic solution seemed viable: to sell the gorgeous Royal Oak house and move permanently to Las Vegas, the only place where they could find steady work. Heart-broken at the thought of leaving the home she loved so much, Julie reluctantly agreed to put the property on the market. The house was listed in May 1970 for $350,000; five months later, when no buyers had come forward, the price had dropped by 15 percent and the property was simultaneously offered as a $2,500 monthly lease.

Painfully aware that she now *needed* to work, Julie returned to the road for a two-week run at the stylish Salon Carnaval supper club in the Sheraton Hotel in San Juan, Puerto Rico, and a three-week stint at the Tropicana, where she headlined again with trombonist Si Zentner. A sojourn to London with Bobby in early June resulted in an episode of a long-running variety show hosted by English comedian Des O'Connor. Broadcast in the United Kingdom later that month and on American screens in July under the *Kraft Music Hall* banner, the show featured Julie performing a new Bobby Troup arrangement of "Daddy," the 1962 Matt Monro hit "Softly, as I Leave You," and a comedic rendition of the 1966 number-one record "Something Stupid" with the host and *Laugh-In* comedian Jo Anne Worley.

Julie came back to the Tropicana in July, with Bobby's trio on the bill, for a second three-week run. By 1970 the hotel was struggling to compete against the larger places on the Strip. When *Los Angeles Times* writer Robert Hilburn toured the Strip during Julie's run, he noted that "it was all rather dull" in the Blue Room until Julie appeared. She still had the power to mesmerize an audience. When one patron continued his too-loud conversation during her show, Julie's reaction was to "just stop" in the middle of the song. "She did everything so perfectly and so subtly," recalled a friend, "that you didn't even know she'd stopped.

All of a sudden, you don't hear any music, and she would say, 'Are you through?!'"

Comedian Tony Russell, who opened for Julie during what became her final engagement at the Tropicana, had a great time watching her performances. "She had that kind of voice that just went right through you; she had that kind of sultry, sexy quality. She was lovely, very friendly, very warm, very nice; a down-to-earth girl. You didn't feel like you had to walk on eggs around her. We would stay for a couple of hours after the show, when the audience was gone, and I'd play the piano and Bobby would play, and we'd sing some songs and talk and bullshit around and drink pretty good!"

A lucrative new advertising deal with Fiat automobiles saw Julie traveling around the United States for introductory sales events prior to her return to Los Angeles's Century Plaza for another two-week run at the three-hundred-seat Westside Room in October. "In this era of raucous, extroverted singers, it's difficult to find the smokey, soft-sell feminine voice," a critic approvingly wrote. Although Julie did her share of trying to belt, it was always the ballads that calmed "a typical night-club audience to the point of actually 'listening.'" *Variety* summed up the performance by stating that "she shows what a supper-club singer is supposed to do; her respect for lyrics . . . and fine sense of the dramatic" made it a pleasant evening. As she ended the last days of her preholiday engagement at the Tropicana in December 1970, with Bobby on board as pianist and arranger, Julie wondered whether this would be her last Christmas in the house she had so lovingly designed and cared for.

Little changed as the calendar turned to 1971. The house remained unsold, so Julie spent most of the year relaxing at home—not that she complained—between engagements in Las Vegas. In late February Julie followed her neighbor, pianist Roger Williams, into the Blue Room when she opened a three-week first run at the Tropicana, accompanied once again by guitarist Don Overberg. "Sheathed in a distractingly open-fronted gown," wrote *Variety*, "the essential London commitment" remained even as she was often obscured by the powerful orchestra.

She was dispirited as the calendar turned from summer to fall. "This kind of work is up and down," she told a reporter in the early 1960s. "Sometimes I think it's the most rewarding thing in the world, if you can communicate with an audience. If you don't communicate, I think it's probably the most frightening thing in the world." Another three weeks in Vegas in front of the same audiences was hard to take, yet it was the only booking on the calendar. With little to look forward to, she had no idea that help would soon arrive—from the unlikeliest of sources.

15

Emergency!

What am I doing here?

—Julie London to journalist Cecil Smith, 1972

"IT CAME OUT OF THE BLUE. I certainly didn't expect it." Jack Webb was on the telephone. Would Julie and Bobby be interested in roles in a new television series he was trying to sell to NBC? The subject was unlikely: stories about the recently authorized, yet still unproven, paramedics of the Los Angeles County Fire Department. The paramedic program, which began in California in late 1969, was still on trial, criticized by ambulance companies, who thought that their business was being stolen, and by doctors, who were convinced that firemen lacked the training to handle medical emergencies in the field.

The pitch combined *Adam-12*, Webb's hit series about the Los Angeles Police Department, with the popular medical drama *Marcus Welby, M.D.*, mixing dramatic paramedic rescues with the actions of dedicated doctors and nurses in the emergency rooms of a Los Angeles hospital. MCA/Universal president Sid Sheinberg was convinced, and Webb asked *Adam-12* creator Robert A. (Bob) Cinader to research the dramatic possibilities. After deflecting the initial resistance of the Los Angeles Fire Department, NBC gave Webb and Cinader the go-ahead to create a pilot.

Julie's relationship with her ex-husband had steadily improved over the years. Not long after she bought a $50,000 getaway house in the Deepwell neighborhood of Palm Springs in the mid-1950s, Jack purchased the property next door so he could be near his growing daughters, surely a sign of a gradual rapprochement. He had often expressed his appreciation to Bobby for the love and dedication he had shown to Stacy and Lisa. The men became business partners in the China Trader restaurant in Toluca Lake, California, where Bobby and his trio had a regular gig beginning in 1966, and Jack had hired Bobby to act in his television shows, including four episodes of the revived *Dragnet* series. Yet if Jack had thought about asking his ex-wife to work for him, he had never mentioned it to her. Now he told them that it was imperative that both of their names be attached to the project if it was to be approved by the network. The roles—registered nurse Dixie McCall and Dr. Joe Early—were as unlikely as the show's premise. Julie called it reverse casting. "Jack has a genius for things like that."

The pilot was scheduled to begin shooting in four weeks. There would have to be a quick turnaround if they accepted the offer, since both Julie and Bobby were Las Vegas bound: she was preparing another three-week run at the Tropicana, and he was completing work with arrangers Billy May and Johnny Mann for a new edition of the hotel's risqué *Folies Bergère* stage show. It really wasn't a difficult decision to make. In 1953 Julie had little hesitation about ending her bad marriage to Jack Webb, but time had passed and old wounds had healed. The girl who was barely out of her teens when she had first gotten married was now a happily remarried, forty-five-year-old woman with five children. She and Jack had matured, and much of the bridge building between Julie and her ex-husband came through the mellowing influence of Bobby Troup. Jack had been a bachelor since 1964, and as he and Bobby became good friends, Julie and the Webb girls became part of the mix. He even had a regular spot at Julie and Bobby's home bar and became a welcome attendee at their annual Christmas Eve party.

The steady income from a successful television series would finally stabilize their finances and go a long way to help them hold on to the

Royal Oak property. Julie welcomed the opportunity to get off the road with open arms. No more frightening moments before going onstage, no more drunks in the audience, no more ennui about a life spent shuttling between ever-smaller gigs. The couple's reply was enthusiastically positive.

⚬⚬⚬

To familiarize themselves with hospital procedures and to make their characters more realistic, Julie and Bobby were sent to Harbor General Hospital near UCLA, to observe procedures in the mobile intensive care unit there. Joining them was the show's male lead, Robert Fuller who, sixteen years earlier, had been among the lucky few to witness Julie's debut performances as a singer, when he stopped for a beer at the 881 Club. When she walked out onto the tiny stage, he "fell apart like a two-dollar shirt." After her guest appearance on *Laramie* a few years later, Robert Fuller, Julie London, and Bobby Troup had become friends. Now as the cast gathered for the cameras to roll on *Emergency!* it was like old-home week.

NBC executives surprised Webb when they announced that *Emergency!* was to begin as a midseason replacement rather than being launched as part of the regular fall 1972 schedule. The two-hour premiere was now set for January 15, 1972, with additional episodes to begin immediately thereafter. Four days before the show was to go before the cameras, only twelve pages of script were ready. There was no one in the business with a more efficient shooting schedule than Jack Webb, so he was the logical choice to helm the pilot. He demurred, saying that it was Bob Cinader's project, but there was no "time to fight with a director." Filming began on November 22, 1971.

It was a tough adjustment for a night owl like Julie London. Working in clubs meant not going to bed until the wee hours of the morning; now five in the morning meant it was time to wake up and get to the studio. The physical and mental adjustments, the complicated medical jargon, and the need to appear like she was actually performing medical procedures was a combination that gave her plenty to worry about.

The first days of the shoot were emotionally and physically exhausting. Her acting muscles had become hardened from lack of use, and she had never had the experience of being directed by her ex-husband, who demanded a lot from his actors. He was "a tough boss," Julie said, although that was nothing new. "He was that way as a husband." The staccato, no-nonsense style of Jack Webb's dramas was well suited to Julie's naturally low-key style, yet her biggest fear was the dialogue. She couldn't even remember her own name, let alone the script. If she blew a line—which often happened—she "blistered the set with four-letter words."

Jack had the perfect solution at hand to ease Julie's fear of the camera. For decades he had used teleprompters to reduce the amount of rehearsal time needed before shooting a scene. He wanted all the actors on *Emergency!* to use the device. While most refused, Julie relied on it, something that was glaringly obvious in the pilot and the balance of the first-season episodes. As the show continued and she became more comfortable with her role and the situation, it became less noticeable; in fact she became so good at using the teleprompter that she mastered the technique of not moving her eyes when reading the screen.

"I'd rather perform on a nice, clean sound stage, but here I am fighting weather and dirt again, just like my early Westerns." Her first day on the set included a complicated sequence filmed on a hillside overlooking the San Fernando Valley. Jack's perfectionist nature didn't make the situation easier; Julie wore out a path on the embankment as the segment was shot over and over. The stress became so acute that she broke out in another case of hives, yet there was no time for rest, not even for a family Thanksgiving.

After the twenty-two days of filming on the pilot ended, shooting began for the eleven episodes of the show's first season two days before Christmas, with two crews running simultaneously to make the already scheduled air dates. Sets were being constructed in one area of the studio while filming was happening on the other side of the walls. "We got started on the series so late it's going to be a full-time involvement just to get it going," Bobby told a journalist. "We'll be doing shows back-to-back from here on out."

The enthusiastic response to an early showing of the two-hour pilot meant that by the time it aired in NBC's *Saturday Night at the Movies* slot, *Emergency!* had already been placed on the regular schedule. Everyone cheered, but their joy was tempered by knowledge of the competition: television's number-one show, *All in the Family.*

The series' first hour-long episode was broadcast on January 22, 1972. "I never expected to be here," marveled Julie, "but now that we're here, I hope we stay." NBC was gambling that the new action series would be a more effective counterprogramming to *All in the Family* than the two situation comedies *Emergency!* had replaced. The show quickly gained popularity, particularly with younger audiences who reacted positively to the exciting rescue sequences. Its ratings steadily increased, and by the end of the season, more than a quarter of all viewers in the time slot were watching the paramedics, which at least put a dent in Archie Bunker's formidable lead.

Although Robert Fuller, Julie, and Bobby received top billing, it was clear by the end of the first season that the real stars of *Emergency!* were the two young, relatively unknown Universal contract actors who played Los Angeles County Fire Station 51 paramedics Johnny Gage and Roy DeSoto. Randolph Mantooth and Kevin Tighe quickly became the idols of teenagers around the country, and it was their ever-growing popularity that sustained the show during its run. Julie didn't mind. She was happy for Randy and Kevin and was content to share the spotlight. The attention that was focused on them relieved her of the pressure to be responsible for the show's success or failure. She and Bobby still got publicity—more than they had received in years.

Initially, the changes in the show were cause for concern. As *Emergency!* was being developed, Jack Webb had told Julie that the paramedic stories might not be enough to hold an audience's interest and that the hospital scenes would be fleshed out to compensate. The pilot clearly laid the groundwork for a personal relationship between Dixie McCall and Robert Fuller's Dr. Kelly Brackett. Although the drama was originally to have been balanced between the paramedics and the hospital staff, it was obvious that young viewers were tuning in each week to see the rescues, not the hospital scenes with the old(er) doctors and Julie. Los Angeles Fire Department staff members who had been assigned to liaise with the program grumbled that it would turn into a soap opera, and after hearing this the romance plotline quickly disappeared as the show concentrated on the rescues and the jokey relationship between the paramedics. Robert Fuller was certain that if Jack Webb had been more involved in the program, he wouldn't have let that happen. But Fuller didn't mind the change and loved that there was just enough being said so that no one would "ever know what Kel and Dixie did when they got off work."

Emergency! became a physical, emotional, and financial lifeline. The steadiness of the work and the chance to get off the road were causes for celebration. Julie may have been surprised at finally finding the situation she'd been looking for, but the routine she and Bobby developed—"get up together, go to work together, come home to spend the evening with the kids"—couldn't be bettered.

Julie reveled in long hours by the pool and time with her children as they and their many friends trooped through the always-open front door. "We really have a ball." The stereo was on twenty-four hours a day, and Julie joined in the fun.

Emergency! star Kevin Tighe became that rare thing—a friend to both Julie *and* Bobby. He spent many happy evenings with the couple. "Whenever I brought over albums by Nina [Simone], Etta James and, early on, Roberta Flack, Julie would instinctively intone the lyrics in a soft harmony, and we'd stay up; Bobby initially at the turn-table, transitioning to other vocalists, other songs into the wee hours."

The young actor accompanied his new friends to local clubs to hear the likes of Sarah Vaughan, Duke Ellington, Billy Eckstine, and pianist Bill Evans, who acted like a kid around Julie. She was an introspective person, very private in her own way, yet warm when she was with people she liked. Singers and musicians like Carmen McRae, Herb Ellis, Jerome Richardson, and Joe Pass turned the annual Christmas party into a real jam session.

Critics were never kind to *Emergency!* They harped on its "dime-novel dialog" and the "deadening rigidity and predictability" of the acting. Julie took little notice. What was important to her was that from its earliest days *Emergency!* had become a family affair. Bobby's daughter Cynnie was the program's script supervisor during its initial season, her actress sister Ronne appeared in three episodes, and October 1972 saw the acting debut of precocious ten-year-old Kelly Troup, who insisted that Dr. Kelly Brackett had been named after her.

A warm, loose relationship developed among the cast and crew, clearly obvious in the numerous bloopers that have made their way into the public sphere. A number of these moments involved Julie's love of salty language. She may not have looked as if "she talked like a sailor," Cynnie Troup laughed, "but she could have quite a mouth on her. She did it so well—it was charming! She wasn't affected; she didn't do things for show." Randolph Mantooth joked that the cast "learned every bad word" they knew from Julie, yet on a serious note, added that she became "a mentor to all of us. She let the words work for her rather than emoting."

The role of former army nurse Dixie McCall was a perfect match for Julie's approach to acting. "My natural style is to play down," she said. "In a hospital, it helps. Doctors and nurses are never supposed to get upset." The strict sense of discipline Dixie showed to the nurses under her charge was softened by her protective nature toward the young paramedics.

Each spring for the next six years, after filming ended for the season, the cast and crew went on hiatus. The break allowed Julie to spend more time with her books and crossword puzzles and the chance to fully enjoy the lives of her growing children. It was also an opportunity to make personal appearances, including some in which she could still be persuaded to sing. One notable occasion was in Louisville, Kentucky, in May of 1973, where she sat on Kevin Tighe's lap to perform "Daddy" for attendees at the Philip Morris Festival of Stars during that year's Kentucky Derby.

Although Julie's Marlboro advertisements had ended years earlier, her connections with the product were still strong, as evidenced by a humorous letter to a tobacco industry executive about how changing cigarette brands was akin to changing husbands. Originally a Pall Mall smoker, she had switched to the brand sponsored by *Dragnet* ("they tasted like dry dog shit") during her marriage to Jack Webb. New man, new cigarette: Parliament ("they were cute").

The hiatus was also an opportunity to return to the lucrative television game show circuit, where she could make more than $1,000 a day (equal to nearly six times that figure today). A season's worth of the syndicated *Celebrity Bowling* could be taped over "one long four-day party," complete with a full bar and food tables. Never at ease among the quipping and glad-handing so integral to these celebrity gab fests, Julie's 1972–1976 appearances on *Hollywood Squares*, *Tattletales*, *Masquerade Party*, *Celebrity Sweepstakes*, *Take My Advice*, and *Match Game* did sometimes provide rare clues into her personality and her relationships.

Two examples: on an episode of *Tattletales*, Julie was asked whether she or her husband was guiltier of not listening to their spouse. Bobby never listened to her, she replied; he agreed—it "absolutely" never worked the other way around. Julie's attitude toward women was typically terse. *Match Game* host Gene Rayburn asked her whether she got along better with men or women. Her one-word response was accompanied by a sly grin: "Men!"

———— ∞ ————

The 1970s passed in a comfortable blur. Julie gladly acknowledged that she wasn't the reason for the success of *Emergency!* Kids found "appeal in the action of the show, the fire engines, the sirens, the equipment, the work of the paramedics." By season three *Emergency!* had settled in as a comfortable second-place ratings success for NBC, besting the competition at ABC while garnering a good share of the audience against the ratings-grabbing *All in the Family* and *M*A*S*H* on CBS. The fourth season, which ended in March of 1975, saw the show breaking into the top thirty Nielsen ratings for the first and only time. A proposed movie version in 1974 never made it beyond the script stage and was canceled due to a writers' strike.

The money was good, and having to work just two or three days a week was a pleasant way to spend her time, but the show's scripts rarely gave Julie much to do beyond a few flashes of humor and the rare occasion of dramatic conflict. It came as a complete surprise when she heard she had been nominated for a Golden Globe Award, but she wasn't shocked when Lee Remick picked up the prize as Best Actress in a Drama Series during the January 26, 1974, ceremony at the Beverly Hilton Hotel.

Julie had not sung much in public since the show began, yet she still received regular requests to perform, even for just one number. If there was anything she missed about her singing career, it was the beautiful gowns. The glamorous image of Julie London on her album covers had faded by the mid-1970s, replaced by the less-than-sexy starched white uniform of Dixie McCall.

It was "silly financially not to cash in on something while the series is on hiatus, or to use the time off to work somewhere," but the thought of nightclubs sent chills up her spine. Everything had to be just right, and how often did that happen? "In a club," she said, "there are three important factors: the room, the band and you. In Vegas, the gambling used to subsidize the shows. Now everything has to pay for itself." In truth the Tropicana was not an option anymore. When the hotel was sold in 1971, as Julie neared the end of her time there, the new owners fired the man who had hired her—entertainment director Maynard Sloate—and dropped the acts he had booked in the Blue Room.

Julie was certain that her status as an actress on a hit television series would lead to opportunities to appear on television variety shows. No one asked. As an interpreter of songs, she was always more amenable to contemporary popular music than her songwriter husband. Her kids had brought a lot of good new songs to Julie's attention. There were a few desultory conversations about making another LP, and she even expressed willingness to revisit the previously scorned arena of country music to do so. Yet nothing came of this avenue either.

"Maybe I'll sing again someday, but for now I only sing when I want to—at home and among close friends," she said in the spring of 1975. When the entire cast of *Emergency!* appeared on Dinah Shore's syndicated daytime talk show later that year, Julie was forced to face the call. Robert Fuller lamented that no one could get her to sing at all. Julie responded that she "sounded pretty good" for the first four years of the show but now she didn't and was visibly put off at Bobby's rejoinder that she did. After some prodding from the host, Julie reluctantly oozed out a few a cappella bars of "Cry Me a River" to *ooh*s and *aah*s from her castmates and the audience. Her reaction was to raise her eyebrows as if to say "really?"

Emergency! concluded its fifth season in the spring of 1976 and was easily renewed to be part of the network's fall schedule. Yet after one hundred episodes, Julie was restless. The lack of variation was a cause for concern. "That moment when you do a scene and you know you've played the hell out of it . . . can urge you on to do more and better; but when you do the same thing all the time, you lose that drive." Still, the boredom of her scenes was alleviated by working with such a congenial cast and crew. During breaks from filming, Julie and Bobby, still dressed in their hospital whites, visited the nearby studio where the *Emergency!* soundtrack was being recorded and hung out while the musicians laid down a few tracks. The joy extended far beyond the final shot of the day. Robert Fuller recalled that if he wasn't at Jack Webb's house after a day's work, he was at Julie and Bobby's warm and welcoming place.

It was "another world," one in which Julie—normally so inside of herself—became a different, more relaxed woman.

The show returned to the air on September 25, 1976, one day before Julie's fiftieth birthday. She was typically sarcastic about the milestone: "I've looked the same since I was 14, except that my waist is a little thicker now and my bottom's closer to the ground." She was content to show up at the Universal lot for a day or two during the week, shoot her largely unimportant-to-the-plot scenes, enjoy the company of her fellow cast members, guest stars, and crew, and collect a nice paycheck. The struggles, it seemed, were over.

While she was forever grateful for the opportunities *Emergency!* had provided, she wasn't above expressing frustration about its limitations. "Whenever there's a scene in the show where I'm not wearing the nurse's uniform, I feel like someone's given me a present." Asked whether she wanted to return to acting in movies instead, Julie revealed her essentially conservative nature. Shocked by the content of contemporary movies and the nudity that had become almost de rigueur on the big screen, she was appalled at the thought of taking her clothes off on camera. "I keep hoping there's a pot of gold at the end of the rainbow. There's always something just around the corner for people to run into. But I haven't the foggiest what—or where—my corner is."

16

"We Said We'd Never Say 'Goodbye'"

I do not believe I need any more than my husband and children and our life together.

—Julie London to the Australian media, 1966

I T WASN'T PARTICULARLY SURPRISING when *Emergency!* was canceled in the spring of 1977 as part of NBC's ultimately fruitless effort to gain an additional year of syndication-friendly episodes for *The Bionic Woman*. Most of the cast had been shocked that the show had lasted as long as it had. Still, it was a bittersweet moment when after 120 episodes *Emergency!* made its final weekly appearance on April 23, 1977. Four months later the cast returned to Universal for a series of two-hour, made-for-television movies. Julie, Bobby, Robert Fuller, and the rest of the Rampart Hospital staff signed deals for the first two installments, "The Steel Inferno" and "Survival on Charter #220," which aired on January 7 and March 25, 1978.*

---

* Much of the location filming for "Survival on Charter #220" was done in the city of Compton, just south of Los Angeles, where many members of the Peck family had settled in the late nineteenth century. Randolph Mantooth and Kevin Tighe completed the balance of their seven-year contracts with the studio and filmed additional movies,

Seven enjoyable years had gone by in an instant, and Julie wasn't sure what was going to happen next. For the moment she was content to stay home and enjoy the financial security the show had brought her. It had always been an unplanned career, so she had no regrets about ignoring the lucrative offers to perform just one more song. "No, I don't do that anymore." She saw herself as the girl next door rather than as a sex symbol and believed that raising her children and living as normal a life as possible was the most important thing she could do.

Julie and Bobby celebrated their twentieth wedding anniversary on New Year's Eve 1979. Two decades had passed in a whirl of activity, travel, and family fun. Even so they had few friends in common: Julie had her girl "buddies," Bobby had his golfing partners. The couple had always lived on a knife-edge, balanced between tension and love as they openly expressed their opinions about each other in sometimes-salty language. Endearments often came in the form of put-downs. Julie berated Bobby for his attitude to contemporary music. "This is a very large world, you know, there's room for all kinds of music, don't you think? You don't have to listen to the things you don't like but wouldn't you be a little angered if someone tried to stop you from listening to the things you wanted to hear?" Although they argued about many things, Bobby declared, "We don't get tired of each other."

Life was meant to be enjoyed, and in 1979 there was cause for further enjoyment after the sale of United Artists Records—which had controlled Julie's catalog (and did little with it) for more than a decade—to the British conglomerate EMI. As the new owners looked at ways to reintroduce her records, all their acquired artists received a royalty boost to 10 percent. "Julie made a hell of a lot of money," recalled Snuff Garrett.

---

which NBC broadcast through July 1979. *Emergency!* continues to have a successful run in syndication.

Hospitality remained the watchword at Julie and Bobby's house, where friends were always welcome. "The front door was never locked until the last person came home. In the daytime, we all walked in and out freely," Tom Williams remembered, largely because everyone knew that Julie would never rouse herself enough to come downstairs to answer the door. Stray people were always showing up on the doorstep to become a part of the extended family, which became the impetus for Jack Webb to dub the house the "orphanage on the hill." Actress Jill Schoelen, whose family had moved into actor Dennis Weaver's former house across the street from Julie and Bobby in the mid-1970s, became a close friend of Kelly Troup. An almost-daily visitor, Jill watched Julie come down the spiral staircase from the second floor and thought it was always like "she was making an entrance." Fascinated by the bedroom closet full of beautiful gowns, the actress called her friend's mother "enormously gifted, quiet, highly intelligent, and a mysterious woman."

Life was centered on the comfortable family room, where everyone gathered for food, drink, games, fun, and uproarious laughter. But mostly music—music everywhere: at the piano, on the stereo, on the walls. Julie spent much of her time listening to music, which she always preferred to singing. Although she remained partial to popular standards and jazz—everyone from singers Kenny Rankin and Michael Franks to pianist Oscar Peterson, guitarist Wes Montgomery, and the driving sounds of tenor saxophonist Don Menza, particularly during his time with the Buddy Rich Big Band—she expressed enjoyment for almost all styles. There was one singer, however, for whom she had no patience: herself. Any request that her own records be put on the stereo was met with a brusque "don't spend time on me!"

Julie made few public references to the 1979 operation that removed her thyroid gland. Whether the procedure was intended to treat cancer, an enlargement of the thyroid, or the hyperthyroidism that had been diagnosed at the beginning of the decade is unclear. All that *was* certain, in Julie's mind, was that the combination of the operation and the wear and tear on her voice caused by chronic smoking and drinking had signaled a definitive end to her singing career.

Old friend Arthur Hamilton expressed surprise at her decision: "I assumed that she would never be able to get away from singing, because [Bobby] would probably say, 'Here, I've got another song for you!'" But home was the only place she wanted to be, where she could lie by the pool and read. "Bobby would have to beg her to go places." It had been more than a decade since Julie had made a recording. She was constantly surprised that anyone still remembered her. "She was quite moved," said a friend, "in her own way, that people would tell her, 'I've never heard anybody like you. I love you and I always will.' That's about all she needed; just to know that everybody liked her. Most people knew how good she was."

Julie was content to remain out of the spotlight. Singing was something she used to do. "If I worked at it six hours a day for three months straight," she told jazz critic Leonard Feather, "I could get it back, but I'm not interested. The only time I miss it is maybe at a party; after a couple of belts I may open my mouth to sing a tune and I shudder." She didn't believe there was any reason for her to return to a recording studio, until one day in the spring of 1981 when she heard the twang of a familiar Texas accent come over the telephone line. It was Snuff Garrett, whose numerous hits for Gary Lewis and the Playboys, Vicki Lawrence, and Cher since his departure from Liberty in the mid-1960s had skyrocketed him to new heights. He was gathering artists for the soundtrack to a new movie, *Sharky's Machine*, starring and directed by his friend Burt Reynolds. "I wanted her to sing a song in the picture, and she said, 'Whatever you want me to do, I'll do it.'"

Julie was—rightly—worried about the state of her voice after the thyroid operation, but the opportunity to work once more with her fun-loving buddy Snuffy was an offer that was too good to resist. The feeling was mutual. "She was great at comebacks," recalled the producer with a raucous laugh. "You'd be saying something, and she'd come back at you—cleverly. Or tell you to 'go fuck yourself,' one of the two!"

The song she was asked to sing was the Rodgers and Hart classic "My Funny Valentine." She was always terrified at the thought of recording something she'd never done before. This was terror magnified to a new degree, even with the rock-solid support of three old friends behind her in the form of guitarist Barney Kessel, double bassist Ray Brown, and drummer Shelly Manne. Julie asked her daughter Lisa to sit opposite her during the session and took strength from her presence. The result was a stark, fragile rendition that sounds as if she and Kessel had seamlessly picked up where they left off when her first album was completed twenty-six years earlier. The self-deprecating singer didn't think much of what she had done. A few vocal flaws in the playback frustrated her so intensely that she was convinced she "couldn't come back to where she had been." Snuff Garrett knew Julie wasn't satisfied but insisted it was only because "her standards were so way out of focus." If "My Funny Valentine" was to be the final recording of Julie London's career, it was an apt coda, filled with the whispered longing that had been the mark of the best of her vintage work. She still "knew how to tell a story."

Bobby Troup, who had garnered five songwriting credits on the *Sharky's Machine* soundtrack, returned to the nightclub scene for the first time in eleven years. While he reveled in the opportunity to revisit old times and old tunes, Julie was content to remain a spectator at his gigs and at the many San Fernando Valley night spots they frequented during the decade. Another aspect of the entertainment world was now occupying her mind. She had fallen in love with a novel called *Crashing*, the 1980 debut of a writer named Enid Harlow. Universal optioned the book for a movie and retained Julie as a consultant on the project, which she hoped to eventually produce. Harlow's novel tells the gripping story of a suburban wife and mother of four children whose feelings of inferiority, weakness, and insecurity have fed a twenty-year addiction to amphetamines. Her husband, a successful Park Avenue internist, is so preoccupied with his career that he never recognizes his wife's pain or helps her find a solution. A tragic death in the family brings her to the point of madness, and only then does assistance arrive in the form of a no-nonsense detoxification specialist, a part that Bobby was certain Julie could have done had she still been interested in acting.

Crashing paralleled aspects of Julie's life. Her inner self had been troubled since childhood, and like the novel's protagonist, she struggled to find the direction and strength to help her achieve her goals. As a young adult, Julie self-medicated with alcohol ("steady sipping all day long," as Enid Harlow described the character's actions) while Jack Webb ignored and belittled her. Now she was watching some of her own children suffer with similar problems. Did she see something in the novel that reflected the behavior of her older daughters? Did she see eighteen-year-old Kelly, who "seemed possessed of a sense of self," and aspects of her teenage boys' personalities in the novel's children? If she did she steadfastly refused to acknowledge it and never fully comprehended the effect that her own problems with alcohol—Julie "loved her screwdrivers"—had on her children.

Julie tried to convince Universal to cast actress Tyne Daly—two years before her breakthrough role in the CBS television drama *Cagney & Lacey*—in the lead role but to no avail. After three years Universal dropped the option on the property during a change in studio personnel.

On December 23, 1982, Julie's daughter Stacy Webb was driving to work at Warner Bros. Studios in Burbank. Turning on the car radio, she heard a broadcaster calmly announce that her father, Jack Webb, had died earlier that morning at his home in West Hollywood. Hysterical, she immediately turned her car around into oncoming traffic and raced to Encino, where she burst into her mother's house. Julie had seen Jack a day earlier; nothing seemed out of place. She struggled to make sense of what her daughter was trying to say as radio broadcasts continuously repeated the story over the course of the day.

It was a somber Christmas gathering two days later as Julie and Bobby honored Jack's memory by placing a bottle of Crown Royal whisky and an overturned glass on the bar at the spot where he usually sat. Julie, Bobby, and Jack's daughters were escorted to Forest Lawn Memorial Park in a police cruiser for the private funeral on the twenty-eighth. Flags were flown at half-mast at all Los Angeles police stations in Webb's honor, and in a first for a nonofficer of the force, a memorial service was held at the Los Angeles Police Academy in Elysian Park, where Webb was saluted by a piper playing "Amazing Grace," a memorial volley from the department's color guard, and a flyover by its Air Support Division.

Jack Webb's death at the age of sixty-two brought forth a flood of memories. In the nearly thirty years since their divorce, Julie had grown to understand him better yet still carried the emotional scars from their years together. Now she recalled with pleasure those early days of infatuation and fun; how his ardent pursuit—knowing that he wanted her so much—and the birth of their daughters had sealed their lives together into a bond that could never be fully broken. Jack's passing reminded Julie of a phrase about marriage in a book she referred to as "her personal philosophy": Kahlil Gibran's *The Prophet*, which she may have been introduced to by the actor Whitfield Connor during the filming of *Tap Roots* in 1947. "You were born together, and together you shall be forevermore. / You shall be together when the white wings of death scatter your days."

Peggy Webber, who had known Julie and Jack since the early 1940s, said Jack's death sent Julie into a spiral of uncertainty. At the funeral she "came up to me and threw her arms around me and said, 'Oh, Peggy, Peggy, I don't know what I should feel! I don't know what I should be thinking!' She was very upset, but she wasn't in tears, she was just . . . twisted. Her emotions were really twisting. She still probably loved him, he was the father of her children—and yes, he had done a lot of dirty things, but at the same time he was trying to make it up."

Jack Webb was honest enough with himself to admit that he hadn't been the best father. His daughter Lisa said he "never came around" as she and her sister Stacy grew older. His bequest of a sizable sum of money to them in his will may have been yet another belated attempt at reconciliation. Julie resented his munificence but recognized that the money was Jack's way of alleviating the guilt he felt at having left the girls when they were so young.

The 1980s passed into the 1990s. Julie remained content with the way her life was panning out and with her loving, yet quirky, family. She and Bobby joyfully shared in the lives of their children, and as far they were concerned, all five were typical adults of their generation. They loved them all for the individuals they had become. While eldest daughter Stacy remained attached to Jack Webb as she found her way through life, Bobby was the only father Lisa had really ever known ("he had a heart of gold"), and she and Julie were more "best friends" than mother and daughter. Kelly and the boys, Reese and Jody, being so close in age acted as something of a team when they were young, doing and getting whatever they wanted. As they grew older, their unique personalities developed. Kelly, said her friend Jill Schoelen, "had the wisdom of Julie and the whimsicalness of Bobby." Reese loved the attention that came with being the son of celebrities, while Jody was content to live his life as if his parents had not been stars.

In 1987 daughter Lisa Breen gave birth to Julie's first grandchild. Lisa and her family rarely missed a weekend at the house where she was raised and in which she got married. As she grew up, Lisa's young daughter Ryann explored the house's "endless nooks and crannies—with no one to stop you doing it" and recalled how her grandmother— "Grandy"—would "tickle my back and sing to me softly until I fell asleep." Yet at the same time as she revealed her love to her family, Julie became increasingly reclusive, rarely spoke to anyone other than family and close friends or even came downstairs from her bedroom if visitors arrived. One family friend said that Julie's daughter Kelly suspected that her mother had become agoraphobic.

In 1995, at the age of sixty-nine, Julie was still a good-looking woman. Her face and figure remained relatively youthful, even if the years of eating poorly and abusing her body with tobacco and alcohol had begun to affect her health. The daily routine of smoking more than three packs of cigarettes and downing five to seven screwdrivers was taking its toll. Julie's doctor diagnosed high blood pressure, and an extended bout with the flu hampered her recovery from a broken ankle that left her hobbling around the house. Ignoring the advice to exercise (it was "against her religion"), the treadmill her doctor recommended gathered dust in her bedroom. Even walking for extended periods of time became an increasingly difficult task.

The medical crisis that seemed almost inevitable finally arrived. "She had very high blood pressure that day," recalled Julie's friend Linda Wheeler, "and they had a nurse come over and check it. They didn't give her anything, but I went up to check on her. She was sitting beside the bed, looking at magazines, but not in a way that was with us. It was the scariest thing." Paramedics quickly arrived on the scene to transport Julie to the hospital, where a CT scan revealed that she had suffered an ischemic stroke. The vital arteries that carry oxygenated blood to the brain had become blocked, and her brain—"the repository of our conscious being and sense of self"—had been severely damaged.

Based on the effects the stroke had on Julie, it is likely to have occurred in the middle cerebral artery, which affected her cerebral cortex and the frontal, parietal, and temporal lobes of the brain. The left-brain stroke resulted in a loss of movement to the right side of the body and expressive aphasia, in which speech comprehension is undiminished but the ability to translate thoughts to speech is heavily compromised.

Her condition stabilized, Julie was transferred to the Screen Actors Guild nursing home in Woodland Hills, where she spent nearly a year undergoing basic rehabilitation. There wasn't much she was capable of beyond repeating numbers out loud . . . one, two, three, four, five . . . as if she were recalling that memorable evening when she met Bobby and sang about counting her fingers. Yet close friends could still bring out the sarcastic humor that those who knew Julie well would always treasure.

The family hired a caretaker to provide basic comforts upon her return to Encino, but Julie disdained all calls to undergo physical therapy sessions that could strengthen her mind and body. It was the stance she had always taken: what was going to come was going to come. She had few goals before the stroke; why should she change now? The unwillingness to help herself recover was a sharp contrast to the dogged resilience of Bobby Troup's ex-wife, Cynthia, who had her right leg amputated in 1977 yet was determined to live a normal life.

Within months of the stroke, Julie broke both of her hips in separate accidents (falls are common after strokes) and subsequently spent most of her time as an invalid in a wheelchair, just as her parents had been in *their* final years. By April of 1996, however, Julie and Bobby had become adjusted to her disability, and life had returned to a semblance of normality. Blithely ignoring the advice of her doctors, she returned to her old ways. A writer who came to interview Bobby recalled that, as the two men left the house to go to lunch, Julie yelled at her husband in a raspy voice from an upstairs window, "Could you get me some Parliaments!?" Bobby, who once remarked that he knew he wasn't the "master of the house," took Julie's demands as he always had—with unfailing good humor.

For her entire adult life before the incapacitating stroke, Julie "would tell you when you were full of shit." Although often applied, that bluntness did not seem to have much of an effect on Julie's oldest daughter. Stacy Webb remained beyond Julie's grasp, and her troubles seemed insurmountable. For years both Julie and Bobby had attended psychological counseling with her, yet no matter what they did, it never seemed to be good enough. Stacy never fully reached her potential, and her death at the age of forty-six on the evening of September 27, 1996, seemed to some—including her mother—almost inevitable. At an intersection near her home in Twenty-Nine Palms (Riverside County), Stacy's truck overturned after a collision with a California Highway Patrol car, and she died about an hour later at Desert Hospital in Palm SpringsDaniel Moyer, Stacy's fiancé and the coauthor of a 2001 biography of Jack Webb, has suggested that her death might have been due to her misjudgment of the patrol vehicle's speed rather than to her implied alcoholic impairment, as suggested by the official police report and published articles on the crash. (Moyer's mother is Jackie Loughery, Jack Webb's third wife.)

For a time Bobby considered whether he should leave Julie in the dark about Stacy's death. Julie displayed no visible reaction after he reluctantly broke the news, although Bobby's daughter Cynnie is certain that "there was a lot more going on; she just [couldn't] communicate, but there was a lot of feeling." Perhaps Stacy's passing brought Julie a sense of relief. Her daughter was now "out of harm's way" and at peace.

Julie London never fully recovered from the 1995 stroke, yet at least one family member believed that she "really got what was going on" around her. "She didn't talk very much," Cynnie Troup recalled, "but I had the feeling that the way she kind of rolled her eyes if my dad would do something, that she was aware of things." Now in his thirties, Julie's son Jody was one of the few people who could rouse her from the visible frustration of not being able to express her needs and feelings in words. Julie could function, but "she wasn't Julie," mused Robert Fuller. "It was the end of a beautiful, beautiful time."

Yet even confined to a wheelchair, she retained her dignity. When *Newsweek* music critic Karen Schoemer came to Encino on the warm afternoon of April 20, 1998, Julie was watching a television soap opera but was perfectly groomed for the occasion. Schoemer noted the "achingly slow, deliberate motion" of the singer's manicured hands as she picked up her pack of Carlton Menthol 100s. Julie was diminished but still strong. Aware and engaged as the writer asked the couple questions about their careers, Julie's ability to articulate her thoughts had diminished to the point where Bobby provided most of the answers—"she forgets," he said—while Julie's responses were infrequent and brief. Julie didn't think about her singing and her records anymore, yet as the trio sat in the gradually darkening room and listened to the exquisite *Easy Does It* album, she could still recall with joy how much she loved the way John Gray played the guitar.

On Tuesday, February 2, 1999, after complaining of breathing problems, Bobby Troup was rushed to Sherman Oaks Hospital. Doctors diagnosed pneumonia. "He was a bit uncomfortable," recalled one of his daughters, "but certainly didn't know he was about to die, and I don't think [the doctors] did either." He seemed on the road to recovery by Saturday night, yet the following day, his condition deteriorated. "He would have died had he not been in the hospital and had the machines to keep him alive [and] resuscitate him. Julie was absolutely right there; she never left his side, and only left once or twice." After ruling out heart surgery as an unnecessary step, the family opted to wait twenty-four hours before making any further decisions on treatment. Old friends Tom Williams and Al Viola came by to provide comfort. Suddenly "somebody came out—it was like a movie—and it was 'Code Blue!' and people were running in and out of the room."

Bobby Troup, who had given so much pleasure to so many with his words and music and whose undying love and dogged persistence in the face of endless resistance had turned Julie London into a singer, passed away at 7:25 PM on February 7, 1999. He was eighty years old. No one really could comprehend what Julie thought of Bobby's passing, but she had already—succinctly—expressed her innermost feelings about her husband: "He made it all possible."

On February 22, a few days after the service at Forest Lawn Memorial Park, a memorial tribute concert was held at the Moonlight Tango Café on Ventura Boulevard. Julie was there, in her wheelchair, grief stricken and unable to speak, as many of Bobby's friends and musical colleagues gathered to pay their respects through song and to tell stories about the man they loved. Tom Williams was there, along with musicians Herm

Saunders, Page Cavanaugh, Al Viola, Lou Levy, and Jack Sheldon (who had played "Taps" from the back of a pickup truck at Forest Lawn), songwriters Jack Segal, Ray Evans, and Jay Livingston, bandleader Les Brown, arranger/composer Neal Hefti, actor Kent McCord (*Adam-12*), and Bobby's *Emergency!* pals Kevin Tighe, Randolph Mantooth, and Robert Fuller. Also in attendance were representatives from the Route 66 Association and from the Montford Point Marines who had served under Bobby during World War II. Rosemary Clooney capped off the event with a moving a cappella performance of "My Buddy."

Snuff Garrett called Bobby "one of the cleverest, funniest people" he had ever known. Now that laughter was gone from the life of Julie London. Friends and family gathered around as she grieved for the man she had loved for more than forty years. Kevin Tighe stayed at the house for a while to keep her company while he sorted out the reams of Bobby's music and lyrics that had been stuffed into a hallway desk drawer.

As if to put a seal on the final years of Julie London's life, doctors discovered a tumor in her lungs. There was little point to putting an already weakened woman through cancer treatment, yet her daughter Kelly—who had been diagnosed with cancer around the same time—shared her mother's gift for irony and her sharp sense of humor in the face of painful reality and jokingly said they could do chemotherapy together.

The pain during the next eighteen months of Julie's life was obvious, but the old Julie—the tough Julie—was still in ample evidence. "She was starting to ask for cigarettes again. She'd gone a long time without doing that. She wasn't asking for drinks anymore, [though] when she was asking for cigarettes, then she'd want a little bit of a drink—she wouldn't drink much of it. She was in another space altogether."

It had been a typically warm mid-October day in Southern California, stirring memories of the beautiful evenings she had so often enjoyed with her children, Bobby, and their close friends at the comforting "house on the hill." Julie's caregiver helped her get dressed up and fixed her hair before rolling her patient's wheelchair into the living room. Asked if she wanted to hear some music, Julie whispered, "Ray Charles." As the music of his hit recording of Buck Owens's "Crying Time" drifted through the air, "huge tears came down the side of her face."

The caregiver returned later in the evening to put her to bed. Once she was tucked in, she began to choke. Childhood friend Caroline Woods and Linda Wheeler, who had known and adored Julie for more than thirty years, rushed into the bedroom. Standing by her side, Julie gave them a look, as if to say "I'm going." The children, who had taken turns to constantly be by their mother's side during her illness, were hastily called, but the heavy traffic that plagues Los Angeles even at night allowed only Jody—always her most loyal family companion—to arrive in time to leap in the back of the ambulance for the two-mile drive, sirens roaring and lights blazing—just like it was an episode of *Emergency!*—to Encino-Tarzana Medical Center.

Julie London took her last breath at 5:30 on the morning of October 18, 2000. It would have been Bobby Troup's eighty-second birthday. The time had arrived for her to fade into the enveloping darkness.

Following cremation Julie was interred in the Columbarium of Providence at Forest Lawn Memorial Park in the Hollywood Hills. As befitted the private person she had always been, only her family and a small group of friends was in attendance to reluctantly say good-bye. The plaque that commemorates their memories of Julie and Bobby reads, "And their graves were side by side."

Epilogue

Echoes

JULIE LONDON'S NEAR-TOTAL RETREAT from the public eye after her last appearance on *Emergency!* in 1978 left her largely unaware of the renewed interest in her music that had begun to quietly bubble during the following decade. While her original audience retained their memories of the singer during her prime and lovingly cherished their now worn copies of her original records, a new generation—some who knew her as Dixie McCall, others who knew nothing at all about her—stumbled upon Julie London's largely hidden past.

This group—broadly defined as the "cocktail nation" (a phrase coined by a member of Combustible Edison, one of the leading retro-lounge acts of the era)—was infatuated by the popular culture of the United States during the decades following the Second World War. Sometimes seriously, often with a touch of irony or humor, they looked to the books, movies, television shows, architecture, and fashion of the 1950s and 1960s as a welcome contrast to contemporary society. They also rediscovered the music of the period that existed side by side with rock 'n' roll—sounds that, with their casual ease and memorable melodies, were the antithesis of rap, grunge, and other genres of popular music in the 1980s and 1990s. This obsessive search for ever-more obscure artists eventually led to Julie London.

As had been the case in the 1950s, Julie's album covers were the come-on, and perhaps many of her records were bought for no other reason than that the pictures made a great wall decoration. But the act of buying and playing old vinyl LPs filled with the sounds of so-called space-age bachelor pad music was also "a vote for a smoother, wittier, more stylish world than the one we've landed up with." Julie's relaxed voice and the ultracool persona that came through the speakers quietly spoke to new sets of ears.

The first significant reconsideration of her work was the top-forty UK success of a new rendition of "Cry Me a River" by Mari Wilson in 1983. The English singer attributed her interest in Julie to a teenage viewing of a BBC television broadcast of *The Girl Can't Help It*. She was "so cool," said Wilson. "People talk about Ella Fitzgerald and Sarah Vaughan but for me Julie had something else. She has that thing of sounding like she's smiling when she's singing anything up tempo or swing. It's like she has a sense of irony in her voice. I'm not interested or moved by vocal pyrotechnics or scatting, just sell me the mood and the story with your voice please, and that's what Julie does."

Six years later came a potent tribute to Julie London in the form of actress Michelle Pfeiffer in her Academy Award–nominated performance as lounge singer Susie Diamond in writer/director Steve Kloves's *The Fabulous Baker Boys*. Whether asking the pianist played by Jeff Bridges to keep the tempo "real slow" before auditioning with a whispered "More than You Know," letting loose with a blistering expletive on a live microphone, or slithering across a piano top during a sexy rendition of "Makin' Whoopee," Pfeiffer effectively captured some of the essence of Julie's style.

During the same decade, one of Julie's biggest fans scoured thrift shops to collect everything he could find by the singer he treasured for the "emotions, value, and quality" she put into her recordings. By 1991 James Austin was on the A&R staff of the Los Angeles–based reissue label Rhino Records, a company known for its off-the-wall releases. What about a Julie London compilation, he asked?

After getting the green light to work on the project, he was told by Capitol Records, which now owned the Liberty Records master tapes, that he'd need Julie's permission to release the record, so he called Bobby Troup, who assured him that no permission was needed but that Julie wasn't going to be thrilled about anyone dredging up her past. Austin had respect for that attitude; some artists aren't interested in what they've done. But she didn't say no, he recalled . . . she just didn't say yes.

After scouring the vaults for the best of the best, he put together the lovingly crafted *Time for Love: The Best of Julie London*, an eighteen-song collection that spanned the singer's career from 1955's "Cry Me a River" to 1967's *Nice Girls Don't Stay for Breakfast*. Julie loved the recording, he later found out, but Bobby still teased that she was "gonna kill" the producer for putting it on the market.

The slow flame of the burgeoning Julie London revival was fanned with the compact disc reissue of the two *Julie Is Her Name* albums by EMI the following year. But it was the 1993 release of "Cry Me a River" by Combustible Edison as a single and as part of their debut album, *I, Swinger!*, on the Seattle-based Sub Pop label (home of grunge heroes Nirvana) that got EMI and Capitol to sit up and think about the revenue potential of Julie's back catalog. In 1996 a series of discs that combined two of Julie's LPs hit the market in the United Kingdom. The releases—part of a broader attempt to exploit the Capitol vaults that included the top names on the label (Peggy Lee, Dean Martin, June Christy, Nat King Cole)—were welcomed with open arms by Julie London fans around the world. Although the pairings had no discernible logic to them and were often mastered from substandard sources, the discs provided access to much of Julie's catalog that had previously only been available on hard-to-find vinyl. Due to poor sales, the series petered out a few years later, having only gathered half of her albums.

While the Capitol Records vaults contained many big hits by big stars, they were ripe for the picking, filled with a mass of dormant master tapes from more obscure artists, most of which had barely seen the light of day since the 1960s. This unearthing, which became the major source of renewed exposure to—and publicity for—Julie London's recordings, also began in 1996, in the midst of the so-called lounge revival, with the launch of the elaborately packaged, multivolume Ultra-Lounge series. The popular compilations, which eventually reached more than twenty-five volumes, began with six discs that largely featured instrumental exotica from the likes of Martin Denny and Les Baxter and easy-listening mood music from bandleaders Billy May and Nelson Riddle.

Volumes four through six—*Bachelor Pad Royale*; *Wild, Cool & Swingin'*; and *Rhapsodesia*—introduced more singers to the mix, including Julie's recordings of "Black Coffee," "You'd Be So Nice to Come Home To," and "Go Slow." Other tracks from her catalog—with the notable exception of "Cry Me a River"—eventually reaching a total of fourteen songs, were featured on *Bossa Novaville*, *Cha-Cha de Amor*, three volumes of *Christmas Cocktails*, a second disc of *Wild, Cool & Swingin'*, *Cocktails with Cole Porter*, two volumes of *On the Rocks* (a collection of rock 'n' roll songs done by middle-of-the-road, or MOR, artists), the *Tiki Sampler*, and *Bottoms Up!*

When the series reached its end three years later with six discs devoted entirely to individual performers, Julie's popularity had reached such a level that she merited her own edition of the *Wild, Cool & Swingin' Artist Collection* alongside the likes of Bobby Darin, Wayne Newton, and the Las Vegas lounge duo of Louis Prima and Keely Smith. She had joined the ranks of Peggy Lee, Judy Garland, Nancy Wilson, Lena Horne, June Christy, and Jo Stafford as one of Capitol's Great Ladies of Song.

Julie London's bona fide credentials as "the first lady of cocktail music" were solidified by her marriages to Jack Webb and Bobby Troup, fellow cultural icons with their own stories to be told. To this group of eager listeners, Julie's "smooth, conversational phrasing and clear diction" made her "in spirit, if not in breadth of talent, the female Sinatra."

In *The Cocktail: The Influence of Spirits on the American Psyche*, a popular book about all things drinking published in 1995, cultural historian Joseph Lanza devoted an entire section ("Sirens of the Cold War") to Julie. He described the singer as "a blend of Dionysian flesh and Detroit steel, streamlined car and cocktail shaker combined," with a "distilled style" and "slow-motion [vocal] delivery that evokes Salvador Dali's melting clocks."

Even at the height of her career, Julie London had never been a fan of Julie London. In the isolation and impaired physical and mental condition of her final years, she professed to have no knowledge that she had captured new eyes and ears, younger people who often wondered what had become of that mysterious figure whose beauty and whispered voice had also ensnared an earlier generation.

In the years since her death, Julie London's unique voice and ability to define a song continues to be recognized. Her iconic recording of "Cry Me a River" was added to the Grammy Hall of Fame by the National Academy of Recording Arts and Sciences in 2001, and fifteen years later the same recording was named to the Library of Congress's National Recording Registry, where her disc joined classics by musical icons like Billie Holiday, Ella Fitzgerald, Frank Sinatra, and Louis Armstrong.

Julie's recordings have also become ripe for the picking by astute music supervisors for film and television soundtracks. The first notable appearance was the use of "Cry Me a River" in the 1993 television adaptation of *Tales of the City*, Armistead Maupin's bestselling novel about life in San Francisco during the 1970s. Thirteen years later, the same song was more prominently featured on the personal jukebox of the mysterious antihero of the dystopian fantasy *V for Vendetta*. "Fly Me to the Moon" appeared on the soundtrack of the hit film *Bridget Jones's Diary* (2001) and was heard again in 2007 during the first season of AMC's influential television series *Mad Men*, about the Madison Avenue advertising business of the 1950s and 1960s. Even the more obscure corners of her catalog were revived. "Gone with the Wind" showed up in *The Notorious Bettie Page*, a 2006 film about the popular yet mysterious pinup of the 1950s, while "Must Be Catchin'" was distinctly heard in the 2011 pilot episode of the short-lived ABC period series *Pan Am*. "Chances Are" got some airtime in the Starz television series *Magic City*, set in the Florida hotel/mob scene of the early 1960s, while the unlikely "Yummy, Yummy, Yummy" was used in a 2001 episode of the HBO series *Six Feet Under*.

This activity belies the fragile state of Julie London's catalog, which remains frustratingly incomplete. In 2012 the hundreds of recordings she made for Liberty Records between 1955 and 1969 became a minor cog in the gigantic Universal Music Group (UMG), itself part of the French media conglomerate Vivendi. Although almost all of Julie's commercially released songs can now be found in digital format on platforms such as iTunes or Amazon, they—as well as many obscure tracks and unreleased recordings—remain ripe for remastering and reissue in the annotated box sets that were once common during the heydays of the predownload record business. With the major industry players—including UMG—concentrating on the name brands in their back catalogs (Frank Sinatra and Miles Davis are among the few artists from Julie's era to make this list), perhaps the only chance that Julie London's music has to achieve this level of respect is for an intrepid independent record label to invest its time and money on discovering and documenting her work. Is anyone listening?

Julie London could have been a star for the ages, one who was remembered as that rare thing: a performer who successfully crossed and recrossed the barriers between acting and singing. That sort of success did not come. Her innate reluctance to exert herself as an actress—to stretch beyond her limitations—and, some would say, her lack of ability, meant that she remained a middle-level star. Clearly, she wanted to work as little as possible and therefore was largely content to leave her career up to the whims of chance. By her own definition, Julie London was happy to be known as a wife, a mother, or a friend rather than as a singer, an actress, or a celebrity.

But did she *ever* look back and wonder how she had been able to find her place in the sun? Did she *ever* think about what her life would have been like had she made even a few different decisions? Probably. Yet there is little doubt that Julie London would surely have dismissed any extended praise of her work as a singer or actress with a deep shrug of the shoulders, a long drag on her cigarette, a sip of her vodka and orange juice, and a well-placed expletive.

For all her success as an interpreter of lyrics, in the end a snatch of dialogue from her 1956 movie *The Girl Can't Help It* may shine a light onto the woman behind the facade and help us understand why she was not reluctant to slip away from fame into a self-imposed obscurity. "If a girl's gonna make it big in show business," talent agent Tom Miller says as he recalls his reluctant star, "she's got to be vitally interested in it." A teenaged Gayle Peck may have vowed to become a star one day, yet it was the older and wiser Julie London who had the final words on her career. "You gotta have the ego for it. And I never really did."

Appendix 1: Discography

US Albums

1955—*Julie Is Her Name.* Liberty LRP-3006 (mono), LST-7027 (stereo).
Songs: Cry Me a River (Hamilton); I Should Care (Weston/Stordahl/Cahn); I'm in the Mood for Love (McHugh/Fields); I'm Glad There Is You (Madeira/Dorsey); Can't Help Lovin' That Man (Kern/Hammerstein); I Love You (Porter); Say It Isn't So (Berlin); It Never Entered My Mind (Rodgers/Hart); Easy Street (Jones); 'S Wonderful (Gershwin/Gershwin); No Moon at All (Evans/Mann); Laura (Mercer/Raksin); Gone with the Wind (Wrubel/Magidson).
Producer: Bobby Troup. Engineer: John Neal. Musicians: Barney Kessel (guitar), Ray Leatherwood (bass). Photography: Phil Howard. Recorded at Western Recorders, Hollywood, August 8–9, 1955.

1956—*Lonely Girl.* Liberty LRP-3012 (mono), LST-7029 (stereo).
Songs: Lonely Girl (Troup); Fools Rush In (Bloom/Mercer); Moments Like This (Lane/Loesser); I Lost My Sugar in Salt Lake City (René/Lange); It's the Talk of the Town (Symes/Neiburg/Livingston); What'll I Do (Berlin); When Your Lover Has Gone (Swan); Don't Take Your Love from Me (Nemo); Where or When (Rodgers/Hart); All Alone (Berlin); Mean to Me (Ahlert/Turk); How Deep Is the Ocean (Berlin); Remember (Berlin).
Producer: Bobby Troup. Engineer: John Neal. Musician: Al Viola (guitar). Photography: Ray Jones. Recorded at Western Recorders, Hollywood, April 1956.

1956—*Calendar Girl.* Liberty SL-9002 (mono; never released in stereo).
Songs: June in January (Rainger/Robin); February Brings the Rain (Troup); Melancholy March (Saunders/Langdon); I'll Remember April (Raye/de Paul/Johnston); People Who Are Born in May (Brent); Memphis in June (Webster/Carmichael); Sleigh Ride in July (Burke/Van Heusen); Time for August (Hamilton); September in the Rain (Warren/Dubin); This

237

October (Troup); November Twilight (King/Webster); Warm December (Russell); The Thirteenth Month (Hamilton).

Arranger/conductor: Pete King. Producer: Bobby Troup. Engineers: John Palladino, John Kraus. Musicians: Frank Beach, Maurie Harris, Ralph Fera, Conrad Gozzo, Cecil Read (trumpet); Si Zentner, Dick Nash, Marshall Cram, Murray McEachern, Lloyd Ulyate (trombone); Vincent DeRosa (French horn); Jules Jacob, Arthur "Skeets" Herfurt, Dale Issenhuth, Bill Ulyate, Gene Cipriano, Marty Berman, Herman Gunkler, Russ Cheever, Ethmer Roten, Harry Klee (reeds); Ann Stockton (harp); Buddy Cole, Mark McIntyre (piano); Howard Roberts, Bob Bain, Al Hendrickson, Vince Terri (guitar); Red Callender, Phil Stephens (bass); Milt Holland, Jack Sperling (drums); Frank Flynn (percussion); Felix Slatkin, Paul Shure, Eudice Shapiro, Israel Baker, Erno Neufeld, Lou Raderman, George Berres, Marvin Limonick, Kurt Dieterle, Marshall Sosson (violin); Alvin Dinkin, Alexander Neimann (viola); Eleanor Slatkin, Kurt Reher, Joseph DiTullio (cello). Photography: Gene Lester. Recorded at Capitol Studios, Hollywood, May–August 1956.

1957—*About the Blues.* Liberty LRP-3043 (mono), LST-7012 (stereo).

Songs: Basin Street Blues (Williams); I Gotta Right to Sing the Blues (Arlen/Koehler); A Nightingale Can Sing the Blues (Marks/Charles); Get Set for the Blues (Karnes); Invitation to the Blues (Fisher/Roberts/Gershwin); Bye Bye Blues (Gray/Hamm/Bennett/Lown); Meaning of the Blues (Troup/Worth); About the Blues (Hamilton); Sunday Blues (Adelson/Clarkson); The Blues Is All I Ever Had (Troup); Blues in the Night (Arlen/Mercer); Bouquet of Blues (Hamilton).

Arranger/conductor: Russ Garcia. Producer: Bobby Troup. Engineers: Ted Keep, Sherwood Hall, Val Valentin. Musicians: Willie Smith (alto saxophone), Maynard Ferguson (trumpet), Barney Kessel (guitar), Shelly Manne (drums). Photography: Alex de Paola. Recorded at Radio Recorders, Hollywood, late 1956–early 1957.

1957—*Make Love to Me.* Liberty LRP-3060 (mono), LST-7060 (stereo).

Songs: If I Could Be with You (Johnson/Creamer); It's Good to Want You Bad (Troup); Go Slow (Garcia/Kronk); A Room with a View (Swan/Stillman); The Nearness of You (Washington/Carmichael); Alone Together (Dietz/Schwartz); I Wanna Be Loved (Rose/Heyman/Green); Snuggled on Your Shoulder (Lombardo/Young); You're My Thrill (Gorney/Clare); Lover Man (Davis/Ramirez/Sherman); Body and Soul (Heyman/Sour/Green/Eyton); Make Love to Me (Gannon/Mann/Weiss).

Arranger/conductor: Russ Garcia. Producer: Simon Jackson. Engineer: Ted Keep. Musicians: Al Viola (guitar). Photography: Garrett-Howard. Recorded at Liberty Studios, Hollywood, spring/summer 1957.

1958—*Julie*. Liberty LRP-3096 (mono), LST-7004 (stereo).

Songs: Somebody Loves Me (Gershwin/MacDonald/DeSylva); Dream of You (Lunceford/ Oliver/Moran); Daddy (Troup); Bye Bye Blackbird (Henderson/Dixon); Free and Easy (Mancini/Troup); All My Life (Stept/Mitchell); When the Red, Red Robin Comes Bob, Bob, Bobbin' Along (Woods); Midnight Sun (Mercer/Hampton/Burke); You're Getting to Be a Habit with Me (Warren/Dubin); Don'cha Go 'Way Mad (Mundy/Stillman/Jacquet); (Back Home Again in) Indiana (Hanley/MacDonald); For You (Dubin/Burke).

Arranger/conductor: Jimmy Rowles. Producer: Bobby Troup. Engineer: Ted Keep. Musicians: Georgie Auld (tenor saxophone); Benny Carter (alto saxophone); Pete Candoli, Jack Sheldon (trumpet); Buddy Collette, Bud Shank (reeds); Jimmy Rowles (piano); Al Hendrickson (guitar); Mel Lewis (drums). Cover design: Charles Ward. Recorded at Liberty Studios, Hollywood, October 1957.

1958—*Julie Is Her Name, Volume 2*. Liberty LRP-3100 (mono), LST-7100 (stereo).

Songs: Blue Moon (Rodgers/Hart); What Is This Thing Called Love (Porter); How Long Has This Been Going On (Gershwin/Gershwin); Too Good to Be True (Boland); Spring Is Here (Rodgers/Hart); Goody Goody (Mercer/Malneck); The One I Love Belongs to Somebody Else (Jones/Kahn); If I'm Lucky (Myrow/De Lange); Hot Toddy (Flanagan/ Hendler); Little White Lies (Donaldson); I'll Guess I'll Have to Change My Plan (Schwartz/ Dietz); I Got Lost in His Arms (Berlin).

Producer: Bobby Troup. Engineer: Ted Keep. Musicians: Howard Roberts (guitar), Red Mitchell (bass). Photography: Garrett-Howard. Recorded at Liberty Studios, Hollywood, July 8, 10–11, 17–19, 1958.

1958—*London by Night*. Liberty LRP-3105 (mono), LST-7105 (stereo).

Songs: Well, Sir (Troup/Lehmann); That's for Me (Rodgers/Hammerstein); Mad About the Boy (Coward); In the Middle of a Kiss (Coslow); Just the Way I Am (Troup); My Man's Gone Now (Gershwin/Heyward); Something I Dreamed Last Night (Fain/Yellen/Magidson); Pousse Café (Hagen/Spencer); Nobody's Heart (Rodgers/Hart); The Exciting Life (Hagen/ Spencer); That Old Feeling (Brown/Fain); Cloudy Morning (Fisher/McCarthy Jr.).

Arranger/conductor: Pete King. Producer: Bobby Troup. Engineer: Ted Keep. Musicians: Al Viola, Howard Roberts (guitar); Red Callender (bass); Felix Slatkin (violin); Alvin Dinkin (viola); Eleanor Slatkin (cello); Kurt Reher (cello). Photography: Garrett-Howard. Recorded at Liberty Studios, Hollywood, May 1957–November 1958.

Note: An outtake from the sessions, a Latin-flavored rendition of Cole Porter's "Night and Day," was released on *Julie London to Her Fans*, a 1962 Italian compilation.

1959—*Swing Me an Old Song*. Liberty LRP-3119 (mono), LST-7119 (stereo).

Songs: Comin' Thru the Rye (traditional); Cuddle Up a Little Closer (Harbach/Hoschna); After the Ball (Harris); Be My Little Baby Bumble Bee (Murphy/Marshall); Camptown

Races (Foster); Old Folks at Home (Foster); Downtown Strutters' Ball (Brooks); How Come You Do Me Like You Do (Bergere/Austin); Row, Row, Row (Jerome/Monaco); By the Beautiful Sea (Atteridge/Carroll); Bill Bailey, Won't You Please Come Home? (Cannon); Three O'Clock in the Morning (Terriss/Robledo).

Arranger/conductor: Jimmy Rowles. Producer: Bobby Troup. Engineers: Ted Keep, Don Gallese. Musicians: Jack Sheldon (trumpet), Jimmy Rowles (piano), Al Viola (guitar). Photography: Garrett-Howard. Recorded at Liberty Studios, Hollywood, April/May 1959.

1959—*Your Number Please.* Liberty LRP-3130 (mono), LST-7130 (stereo).

Songs: Makin' Whoopee (Kahn/Donaldson); It Could Happen to You (Burke/Van Heusen); When I Fall in Love (Young/Heyman); It's a Blue World (Wright/Forrest); They Can't Take That Away from Me (Gershwin/Gershwin); One for My Baby (and One More for the Road) (Arlen/Mercer); Angel Eyes (Brent/Dennis); Love Is Here to Stay (Gershwin/Gershwin); The More I See You (Gordon/Warren); A Stranger in Town (Tormé); Two Sleepy People (Carmichael/Loesser); Learnin' the Blues (Silvers).

Arranger/conductor: André Previn. Arranger: Al Woodbury. Producer: Bobby Troup. Engineers: Bill Putnam, Ted Keep. Musicians: Arthur Cleghorn (flute); Wilbur Schwartz (flute); Arnold Koblenz (oboe); John Cave, Richard Perissi, Sinclair Lott (French horn); Catherine Gotthoffer (harp); André Previn (piano); Monty Budwig (bass); Frank Capp (drums); Lou Raderman, Dan Lube, Victor Arno, David Frisina, Eudice Shapiro, George Kast, William Miller, Alfred Lustgarten, Lisa Minghetti, Mort Herbert, Sam Freed, Anatol Kaminsky (violin); Virginia Majewski, Cecil Figelski, Allan Harshman, Robert Ostrowsky (viola); Edgar Lustgarten, Raphael Kramer, Kurt Reher, Armand Kaproff (cello). Photography: Garrett-Howard. Recorded at United Recording and Liberty Studios, Hollywood, August/September 1959.

1960—*Julie at Home.* Liberty LRP-3152 (mono), LST-7152 (stereo).

Songs: You'd Be So Nice to Come Home To (Porter); Lonesome Road (Austin/Shilkret); They Didn't Believe Me (Kern/Reynolds); By Myself (Dietz/Schwartz); The Thrill Is Gone (Brown/Henderson); You've Changed (Carey/Fischer); Goodbye (Jenkins); Sentimental Journey (Green/Brown/Homer); Give Me the Simple Life (Ruby/Bloom); You Stepped Out of a Dream (Kahn/Brown); Let There Be Love (Rand/Grant); Everything Happens to Me (Adair/Dennis).

Producer: Si Waronker. Engineer: John Kraus. Musicians: Jimmy Rowles (piano), Emil Richards (vibraphone), Al Viola (guitar), Don Bagley (bass), Earl Palmer (drums), Bob Flanigan (trombone on "By Myself" and "You Stepped Out of a Dream"). Photography: Garrett-Howard. Recorded at Julie London's house, Encino, January 1960.

1960—*Around Midnight.* Liberty LRP-3164 (mono), LST-7164 (stereo).

Songs: 'Round Midnight (Monk/Hanighen/Williams); Lonely Night in Paris (Troup/Alcivar); Misty (Garner/Burke); Black Coffee (Burke/Webster); Lush Life (Strayhorn); In the

Wee Small Hours of the Morning (Hilliard/Mann); Don't Smoke in Bed (Robison); You and the Night and the Music (Dietz/Schwartz); Something Cool (Barnes); How About Me (Berlin); But Not for Me (Gershwin/Gershwin); The Party's Over (Styne/Comden/Green). Arranger/conductor: Dick Reynolds. Producer: Si Waronker. Engineer: John Kraus. Musician: Al Viola (guitar). Photography: Garrett-Howard. Recorded at Capitol Studios, Hollywood, June/July 1960.

1960—*Send for Me.* Liberty LRP-3171 (mono), LST-7171 (stereo).
Songs: Evenin' (Parish/White); What's Your Story, Morning Glory (Williams/Webster/Lawrence); Get on the Right Track (Turner); I Must Have That Man (McHugh/Fields); Tain't What You Do (It's the Way That Cha Do It) (Oliver/Young); Baby Come Home (Troup/Rowles); Every Day (I Have the Blues) (Chatman/York); Yes Indeed (Oliver); Gee Baby Ain't I Good to You (Redman/Razaf); Cheatin' on Me (Pollack/Yellen); Trav'lin' Light (Mercer/Mundy/Young); Send for Me (Jones).
Arranger/conductor: Jimmy Rowles. Producer: Si Waronker. Engineer: Bones Howe. Musician: Jack Sheldon (trumpet). Photography: Garrett-Howard. Recorded at Radio Recorders, Hollywood, late 1960.

1961—*Whatever Julie Wants.* Liberty LRP-3192 (mono), LST-7192 (stereo).
Songs: Why Don't You Do Right (McCoy); My Heart Belongs to Daddy (Porter); Hard Hearted Hannah (Yellen/Ager/Bigelow/Bates); Do It Again (Gershwin/DeSylva); Take Back Your Mink (Loesser); Diamonds Are a Girl's Best Friend (Styne/Robin); Daddy (Troup); An Occasional Man (Martin/Blane); Love for Sale (Porter); Always True to You in My Fashion (Porter); There'll Be Some Changes Made (Higgins/Overstreet); Tired (Roberts/Fisher).
Arranger: Dick Reynolds ("Do It Again"). Producer/conductor: Felix Slatkin. Photography: Garrett-Howard. Recorded at United Recording, Hollywood, spring 1961.

1962—*Sophisticated Lady.* Liberty LRP-3203 (mono), LST-7203 (stereo).
Songs: Sophisticated Lady (Ellington/Mills/Parish); Blame It on My Youth (Heyman/Levant); Make It Another Old Fashioned Please (Porter); You're Blasé (Sievier/Hamilton); Bewitched (Rodgers/Hart); Spring Can Really Hang You Up the Most (Wolf/Landesman); Remind Me (Fields/Kern); When She Makes Music (Segal/Fisher); When the World Was Young (Mercer/Philippe-Gerard); If I Should Lose You (Rainger/Robin); Where Am I to Go (Troup/Dennis); Absent Minded Me (Merrill).
Producer: Si Waronker. Photography: Garrett-Howard. Recorded at United Recording, Hollywood, late 1961.

1962—*Love Letters.* Liberty LRP-3231 (mono), LST-7231 (stereo).
Songs: Love Letters (Young/Heyman); The Second Time Around* (Cahn/Van Heusen); I Loves You, Porgy (Gershwin/Gershwin/Heyward); What a Diff'rence a Day Made (Adams/

Grever); Never on Sunday* (Towne/Hadjidakis); I Miss You So (Henderson/Scott/Robin); All the Way (Cahn/Van Heusen); Come on-a My House (Bagdasarian/Saroyan); Hey There (Adler/Ross); And That Reminds Me (Stillman/Bargoni); Fascination* (Manning/Marchetti); Broken-Hearted Melody (David/Edwards).

Arranger: Ernie Freeman(*). Producer: Snuff Garrett. Engineers: Eddie Brackett, Jim Economides. Musician: Barney Kessel (guitar). Photography: Garrett-Howard. Recorded at United Recording, Hollywood, March 1962, except "Come on-a My House" (ca. October 1958).

1962—*Love on the Rocks*. Liberty LRP-3249 (mono), LST-7249 (stereo).
Songs: How Did He Look (Silver/Shelley); What's New (Burke/Haggart); The End of a Love Affair (Redding); A Cottage for Sale (Conley/Robison); Where Are You? (Adamson/ McHugh); Willow Weep for Me (Ronell); Guess Who I Saw Today (Grand/Boyd); Where Did the Gentleman Go (Troup); Don't Worry 'Bout Me (Koehler/Bloom); I'll Be Seeing You (Kahal/Fain); The Man That Got Away (Arlen/Gershwin); Love on the Rocks (Forest/Hughes).

Arranger/conductor: Pete King. Producer: Snuff Garrett. Musicians: Jack Sheldon (trumpet), John Gray (guitar), Chuck Berghofer (bass), Kenny Hume (drums). Photography: Studio Five. Recorded at Universal Recording, Chicago (backing tracks), and United Recording, Hollywood (overdubs), August/September 1962.

1963—*Latin in a Satin Mood*. Liberty LRP-3278 (mono), LST-7278 (stereo).
Songs: Frenesi (Dominguez/Charles/Russell); Be Mine Tonight (Skylar/Lara); Yours (Gamse/ Sherr/Roig); Besame Mucho (Velázquez/Skylar); Adios (Woods/Madriguera); Sway (Gimbel/ Ruiz); Perfidia (Leeds/Dominguez); Come Closer to Me (Stewart/Farres); Amor (Ruiz/Skylar/Mendez); Magic Is the Moonlight (Pasquale/Grever); You Belong to My Heart (Gilbert/ Lara); Vaya Con Dios (Pepper/Russell/James).

Arranger/conductor: Ernie Freeman. Producer: Snuff Garrett. Engineers: Eddie Brackett, Walt Payne. Photography: Garrett-Howard. Recorded at United Recording, Hollywood, late 1962.

1963—*The End of the World* (aka *The Good Life*). Liberty LRP-3300 (mono), LST-7300 (stereo).
Songs: The End of the World (Dee/Kent); I Wanna Be Around (Mercer/Vimmerstedt); Call Me Irresponsible (Cahn/Van Heusen); Our Day Will Come (Hilliard/Garson); I Left My Heart in San Francisco (Cory/Cross); Fly Me to the Moon (Howard); Days of Wine and Roses (Mancini/Mercer); I Remember You (Mercer/Schertzinger); My Coloring Book (Ebb/Kander); Chances Are (Allen/Stillman); Slightly Out of Tune (Desafinado) (Hendricks/ Cavanaugh/Jobim/Mendonça); The Good Life (Distel/Reardon).

Arranger/conductor: Ernie Freeman. Producer: Snuff Garrett. Engineer: Dave Hassinger. Photography: Virgil Apger. Recorded at RCA, Hollywood, spring 1963, except "Slightly Out of Tune (Desafinado)" (August/September 1962).

1963—*The Wonderful World of Julie London.* Liberty LRP-3324 (mono), LST-7324 (stereo).

Songs: I'm Coming Back to You (Warren/Kent); Soft Summer Breeze (Heywood/Spencer); Can't Get Used to Losing You (Pomus/Shuman); A Taste of Honey (Scott/Marlow); Little Things Mean a Lot (Stutz/Lindeman); In the Still of the Night (Porter); Love for Sale (Porter); When Snow Flakes Fall in the Summer (Weil/Mann); How Can I Make Him Love Me? (Pomus/Shuman); Say Wonderful Things (Newell/Green); Guilty Heart (DeVorzon/Haskell/Perry); (I Love You) And Don't You Forget It (Mancini/Stillman).

Arranger/conductor: Ernie Freeman. Producer: Snuff Garrett. Engineer: Eddie Brackett. Photography: Studio Five. Recorded at United Recording, Hollywood, summer 1963.

1964—*You Don't Have to Be a Baby to Cry* (aka *Julie London*). Liberty LRP-3342 (mono), LST-7342 (stereo).

Songs: Since I Fell for You (Johnson); Night Life (Nelson); Charade (Mancini/Mercer); You Don't Have to Be a Baby to Cry (Merrill/Shand); Wheel of Fortune (Benjamin/Weiss); Wives and Lovers (Bacharach/David); Fools Rush In (Mercer/Bloom); That Sunday (That Summer) (Weiss/Sherman); I Wish You Love (Beach/Trenet); There! I've Said It Again (Evans/Mann); All About Ronnie (Greene); I Want to Find Out for Myself (Dee/Kent).

Arranger/conductor: Ernie Freeman. Producer: Snuff Garrett. Engineer: Dave Hassinger. Musicians: Jack Sheldon (trumpet), Plas Johnson (tenor saxophone). Photography: Studio Five. Recorded at RCA, Hollywood, late 1963.

1964—*In Person at the Americana.* Liberty LRP-3375 (mono), LST-7375 (stereo).

Songs: Opening/Lonesome Road (Austin/Shilkret); Send for Me (Jones); My Baby Just Cares for Me (Kahn/Donaldson); The Trolley Song (Martin/Blane); Daddy (Troup); Medley: Basin Street Blues (Williams)/St. Louis Blues (Handy)/Baby, Baby All the Time (Troup); Kansas City (Lieber/Stoller); Bye Bye Blackbird (Dixon/Henderson); By Myself (Dietz/Schwartz); I Love Paris (Porter); Gotta Move (Matz); Cry Me a River (Hamilton); The Man That Got Away/Closing (Arlen/Gershwin).

Arranger: Don Bagley. Vocal arranger: Ken Albers. Producer: Snuff Garrett. Engineers: Tom Dowd, Dave Hassinger. Musicians: Don Bagley (bass), Sal Salvador (guitar), Jerome Richardson (reeds). "The Casuals": Cal Sexton, Bob Anson, Ron Parry, Don McLeod (vocals). Photography: Burt Goldblatt. Recorded at the Royal Box, Americana Hotel, New York, April 1964.

1965—*Our Fair Lady.* Liberty LRP-3392 (mono), LST-7392 (stereo).

Songs: Theme from a Summer Place (Discant/Steiner); As Time Goes By (Hupfeld); More (Theme from Mondo Cane) (Newell/Ortolani/Oliviero); An Affair to Remember (Adamson/McCarey/Warren). *Note:* only the four songs not previously released are listed.

Arranger/conductor: Richard Wess. Producer: Snuff Garrett. Engineer: Dave Hassinger. Musicians: Gene Cipriano, Paul Horn (reeds); Ernie Freeman (piano); Tommy Allsup, John Gray (guitar); Red Callender (bass); Earl Palmer (drums); Julius Wechter (percussion); William Kurasch, Israel Baker, Ralph Schaeffer, Leonard Malarsky, Stanley Plummer, John de Voogdt, Tibor Zelig, Sidney Sharp (violin); Joseph DiFiore, Alexander Neimann (viola); Irving Lipschultz, Joseph Saxon (cello). Cover design: Studio Five. Recorded at RCA, Hollywood, October 9 and 10, 1964.

1965—*Feeling Good.* Liberty LRP-3416 (mono), LST-7416 (stereo).
Songs: My Kind of Town (Cahn/Van Heusen); Girl Talk (Hefti/Troup); King of the Road (Miller); I Bruise Easily (Manley); Feeling Good (Bricusse/Newley); Watermelon Man (Hancock); She's Just a Quiet Girl (Mae) (Ortolani/Vance); Summertime (Gershwin/Heyward); Hello Dolly! (Herman); Won't Someone Please Belong to Me (Troup).
Arranger/conductor: Gerald Wilson. Producer: Richard Bock. Musicians: Jack Wilson (piano, organ), Teddy Edwards (tenor saxophone), John Gray (guitar), Jimmy Bond (bass), Earl Palmer (drums), Tom Williams (vocal on "King of the Road"). Photography: Fred Seligo. Recorded at Liberty Records (former Pacific Jazz Studios), Los Angeles, summer 1965.

1965—*All Through the Night.* Liberty LRP-3434 (mono), LST-7434 (stereo).
Songs: I've Got You Under My Skin (Porter); You Do Something to Me (Porter); Get Out of Town (Porter); All Through the Night (Porter); So in Love (Porter); At Long Last Love (Porter); Easy to Love (Porter); My Heart Belongs to Daddy (Porter); Ev'ry Time We Say Goodbye (Porter); In the Still of the Night (Porter).
Arranger: Russ Freeman. Producer/Engineer: Richard Bock. Musicians: Bud Shank (alto saxophone, flute), Russ Freeman (piano), Joe Pass (guitar), Monty Budwig (bass), Colin Bailey (drums). Photography: Fred Seligo. Recorded at Liberty Records (former Pacific Jazz Studios), Los Angeles, July 12, 13, and 16, 1965.

1966—*For the Night People.* Liberty LRP-3478 (mono), LST-7478 (stereo).
Songs: Won't You Come Home Bill Bailey? (Cannon); I Got It Bad (and That Ain't Good) (Ellington/Webster); Saturday Night (Is the Loneliest Night in the Week) (Cahn/Styne); God Bless the Child (Herzog Jr./Holiday); Am I Blue? (Akst/Clarke); Dream (Mercer); Here's That Rainy Day (Burke/Van Heusen); When the Sun Comes Out (Arlen/Koehler); Can't Get Out of This Mood (McHugh/Loesser); I Hadn't Anyone Till You (Noble); I'll Never Smile Again (Lowe).
Arranger: Don Bagley. Producer: Calvin Carter. Engineer: Joe Sidore. Musicians: Don Bagley (bass), John Gray (guitar), Jack Sheldon (trumpet). Photography: Color-Sonics Inc. Recorded at Western Recorders, Hollywood, summer 1966.

1967—*Nice Girls Don't Stay for Breakfast.* Liberty LRP-3493 (mono), LST-7493 (stereo). Songs: Nice Girls Don't Stay for Breakfast (Troup/Leshay); When I Grow Too Old to Dream (Romberg/Hammerstein); I've Got a Crush on You (Gershwin/Gershwin); Everything I Have Is Yours (Adamson/Lane); You Made Me Love You (McCarthy/Monaco); Baby, Won't You Please Come Home (Warfield/Williams); I Didn't Know What Time It Was (Rodgers/Hart); Give a Little Whistle (Washington/Harline); I Surrender, Dear (Clifford/Barris); You Go to My Head (Gillespie/Coots); There Will Never Be Another You (Warren/Gordon); Mickey Mouse (Dodd).
Arranger: Don Bagley. Producer: Calvin Carter. Engineers: Joe Sidore, Chuck Britz. Musicians: Don Bagley (bass), John Gray (guitar), Jack Sheldon (trumpet), Bob Cooper (tenor saxophone). Photography: Studio Five. Recorded at Western Recorders, Hollywood, fall 1966.

1967—*With Body and Soul.* Liberty LRP-3514 (mono), LST-7514 (stereo).
Songs: The Comeback (Fraser); Come on By (Badale/Simon); C. C. Rider (traditional); Romance in the Dark (Green); I Got a Sweetie (Charles); You're No Good (Ballard Jr.); Alexander's Ragtime Band (Berlin); If You Want This Love (Knight); Looking Back (Otis/Benton/Hendricks); Treat Me Good (Scott/Radcliffe); Straight Shooter (Phillips).
Arranger: Kirk Stuart. Producer: Calvin Carter. Engineers: Lanky Linstrot. Musicians: Kirk Stuart (piano). Photography: Gene Trindl. Recorded at United Recording, Hollywood, summer 1967.

1968—*Easy Does It.* Liberty LST-7546 (stereo, no mono release).
Songs: Show Me the Way to Go Home* (King); Me and My Shadow* (Dreyer/Jolson/Rose); This Can't Be Love* (Rodgers/Hart); Spring Will Be a Little Late This Year** (Loesser); Soon It's Gonna Rain* (Jones/Schmidt); I'll See You in My Dreams** (Kahn/Jones); April in Paris (Duke/Harburg); Bidin' My Time (Gershwin/Gershwin); The Man I Love (Gershwin/Gershwin); It Had to Be You (Kahn/Jones); We'll Be Together Again (Laine/Fischer); The One I Love Belongs to Somebody Else (Kahn/Jones).
Arrangers: Kirk Stuart, Don Bagley (*), Allyn Ferguson (**). Producer: Calvin Carter. Engineer: Lanky Linstrot. Musicians: Don Bagley (bass), John Gray (guitar), Kirk Stuart (piano, organ), Earl Palmer (drums). Photography: John Engstead. Recorded at United Recording and Liberty Studios (former Pacific Jazz Studios), Hollywood, October/November 1967.

1969—*Yummy, Yummy, Yummy.* Liberty LST-7609 (stereo, no mono release).
Songs: Stoned Soul Picnic (Nyro); Like to Get to Know You (Scharf); Light My Fire (Morrison/Manzarek/Krieger/Densmore); It's Nice to Be with You (Goldstein); Sunday Mornin' (Guryan); Hushabye Mountain (Sherman/Sherman); The Mighty Quinn (Dylan); Come to Me Slowly (Guryan); And I Love Him (Lennon/McCartney); Without Him (Nilsson); Yummy, Yummy, Yummy (Resnick/Levine); Louie Louie (Berry).

Arranger/conductor/producer: Tommy Oliver. Engineers: Bruce Ellison, Ami Hadani. Musicians: Bob Knight (trombone); Bill Perkins, Jim Horn (reeds); Michel Rubini (piano); Al Casey, Neil Levang, Mike Deasy, Lou Morell (guitar); Lyle Ritz (electric bass); John Guerin, Hal Blaine (drums); Gary Coleman, Dale Anderson (percussion); Wilbert Nuttycombe, James Getzoff, Leonard Malarsky, Paulo Alencar, Ralph Schaeffer, William Kurasch, Harry Bluestone, Sidney Sharp, Israel Baker (violin); Harry Hyams, Joseph DiFiore, Leonard Selic, Philip Goldberg, Louis Kievman (viola); Armand Kaproff, Jesse Ehrlich (cello). Photography: John Engstead. Recorded at T.T.G. Recorders, Hollywood, August/September 1968.

US Singles and EPs

1955—Cry Me a River (Hamilton) b/w 'S Wonderful (Gershwin/Gershwin). Liberty 55006.

1956—Baby, Baby All the Time (Troup) b/w Shadow Woman (Hamilton). Liberty 55009. Arranger/conductor: Russ Garcia.

1956—Lonely Girl (Troup) b/w September in the Rain (Warren/Dubin). Liberty 55025. Arranger/conductor: Pete King. The A-side adds strings to the album version.

1956—Now Baby Now (Cahn/Brodsky) b/w Tall Boy (Kayne). Liberty 55032. Arranger/conductor: Pete King.

1957—The Boy on a Dolphin (Webster/Friedhofer) b/w Meaning of the Blues (Troup/Worth). Liberty 55052. Arranger/conductor: Howard Roberts (A), Russ Garcia (B). The B-side has a different vocal than the version released on *About the Blues*.

1957—It Had to Be You (Kahn/Jones) b/w Dark (Greines). Liberty 55076. With the Spencer-Hagen Orchestra.

1957—Saddle the Wind (Livingston/Evans) b/w I'd Like You for Christmas (Troup). Liberty 55108. Conductor: Johnny Mann.

1958—The Freshmen (Troup/London) b/w Tell Me You're Home (Troup). Liberty 55131. Conductors: Dick Reynolds (A), Johnny Mann (B).

1958—Voice in the Mirror (Troup/London) b/w It's Easy (Bagdasarian). Liberty 55139. Conductor: Pete King (A).

1958—Man of the West (Troup) b/w Blue Moon (Rodgers/Hart). Arranger: Howard Roberts (B). Liberty 55157.

1959—Come on-a My House (Bagdasarian/Saroyan) b/w My Strange Affair (Troup). Liberty 55175.

1959—Must Be Catchin' (Stanley) b/w Something I Dreamed Last Night (Fain/Yellen/Magidson). Liberty 55182. Arranger/conductor: Pete King (B).

1959—Comin' Thru the Rye (traditional) b/w Makin' Whoopee (Donaldson/Kahn). Liberty 55216. Arrangers/conductors: Jimmy Rowles (A), André Previn (B).

1959—Cry Me a River (Hamilton) b/w It's a Blue World (Wright/Forrest). Liberty 55227. Conductor: Felix Slatkin (A). Arranger/conductor: André Previn (B). The A-side adds strings to the original recording.

1960—In the Wee Small Hours of the Morning (Hilliard/Mann) b/w Time for Lovers (Rustigian). Liberty 55269. Producer: Si Waronker. Arranger/conductor: Dick Reynolds.

1961—Send for Me (Jones) b/w Evenin' (Parish/White). Liberty 55300. Producer: Si Waronker. Arranger/conductor: Jimmy Rowles.

1961—Every Chance I Get (Stanley) b/w Sanctuary (Keith/Bergman/North). Liberty 55309. Producer: Felix Slatkin. Arranger/conductor: Dick Reynolds.

1961—My Darling, My Darling (Loesser) b/w My Love, My Love (Haymes/Acquaviva). Liberty 55337. Producer: Clyde Otis. Arranger/conductor: Belford Hendricks.

1962—Slightly Out of Tune (Desafinado) (Hendricks/Cavanaugh/Jobim/Mendonça) b/w Where Did the Gentleman Go (Troup). Liberty 55512. Producer: Snuff Garrett. Arranger/conductor: Ernie Freeman (A), Pete King (B).

1963—I'm Coming Back to You (Warren/Kent) b/w When Snow Flakes Fall in the Summer (Weil/Mann). Liberty 55605. Producer: Snuff Garrett. Arranger/conductor: Ernie Freeman.

1964—I Want to Find Out for Myself (Dee/Kent) b/w Guilty Heart (DeVorzon/Haskell/Perry). Liberty 55666. Producer: Snuff Garrett. Arranger/conductor: Ernie Freeman.

1964—The Boy from Ipanema (Jobim/Gimbel) b/w My Lover Is a Stranger (Segal/Fisher). Liberty 55702. Arranger/conductor: Don Bagley. Producer: Snuff Garrett. Musicians: Plas Johnson (tenor saxophone, flute), Jimmy Rowles (piano), John Gray (guitar), Don Bagley (bass), Shelly Manne (drums), Emil Richards (vibraphone, percussion).

1964—You're Free to Go (Robertson/Herscher) b/w We Proved Them Wrong (Keller/Kolber). Liberty 55759. Arranger/conductor: Richard Wess (A), Ernie Freeman (B). Producer: Snuff Garrett.

1965—Girl Talk (Hefti/Troup) b/w Won't Someone Please Belong to Me (Troup). Liberty 55830. Arranger/conductor: Gerald Wilson. Producer: Richard Bock.

1966—Nice Girls Don't Stay for Breakfast (Troup/Leshay) b/w Won't You Come Home Bill Bailey? (Cannon). Liberty 55911. Arranger: Don Bagley. Producer: Calvin Carter.

1967—Mickey Mouse March (Dodd) b/w Baby, Won't You Please Come Home (Warfield/Williams). Liberty 55966. Arranger: Don Bagley. Producer: Calvin Carter.

1968—Yummy, Yummy, Yummy (Resnick/Levine) b/w Come to Me Slowly (Guryan). Liberty 56074. Arranger/conductor/producer: Tommy Oliver.

1968—Louie Louie (Berry) b/w Hushabye Mountain (Sherman/Sherman). Liberty 56085. Arranger/conductor/producer: Tommy Oliver.

1969—Too Much of a Man (Kingston) b/w Sittin' Pretty (Gentry/Gordon). Liberty 56112 (unreleased). Arranger/producer: Tommy Oliver. Musicians: Ollie Mitchell (trumpet); David Duke (French horn); Jim Horn (reeds); Michel Rubini (piano); David Cohen, Neil Levang (guitar); Bob West (bass); John Guerin, Alan Estes (drums); Tommy Morgan (harmonica); Ralph Schaeffer, Mischa Russell, Henry Ferber, Tibor Zelig, James Getzoff, Assa Drori (violin); Louis Klevman, Joseph DiFiore (viola); Jesse Ehrlich, Raymond Kelley (cello).

Miscellaneous Recordings of Note

1955 Bethlehem demo recordings—A Foggy Day (Gershwin/Gershwin); You're Blasé (Sievier/Hamilton); Don't Worry 'Bout Me (Koehler/Bloom); Sometimes I Feel Like a Motherless Child (traditional). Musicians: Bobby Troup (piano, celeste), Buddy Collette (alto flute), Howard Roberts (guitar), Bob Enevoldsen (bass), Don Heath (drums). Recorded at Radio Recorders, Los Angeles, March 2, 1955.

1956—I'll Cry Tomorrow (North/Mercer). Liberty LSX-1001. Arranger/conductor: Russ Garcia. Nonalbum track on an EP with three other tracks released elsewhere.

1981—My Funny Valentine (Rodgers/Hart). Warner Bros. BSK-3653. Producer: Snuff Garrett. Engineer: Grover Helsley. Musicians: Barney Kessel (guitar), Ray Brown (bass), Shelly Manne (drums). For *Sharky's Machine* soundtrack.

1991—*Time for Love: The Best of Julie London* (compilation). Rhino R2 70737.

1993—*Les Brown and His Band of Renown*. Hindsight HCD252. Airchecks of *The Les Brown Show* recorded for the US Marine Corps Reserve in 1957. Julie sings "Sunday Blues," "This October," "September in the Rain," and "Tall Boy" accompanied by Brown's band, including Dave Pell (tenor saxophone), Ronny Lang (alto saxophone), Ray Sims (trombone), Don Fagerquist (trumpet), Donn Trenner (piano), and Tony Rizzi (guitar).

1999—*The Artist Collection: Julie London* (compilation, part of the Ultra-Lounge Wild, Cool & Swingin' series). Capitol CDP7243 5 20331 2 6. Julie has a number of songs on other volumes in the Ultra-Lounge series, including the previously unreleased recording of Irving Berlin's "I've Got My Love to Keep Me Warm" on the 2004 compilation *Christmas Cocktails, Part Three*.

2005—*The Very Best of Julie London* (compilation). Capitol 09463-12129-2-5.

2013—*Live at New Latin Quarter*. NLQ Entertainments, Japan MMV-1004. Two tracks from this May 1964 recording in Tokyo were released in 2010 on *The Jazz & Blues Collection, Volume 1* (WhiteHouse Records).

2016—*Julie London in Tokyo 1964*. SSJ Records, Japan XQAM-1082. The audio portion of the *Julie London in Japan* television program, taped on May 28, 1964.

Appendix 2: Filmography

Movies and Television (as an actress)

Nabonga. 1944. PRC. Producer: Sigmund Neufeld. Director: Sam Newfield. Screenplay: Fred Myton. Cast: Buster Crabbe, Fifi D'Orsay, Barton MacLane, Julie London (hereafter cited as JL), Ray Corrigan.

Janie. 1944. Warner Bros. Producer: Alex Gottlieb. Director: Michael Curtiz. Screenplay: Agnes Christine Johnston, Charles Hoffman. Cast: Robert Hutton, Edward Arnold, Ann Harding, Joyce Reynolds, Alan Hale, Robert Benchley, Hattie McDaniel. (JL uncredited.)

Billy Rose's Diamond Horseshoe. 1945. 20th Century Fox. Producer: William Perlberg. Director: George Seaton. Screenplay: George Seaton, suggested by the play *The Barker* by John Kenyon Nicholson. Cast: Betty Grable, Dick Haymes, Phil Silvers, William Gaxton, Beatrice Kay, Margaret Dumont. (JL uncredited.)

On Stage Everybody. 1945. Universal. Producers: Lou Goldberg, Warren Wilson. Director: Jean Yarbrough. Screenplay: Warren Wilson, Oscar Brodney. Cast: Peggy Ryan, Jack Oakie, JL, Esther Dale, Wallace Ford, Milburn Stone.

Solid Senders. 1945. Universal. Director: Will Cowan. Cast: Jan Garber, JL, Lorraine Kruger, Jimmie Dodd. (Short subject.)

Night in Paradise. 1946. Universal. Producer: Walter Wanger. Director: Arthur Lubin. Screenplay: Ernest Pascal, from the book *The Peacock's Feather* by George S. Hellman. Cast: Merle Oberon, Turhan Bey, Thomas Gomez, Gale Sondergaard, Ray Collins. (JL uncredited.)

Science Spins a Yarn. 1946. Cast: Regis Toomey, Lois Austin, Johnny Calkins, JL. (Industrial film for the American Viscose Corporation.)

The Red House. 1947. United Artists. Producer: Sol Lesser. Director: Delmer Daves. Screenplay: Delmer Daves, from the novel by George Agnew Chamberlain. Cast: Edward G. Robinson, Lon McCallister, Judith Anderson, Rory Calhoun, Allene Roberts, JL, Ona Munson.

249

Tap Roots. 1948. Universal. Producer: Walter Wanger. Director: George Marshall. Screenplay: Alan LeMay, Lionel Wiggam, based on the novel by James Street. Cast: Van Heflin, Susan Hayward, Boris Karloff, JL, Whitfield Connor, Ward Bond, Richard Long.

Task Force. 1949. Warner Bros. Producer: Jerry Wald. Director: Delmer Daves. Screenplay: Delmer Daves. Cast: Gary Cooper, Jane Wyatt, Wayne Morris, Walter Brennan, JL, Bruce Bennett, Jack Holt.

Return of the Frontiersman. 1950. Warner Bros. Producer: Saul Elkins. Director: Richard L. Bare. Screenplay: Edna Anhalt. Cast: Gordon MacRae, JL, Rory Calhoun, Jack Holt.

The Fat Man. 1951. Universal. Producer: Aubrey Schenck. Director: William Castle. Screenplay: Harry Essex, Leonard Lee, from a story by Leonard Lee. Cast: J. Scott Smart, JL, Rock Hudson, Clinton Sundberg, Jayne Meadows, Emmett Kelly.

Armstrong Circle Theatre (TV), "Hit a Blue Note." 1954. NBC. Teleplay: Anne Howard Bailey. Cast: Carol Bruce, JL, Walter Matthau.

The Fighting Chance. 1955. Republic. Producer: Herbert J. Yates. Director: William Witney. Screenplay: Houston Branch, from a short story by Robert Blees. Cast: Rod Cameron, JL, Ben Cooper, Taylor Holmes, Howard Wendell.

Crime Against Joe. 1956. United Artists. Producer: Howard W. Koch. Director: Lee Sholem. Screenplay: Robert C. Dennis, based on a story by Decla Dunning. Cast: John Bromfield, JL, Henry Calvin, Patricia Blake, Joel Ashley.

The Girl Can't Help It. 1956. 20th Century Fox. Producer: Frank Tashlin. Director: Frank Tashlin. Screenplay: Frank Tashlin, Herbert Baker. Cast: Tom Ewell, Jayne Mansfield, Edmond O'Brien, Henry Jones, JL, Ray Anthony, Fats Domino, Abbey Lincoln, Nino Tempo, Eddie Cochran, Gene Vincent, Little Richard, the Platters, the Treniers.

Drango. 1957. United Artists. Producer: Hall Bartlett. Directors: Hall Bartlett, Jules Bricken. Screenplay: Hall Bartlett. Cast: Jeff Chandler, Joanne Dru, JL, Donald Crisp, John Lupton, Ronald Howard.

The Great Man. 1957. Universal. Producer: Aaron Rosenberg. Director: José Ferrer. Screenplay: José Ferrer, Al Morgan, based on the book by Al Morgan. Cast: José Ferrer, Dean Jagger, Keenan Wynn, JL, Joanne Gilbert, Ed Wynn, Jim Backus.

Zane Grey Theatre (TV), "A Time to Live." 1957. CBS. Producer: Hal Hudson. Director: Lewis Foster. Teleplay: Aaron Spelling, from a story by Joseph Chadwick. Cast: Ralph Meeker, JL, John Larch.

Playhouse 90 (TV), "Without Incident." 1957. CBS. Producer: Charles Marquis Warren. Director: Charles Marquis Warren. Teleplay: David Victor, Herbert Little Jr., from a story by Charles Marquis Warren. Cast: Errol Flynn, Ann Sheridan, John Ireland, JL.

Saddle the Wind. 1958. MGM. Producer: Armand Deutsch. Director: Robert Parrish. Screenplay: Rod Serling, from a short story by Thomas Thompson. Cast: Robert Taylor, JL, John Cassavetes, Donald Crisp, Charles McGraw, Royal Dano.

A Question of Adultery. 1958. Eros/Connaught Place/Raystro Productions (UK). Producer: Raymond Stross. Director: Don Chaffey. Screenplay: Anne Edwards, with additional scenes by Denis Freeman. Cast: JL, Anthony Steel, Basil Sydney, Donald Houston, Anton Diffring.

Voice in the Mirror. 1958. Universal. Producer: Gordon Kay. Director: Harry Keller. Screenplay: Lawrence B. Marcus. Cast: Richard Egan, JL, Walter Matthau, Arthur O'Connell, Troy Donohue, Mae Clarke.

Man of the West. 1958. United Artists. Producer: Walter M. Mirisch. Director: Anthony Mann. Screenplay: Reginald Rose, based on the novel *The Border Jumpers* by Will C. Brown. Cast: Gary Cooper, JL, Lee J. Cobb, Arthur O'Connell, Jack Lord, Royal Dano.

Night of the Quarter Moon. 1959. MGM. Producer: Albert Zugsmith. Director: Hugo Haas. Screenplay: Frank Davis, Franklin Coen. Cast: JL, John Drew Barrymore, Anna Kashfi, Dean Jones, Agnes Moorehead, Nat King Cole, Cathy Lee Crosby, Ray Anthony, Jackie Coogan, Charles Chaplin Jr.

The David Niven Show (TV), "Maggie Malone." 1959. NBC. Producer: Vincent M. Fennelly. Director: Lewis Allen. Teleplay: Richard Carr, John Robinson. Cast: JL, Steve Brodie, Stacy Harris, Regis Toomey.

Adventures in Paradise (TV), "Mission to Manila." 1959. ABC. Producer: Richard Goldstone. Director: Bernard Girard. Teleplay: Richard H. Landau. Cast: Gardner McKay, JL, Thomas Gomez, Anna May Wong.

The Wonderful Country. 1959. United Artists. Producer: Chester Erskine. Director: Robert Parrish. Screenplay: Robert Ardrey, from the book by Tom Lea. Cast: Robert Mitchum, JL, Gary Merrill, Pedro Armendariz, Jack Oakie, Albert Dekker, Charles McGraw, LeRoy "Satchel" Paige.

The 3rd Voice. 1960. 20th Century Fox. Producers: Hubert Cornfield, Maury Dexter. Director: Hubert Cornfield. Screenplay: Hubert Cornfield, from the novel *All the Way* by Charles Williams. Cast: Edmond O'Brien, JL, Laraine Day, Olga San Juan, George Eldredge.

Laramie (TV), "Queen of Diamonds." 1960. NBC. Producer: John C. Champion. Director: Lesley Selander. Teleplay: Jerry Adelman, from a story by Daniel B. Ullman. Cast: Robert Fuller, John Smith, JL, Claude Akins.

Rawhide (TV), "Incident at Rojo Canyon." 1960. CBS. Producer: Charles Marquis Warren. Director: Ted Post. Teleplay: Budd Bankson, Steve Raines. Cast: Eric Fleming, Clint Eastwood, Sheb Wooley, JL, Bobby Troup.

Michael Shayne (TV), "Die Like a Dog." 1960. NBC. Producer: Joseph Hoffman. Teleplay: Robert Bloomfield. Cast: Richard Denning, Jerry Paris, JL.

Dan Raven (TV), "Tinge of Red." 1960. NBC. Producers: Lewis Reed, Tony Barrett. Director: Philip Leacock. Teleplay: Al C. Ward. Cast: Skip Homeier, Dan Barton, Quinn K. Redeker, JL, Gavin MacLeod.

The George Raft Story. 1961. Allied Artists. Producer: Ben Schwalb. Director: Joseph Newman. Screenplay: Crane Wilbur, Daniel Mainwaring. Cast: Ray Danton, Jayne Mansfield, JL, Barrie Chase, Barbara Nichols, Neville Brand, Frank Gorshin.

Hong Kong (TV), **"Suitable for Framing."** 1961. ABC. Producer: Herbert Hirschman. Director: Stuart Rosenberg. Teleplay: Art Wallace. Cast: Rod Taylor, Lloyd Bochner, JL.

The Barbara Stanwyck Show (TV), **"Night Visitor."** 1961. NBC. Producer: Louis F. Edelman. Director: Don Medford. Teleplay: Bob Duncan, Wanda Duncan. Cast: Barbara Stanwyck, Michael Ansara, JL.

Checkmate (TV), **"Good-Bye, Griff."** 1961. CBS. Producer: Dick Berg. Director: Allen H. Miner. Teleplay: Steven Thornley [Ken Pettus], Sheldon Stark, from a story by Steven Thornley. Cast: Anthony George, Sebastian Cabot, Doug McClure, JL, Harry Guardino, Simon Oakland, Lynn Bari.

Follow the Sun (TV), **"Night Song."** 1961. ABC. Producer: William H. Wright. Director: Felix Feist. Teleplay: Harold Jack Bloom. Cast: Barry Coe, Brett Halsey, JL, Charles McGraw, Lawrence Tierney.

The Eleventh Hour (TV), **"Like a Diamond in the Sky."** 1963. NBC. Producer: Sam Rolfe. Director: Jack Arnold. Teleplay: Alfred Brenner. Cast: Wendell Corey, Jack Ging, JL, Herschel Bernardi, Everett Sloane, Russell Johnson.

Dick Powell Theatre (TV), **"Charlie's Duet."** 1963. NBC. Producer: Aaron Spelling. Director: Don Taylor. Teleplay: Richard Carr. Cast: Anthony Franciosa, Cesar Romero, JL, Zsa Zsa Gabor, Jim Backus, Jules Munchin.

Alfred Hitchcock Hour (TV), **"Crimson Witness."** 1965. NBC. Producer: David Friedkin. Director: David Friedkin. Teleplay: Morton Fine, David Friedkin, from a story by Nigel Elliston. Cast: Peter Lawford, JL, Roger C. Carmel, Martha Hyer.

I Spy (TV), **"Three Hours on a Sunday Night."** 1965. NBC. Producers: Morton Fine, David Friedkin. Director: Paul Wendkos. Teleplay: Morton Fine, David Friedkin. Cast: Robert Culp, Bill Cosby, JL, Sheldon Leonard.

The Man from U.N.C.L.E. (TV), **"The Prince of Darkness Affair, Part 2."** 1967. NBC. Producer: Anthony Spinner. Director: Boris Sagal. Teleplay: Dean Hargrove. Cast: Robert Vaughn, David McCallum, Leo G. Carroll, Bradford Dillman, Lola Albright, Carol Lynley, JL, John Carradine.

The Big Valley (TV), **"They Called Her Delilah."** 1968. ABC. Producer: Lou Morheim. Director: Virgil W. Vogel. Teleplay: Ken Pettus, from a story by Lou Morheim. Cast: Barbara Stanwyck, Richard Long, Lee Majors, Peter Breck, Linda Evans, JL, Bobby Troup.

Emergency! (TV series and made-for-TV movies). 1972–1978. NBC. Producers: Robert A. Cinader, Edwin Self, Gino Grimaldi. Cast: Robert Fuller, JL, Bobby Troup, Randolph Mantooth, Kevin Tighe.

Notes

Prologue: Spring/Summer 1955

break a leg: Arnold Hano, "She's on Hand to Provide the Basic Femininity," *TV Guide*, June 17, 1972.

"I was so scared": Pete Martin, "I Call on Julie London," *Saturday Evening Post*, August 17, 1957.

"noise . . . All the faces": Jane Kesner Ardmore, "The Private Blues of Julie London," *Coronet*, June 1958.

additional spotlights: Barney Kessel, "Julie London: A Rare Vocal Treasure," *Inside Jazz* radio program, Oklahoma, ca. mid-1980s.

"The audience thought it": James Bacon, "Ex–Mrs. Jack Webb Rates as Top Singer, Actress," *Bridgeport Post*, February 3, 1957.

"The only thing I remember": Martin, "I Call."

1: God Bless the Child

The pair locked eyes: Julie London and Bobby Troup, interview by Karen Schoemer, Encino, CA, April 20, 1998.

the couple was married: California State Board of Health, Bureau of Vital Statistics, standard certificate of marriage, San Joaquin County, filed November 18, 1925.

"quick to take advantage": J. M. Guinn, *A History of California and an Extended History of Its Southern Coast Counties: Also Containing Biographies of Well-Known Citizens of the Past and Present* (Los Angeles: Historic Record Company, 1907), 2:1452, 1454.

For more than twenty years: Jeanne Woodson Labadie, "Peck & O'Brien Family," ca. 1980.

the Pecks' only child: California State Board of Health, Bureau of Vital Statistics, standard certificate of birth, Sonoma County, filed September 28, 1926.

"bedtime stories": Labadie, "Peck."

watched as her mother: Julie London, interview by Bobby Troup, in *Jazz Book*, vol. 2, Armed Forces Radio Service, ca. summer/fall 1964. Hereafter cited as Troup, *Jazz Book.*

For three years: The Real Julie, Liberty Records publicity pamphlet, 1961.

singing debut: "Golden Mould: Julie London, One of the Nebulae of Hollywood," *Esquire,* November 1943.

"Our whole family kind of": Julie London, interview by Fritz Peerenboom, *Jazz Roundtable,* WOSU radio, Columbus, OH, October 1971. Hereafter cited as Peerenboom, *Jazz Roundtable.*

By the time Gayle: Program for the *California's Hour* broadcast, June 15, 1936 (Troup/ London papers).

"a lost decade": Richard Thompson, e-mail to author, July 19, 2012.

"There wasn't anything": Martin, "I Call."

Jack's tendency toward alcoholism: "Man Arrested After Crash, Woman Hurt," *San Bernardino Sun,* September 13, 1934.

"People thought": Lisa Breen, interview with author, May 9, 2014.

"a gentle, quiet girl": Ardmore, "Private Blues."

"I wasn't what you'd call": Ardmore, "Private Blues."

given the opportunity to perform: Julie London and Bobby Troup, interview by Bill Ballance, KNX Radio, Los Angeles, September 12, 1955. Hereafter cited as Ballance, KNX.

2: Dream

"special diet": Jean Lewis, "Julie London Had Allergy," *Palm Beach Post,* August 8, 1975.

"food on the table": Richard Bauman, "Up to Date . . . with Julie London," *Girl Talk,* n.d. (Troup/London scrapbooks, hereafter cited as TLS).

"One 1941 evening": Daniel Moyer and Eugene Alvarez, *Just the Facts, Ma'am: The Authorized Biography of Jack Webb* (Santa Ana, CA: Seven Locks Press, 2001), 48.

other published versions: Maurice Zolotow, "The True Story of Jack Webb: The Names Have Not Been Changed (Part 3)," *American Weekly,* September 26, 1954.

"had one look at her": Lisa Breen, interview with author, May 9, 2014.

Agents avidly pursued her: Dorothy LaPointe Gurnee, interview in *The Lady's Not a Vamp,* BBC Television, 2006.

"sweet Sue": Jim Bawden, "Amazing Julie London: She Juggled Two Careers in Films and on Records," Harkit Records, June 4, 2012, www.harkitrecords.com/julie_london_ interview.html.

"learn to be a stenographer": Unidentified clipping, January 24, 1957 (TLS).

"one man wallet girl": "Golden Mould."

"the idea of being in love": "Early Lost Loves Reported by Stars," *Seventeen,* June 1961.

When he boasted: Moyer and Alvarez, *Just the Facts,* 50.

"eye-filling blonde": "Feature Reviews: *Nabonga,*" *Boxoffice,* March 11, 1944.

"slink around": *Variety,* February 23, 1944.

the only movie work: Bawden, "Two Careers."

Impressed when he learned: Arthur Hamilton, interview in *The Lady's Not a Vamp*, BBC Television, 2006. Hereafter cited as Hamilton, *Vamp*.

"We sang each other songs": Arthur Hamilton, e-mail to author, August 21, 2011.

"In pictures I made": "Julie London's 1st Job Had Ups, Downs," *Panama City News*, October 18, 1967.

"double features": Moyer and Alvarez, *Just the Facts*, 50.

"a college boy": Peggy Webber, interview with author, March 7, 2013.

another chance encounter: "They Whistle When She Walks," *World's News* (Sydney, Australia), April 6, 1946.

"some promise": Abel Green, "Film Reviews: *On Stage Everybody,*" *Variety*, July 18, 1945.

"strictly type-casting!": Ballance, KNX.

battling during their scenes: Bawden, "Two Careers."

"predatory bobby-soxer": "Julie London: Hollywood Makes a Star of Still Another Elevator Operator," *Life*, February 24, 1947.

"potential Lana Turner": Wanda Hale, "Horror Joined with Realism in 'Red House,'" *New York Daily News* [March 1947] (Edward G. Robinson Collection, "The Red House," box 23:29, USC Cinematic Arts Library).

"practiced siren": Mae Tinee, "Movie Unfolds Fanciful Tale of Haunted House," *Chicago Tribune*, March 22, 1947.

"bad comeback": Bawden, "Two Careers."

"madly in love": Peggy Webber, interview with author, March 7, 2013.

Two days later: "Marriages: Webb-London," *Billboard*, August 2, 1947.

The newlyweds: Graham Kislingbury, Universal Studios press release, August 5, 1947 (*Tap Roots* production files, Universal Collection, USC Cinematic Arts Library).

3: Bouquet of Blues

with little money: Moyer and Alvarez, *Just the Facts*, 50–51.

"good enough actor[s]": "Screen's Unkind to Lads in Gray," *Washington Post*, October 13, 1948.

"very blah": Universal Collection, USC Cinematic Arts Library.

trial separation: "Julie London Confirms Talk of Separation," *Los Angeles Times*, December 24, 1948.

traffic-safety campaign: "Actress Plays Dunce Role in Safety Drive," *Los Angeles Times*, April 7, 1949.

Illness kept Julie off the set: Warner Bros. Pictures Interoffice memorandum from T. C. Wright to R. J. Obringer, May 5, 1949 (Warner Bros. Archives, School of Cinematic Arts, University of Southern California).

"When I got pregnant": Ardmore, "Private Blues."

Julie's pregnancy: Jimmie Fidler, "In Hollywood," *Nevada State Journal*, October 9, 1949.

A scene apparently filmed: Task Force, final shooting script by Delmer Daves, October 22, 1948, 100–105 (Delmer Daves papers at Stanford University, Stanford, CA).

"insisted on going": Peggy Webber, interview with author, March 7, 2013.

a new set of shutters: Lewis, "Allergy."

"sorriest sagebrush sagas": Bosley Crowther, "The Screen: Quartet of Newcomers Arrives," *New York Times,* June 10, 1950.

"as spiritless a heroine": Barn, "'Return of the Frontiersman' Weak Western Almost a Travesty," *Independent Exhibitors Film Bulletin,* June 5, 1950.

a veteran smoker: Julie London and Bobby Troup, interview by Karen Schoemer, Encino, CA, April 20, 1998.

"My career didn't mean a thing": Virginia McPherson, "Julie Drops Film Career to Make Room for Hubby," *Binghamton Press,* October 2, 1950 (Universal Collection, USC Cinematic Arts Library).

"She seemed kind of at loose ends": Peggy Webber, interview with author, March 7, 2013.

"diapers in every bucket": Ibid.

"better and better": Richard Gehman, "New Life for Julie London," *Washington Post,* April 7, 1957.

Jack spent days: Ardmore, "Private Blues."

Jack left for work: "Jack Webb Absent as His Wife Wins Divorce," *Los Angeles Times,* November 26, 1953.

"really wanted to be married": Peggy Webber, interview with author, March 7, 2013.

"I believe we ironed out": "Jack Webb, Wife Become Reconciled," *Sarasota Journal,* June 16, 1953.

Julie asked the court: "Film Actress, 26, Sues Jack Webb for Divorce," *Los Angeles Times,* August 15, 1953.

"often violent": Anne Edwards, *Leaving Home: A Hollywood Blacklisted Writer's Years Abroad* (Lanham, MD: Scarecrow, 2012), 68.

To avoid the noise: Martin, "I Call."

"old-fashioned American": Arno Johansen, "The Comeback of Julie London," *Parade,* March 15, 1959.

"sentenced [herself]": Jane Kesner Ardmore, "Julie London Starts a New Life," unpublished draft of the June 1958 *Coronet* article (author's collection).

her mother's heart: Lisa Breen, interview with author, May 9, 2014.

"no time for marriage": "'Dragnet' Webb's Wife Tells Facts, Wins Divorce," *Lebanon Daily News,* November 26, 1953.

"talking down to me": "Jack Webb Absent."

forty-page financial agreement: Ibid.

4: A Place in the Sun

asked her to comment: "'Dragnet' Director Is Not 'Romantic,'" *Florence Times*, December 10, 1953.

sale of Dragnet: "Jack Webb of 'Dragnet' Cited on Divorce Pay," *Los Angeles Times*, March 10, 1954.

"crushing, frightening": "Julie London Shuns Alimony," *Sarasota Herald-Tribune*, February 21, 1960.

"disloyalty": Ardmore, "Julie London Starts."

"Everyone who has gone through a divorce": Lewis, "Allergy."

she sarcastically responded: Michael "Doc Rock" Kelly, *Liberty Records: A History of the Recording Company and Its Stars, 1955–1971* (Jefferson, NC: McFarland, 1993), 13.

"Stop brooding": Ardmore, "Private Blues."

Commissioned into: Cynthia Hare, *Once I Was a Debutante* (Van Nuys, CA: RonBob, 2012), 66–76.

Upon his discharge: Ibid., 81.

Arriving in Los Angeles: Ibid., 82–85.

"poor man's Nat Cole": Ibid., 93.

"my big downfall": Julie London to Bobby Troup, July 12, 1954 (TLS).

"out of limbo": Ardmore, "Private Blues."

"living room singer": Julie London, interview by John Salisbury, *Sunday Spectacular*, KXL Radio, Portland, OR, July 21, 1968. Hereafter cited as Salisbury, *Sunday Spectacular*.

Julie became too frightened: Martin, "I Call."

5: Cry Me a River

"kicking the idea around": Harrison Carroll, "Behind the Scenes in Hollywood," *New London Evening Day*, November 12, 1954.

"terribly anxious": Troup, *Jazz Book*.

executives were unimpressed: Julie London and Bobby Troup, interview by Karen Schoemer, Encino, CA, April 20, 1998.

"As shy as the smallest bud": "Calling All Cats," *Radio-TV Mirror*, September 1958.

"how sensitive": Kessel, *Inside Jazz.*

"a heck of a job": John Tynan, "Julie London: Cover Girl," *Down Beat*, January 23, 1957.

"My bar bill": Robert Windeler, "For Julie London and Bobby Troup, 'Emergency!' Is Just What the Doctor Ordered," *People*, January 14, 1977.

"just happened to remember": Salisbury, *Sunday Spectacular.*

"I was scared to death": John T. McCullough, "She Cried a River," *Milwaukee Sentinel,* April 29, 1956.

frantically ran to doctors: Ardmore, "Private Blues."

"It was frightening": Salisbury, *Sunday Spectacular.*

"I sneaked in": Ardmore, "Private Blues."

"I was afraid it might throw me": Harrison Carroll, "Behind the Scenes in Hollywood," *New London Evening Day,* July 8, 1955.

"We were lucky": Kelly, *Liberty Records,* 14.

"I would attend parties": Arthur Hamilton, e-mail to author, August 21, 2011.

"Webb called me": Ibid.

"lost in the shuffle": Ballance, KNX.

they didn't have any music: Kessel, *Inside Jazz.*

"degree of warmth": Dorothy Kilgallen, *News-Herald* (Franklin, PA), June 25, 1955.

"plenty of emotion": Mike Gross, "Jocks, Jukes and Disks," *Variety,* October 12, 1955.

"show-wise poise": "Review Spotlight on . . . Popular Records," *Billboard,* October 15, 1955.

Demand for copies: Kelly, *Liberty Records,* 15.

"I remember the excitement": Lenny Waronker, interview with author, July 19, 2012.

resulted in a lawsuit: "Coast Indie Sues Merc on Copy Claim; Asks 150G on 'River' Arrangement," *Variety,* December 21, 1955.

"unknown song": Troup, *Jazz Book.*

"it'll be a smash": "Record Reviews," *Cash Box,* October 15, 1955.

A year later: Tynan, "Cover Girl."

"the sounds and the words": Donald Freeman, "'It's a Man's World'—Julie," *Chicago Tribune,* February 17, 1963.

"the word plebeian*":* Troup, *Jazz Book.*

"Sound was a big deal": Lenny Waronker, interview with author, July 19, 2012.

"dirty appeal": Kelly, *Liberty Records,* 15.

"Anything more powerful": Ralph J. Gleason, "Bittersweet Ballads in a Boudoir Manner," *San Francisco Chronicle,* January 17, 1956.

She was the first woman: Troup, *Jazz Book.*

"combination of simplicity": "Packaged Goods," *Down Beat,* February 22, 1956.

"tight rein": Gleason, "Bittersweet Ballads."

"her comeuppance": "Feature Reviews: *The Fighting Chance,*" *Boxoffice,* June 16, 1956.

"I was sure everyone could hear": Joey Sasso, "Words and Music," n.d. (TLS).

"seductively … and since": New Yorker, January 28, 1956.

"bewitching paradox": June Bundy, "Review Digest: Legit," *Billboard,* January 28, 1956.

"made the warm new Cameo": Nat Hentoff, "Caught in the Act," *Down Beat,* February 22, 1956.

"the same business": "Popular Records," *Miami News,* February 5, 1956.

"rather rare": Benny Goodman, "10 Basic Records Selected from Jazz," n.p., March 4, 1956 (TLS).

"I thought somebody": Salisbury, *Sunday Spectacular*.

"wouldn't speak to me": Troup, *Jazz Book*.

"selling mood": Kelly, *Liberty Records*, 54.

"powerful wallop": "Reviews and Ratings of New Popular Albums," *Billboard*, June 23, 1956.

"soporific": John S. Wilson, "Ethel Merman Sings Her Biography," *New York Times*, October 14, 1956.

"watch it go": "Sleeper of the Week," *Cash Box*, July 14, 1956.

"brought down the house": Julie London and Bobby Troup, interview by Karen Schoemer, Encino, CA, April 20, 1998.

"all of us to suffer": Dorothy Kilgallen, "The Voice of Broadway," *Daytona Beach Morning Journal*, October 29, 1956.

"In those days": Lenny Waronker, interview with author, July 19, 2012.

"it took longer to shoot": Julie London, interview by Edward R. Murrow, *Person to Person*, CBS, September 13, 1957.

"fully broken into recording": Tynan, "Cover Girl."

"Julie and Bobby and I": Arthur Hamilton, e-mail to author, August 23, 2011.

a ballad by Bobby: Bob Bayles, e-mail to author, April 19, 2016.

"If you are male": *Playboy*, ca. 1956 clipping (TLS).

Tashlin had even described: Frank Tashlin, *Do Re Mi*, first-draft screenplay, August 10, 1956 (20th Century Fox Collection, USC Cinematic Arts Library).

A short sequence: Frank Tashlin, *Do Re Mi*, revised screenplay, August 22, 1956 (20th Century Fox Collection, USC Cinematic Arts Library).

Enthusiastic fans: Mickey Blackwell, "The Fans Go Wild over Julie," *Daily Tar Heel*, November 14, 1963.

"meager and witless": Bosley Crowther, "Screen: One-Track Film," *New York Times*, February 9, 1957.

"exploitation bonanza": "Feature Reviews: *The Girl Can't Help It*," *Boxoffice*, December 29, 1956.

"The juxtaposition of the sultry vamp": Martha Saxton, *Jayne Mansfield and the American Fifties* (Boston: Houghton Mifflin, 1975), 85.

6: The Exciting Life

She was uncertain: Earl Wilson, "London's Bridges," *Sarasota Herald-Tribune*, November 25, 1956.

he suggested an experiment: Martin, "I Call."

"whether to be honest": Ardmore, "Private Blues."

Even on the morning: Martin, "I Call."

"spontaneous applause": Dorothy Kilgallen, "Voice of Broadway," *Anderson Daily Bulletin*, June 22, 1956.

Julie reacted to the hype: Earl Wilson, "Julie London Takes the Stand," *Daily Intelligencer* (Doylestown, PA), November 24, 1956.

"digs into a dramatic role": Brog, *Variety*, November 28, 1956.

"second to none": Jay Carmody, "'Great Man' Is 1957's First 10-Best Movie," *Washington Evening Star*, January 17, 1957 (TLS).

"a corrosive, cynical comment": "The New Pictures," *Time*, January 21, 1957.

"a bad, wild girl": Cecil Smith, "Julie London, Torn Between Singing and Acting, Tries Hand at Westerns," *Los Angeles Times*, June 2, 1957.

"girl of the Old West": Jack O'Brian, "Critic Suggests Tomahawks Be Used on TV Indian Drama," *Reading Eagle*, June 7, 1957.

Even with the disagreements: Jack Holland, "Julie London and Bobby Troup . . . Why We're Not Afraid of Marriage," *TV-Radio Life*, June 1, 1957.

"marriage is not": Sheilah Graham, *Bluefield Daily Telegraph*, September 24, 1957.

"at her breathiest": "Reviews and Ratings of New Albums: Popular," *Billboard*, June 10, 1957.

"about the results": Rex Morton, "Julie Is So Tasty!," *New Musical Express*, May 17, 1957 (TLS).

"soft, easy approach": Marc Myers, "Interview: Russ Garcia (Part 2)," *JazzWax*, September 18, 2008.

"didn't come back for a week": Ardmore, "Private Blues."

"never recorded": Russ Garcia, e-mail to author, March 12, 2007.

"single-purposed intimacy": Wally George, "Court of Records," *Los Angeles Times*, August 25, 1957.

"all eyes agog": "Album Cover of the Week," *Billboard*, June 17, 1957.

the summation of her style: Bawden, "Two Careers."

"an absolutely gorgeous woman": Murray Garrett, interview with author, October 27, 2011.

"When you get an artist": Murray Garrett, interview in *The Lady's Not a Vamp*, BBC Television, 2006.

"very similar": Edwin Greines Cohen, interview with author, June 18, 2012.

"I am not my image": Windeler, "Doctor Ordered."

"give it a lot of warmth": Hal Humphrey, "Julie Sounds Good Like a Commercial Should," *Los Angeles Times*, October 28, 1962.

"When Julie sang": Draper Daniels, *Giants, Pigmies, and Other Advertising People* (Chicago: Crain, 1974), 245.

"dream house": "Hollywood Is Awed over Julie London's New $225,000 Home," *Newport Daily News*, January 8, 1960.

"early American den": Jim Mahony, "Behind the Scenes in Hollywood," *Vidette Messenger*, July 29, 1957.

"There was this beautiful place": Bill O'Halloren, "'Let's Try Plasma,'" *TV Guide*, August 16, 1975.

"such a huge house": Peer J. Oppenheimer, "Julie London Sings the Blues," *Family Weekly*, March 15, 1959.

"she would never record": Kelly, *Liberty Records*, 40–41.

Waronker soon declared: "Name Bennett Liberty GM," *Billboard*, March 31, 1958.

"Witch Doctor" . . . quickly paid off: Norris Leap, "Cotton Wouldn't Grow, So He Made Record Sales Spring Up," *Los Angeles Times*, October 29, 1961.

"really strong guy": Lenny Waronker, interview with author, July 19, 2012.

"that hungry": Edwin Schallert, "Julie Carves a New Career Out of Wax," *Los Angeles Times*, October 28, 1956.

"hillbilly and Western": Bob Barnes, "Ex-Farm Boy Directs One of Top U.S. Record Firms," *Corpus Christi Caller Times*, January 7, 1962.

7: Free and Easy

"hip quality": Mike Gross, "Album Reviews," *Variety*, May 21, 1958.

"sultry off-beating": "Review Spotlight on . . . Popular Albums," *Billboard*, May 26, 1958.

"Don't breathe it": Smith, "Torn Between."

"The more wooden [Taylor] got": Gordon F. Sander, *Serling: The Rise and Twilight of Television's Last Angry Man* (New York: Dutton, 1992), 126–27.

"pain in the ass": Marshall Fine, *Accidental Genius: How John Cassavetes Invented American Independent Film* (New York: Miramax, 2005), 63–65.

"was so beautiful": Dorothy Aldridge, "A Character Actor Career Which Began Here Spins a 30-Year Cycle, Climaxing in Colorado," *Colorado Springs Gazette Telegraph*, October 14, 1972.

an indelible impression: Jim Mahony, "Julie London Gets a Bang out of Last Scene of 'Saddle the Wind,'" *Lockport Union Sun & Journal*, August 6, 1957.

Taylor and Cassavetes: Glenn Lovell, *Escape Artist: The Life and Films of John Sturges* (Madison: University of Wisconsin Press, 2008), 143.

"vital facet": *Saddle the Wind* production files (MGM Collection, USC Cinematic Arts Library).

"I gave better dialogue": Joel Engel, *Rod Serling: The Dreams and Nightmares of Life in the Twilight Zone* (Chicago: Contemporary, 1989), 146.

"surprisingly effective": "Feature Reviews: *Saddle the Wind*," *Boxoffice*, March 17, 1958.

"exceptional believability": *Variety*, March 5, 1958.

"a pretty cipher": Moira Walsh, *America*, March 29, 1958.

Stalis Productions: "Julie London Will Do New Independent," *Los Angeles Times*, March 10, 1958.

stream of tears: Ardmore, "Private Blues."

"restrained and effective": James M. Jerauld, "Review: *Voice in the Mirror*," *Motion Picture Daily*, May 21, 1958.

"quietly pathetic": Mae Tinee, "Film About Alcoholism Convincing," *Chicago Tribune*, February 6, 1959.

"sincerity rather than sensationalism": Marjory Adams, "Alcoholic Film at Pilgrim," *Boston Globe*, July 24, 1958.

"hard-hitting": *Variety*, May 21, 1958.

downbeat advertising: Archie Herzoff to Jeff Livingston, June 30, 1958 (Universal Collection, *Voice in the Mirror* production files, USC Cinematic Arts Library).

The couple was more pleased: Leonard Feather, "Troups Move into New Roles," *Los Angeles Times*, July 19, 1981.

"inseparable relationship": Ron Burton, "Film Shop," *Traverse City Record Eagle*, October 11, 1957.

Liberty had asked Barney Kessel: Maurice J. Summerfield, *Barney Kessel: A Jazz Legend* (Blaydon on Tyne: Ashley Mark, 2008), 43.

"You stand out in the hot sun": Bob Thomas, "Movie-Makers Aim for Adult Themes," *Newport Daily News*, July 24, 1958.

140-member cast and crew: "Filming Will Start Monday on Cooper, London Movie," *Modesto Bee and Herald-News*, February 6, 1958.

After settling in: "Gary Cooper Film Will Be Shot in Lode," *Modesto Bee and Herald-News*, January 20, 1958.

got her skirt tangled: "Actress Escapes Harm as Stage Horses Bolt," *Modesto Bee and Herald-News*, February 12, 1958.

"get the bruises": Louella Parsons, "Favorite H'wood Talk Topics," *San Antonio Light*, February 23, 1958.

"Given a choice": "'Fallen Women' Roles All Right, But Julie London Tired of West," *Newport Daily News*, August 13, 1958.

she and Cooper repeatedly flubbed: "The Most ADULT Western of All," *Modern Man*, December 1958.

working agreement: Hedda Hopper, "Looking at Hollywood," *Chicago Tribune*, April 8, 1958.

"considerable figure": Will C. Brown, *The Border Jumpers* (Bath, UK: Chivers Press, 1996), 113.

"her thoughts are her own": Reginald Rose, *Man of the West* [script], ca. January 1958 (Troup/London papers).

Luridly publicized: "Most ADULT."

"shaking for days": Ibid.

a version of the script: Undated script with revisions dated January 14 and January 28, 1958 (Troup/London papers).

"not up to snuff": Glenn Erickson, "Man of the West: A Western We Want to See!," DVD Savant website, www.dvdtalk.com/dvdsavant/s38manwest.html.

"moments of sympathy": John L. Scott, "'Man of West' Proves Shock Type Western," *Los Angeles Times*, October 9, 1958.

"only bit of beauty": Marjory Adams, "Cooper Back in Saddle," *Boston Globe*, October 10, 1958.

"heart-tugging fatalism": Jack Moffitt, "'Man of West' Suspenseful, Offbeat Sagebrush Saga," *Hollywood Reporter*, September 17, 1958.

"grind houses": Bawden, "Two Careers."

"delete all references": *Man of the West* pressbook.

"I've agreed to do pictures": Cecil Smith, "Julie London Career Soars Like Balloon," *Los Angeles Times*, September 21, 1958.

"aware of how honest": Kevin Tighe, e-mail to author, March 10, 2014.

"Suggestive without going overboard": Murray Garrett, interview with author, October 27, 2011.

"We've got to get more sex": Anna Kashfi Brando and E. P. Stein, *Brando for Breakfast* (New York: Crown, 1979), 132.

Alice Rhinelander case: Mark J. Madigan, "Miscegenation and 'the Dicta of Race and Class': The Rhinelander Case and Nella Larsen's *Passing*," *Modern Fiction Studies* 36, no. 4 (Winter 1990): 523–29.

admirably muted: Howard Thompson, "Racial Love Story," *New York Times*, March 5, 1959.

"emotional depths": Charles Stinson, "'Quarter Moon' Now on Many Area Screens," *Los Angeles Times*, April 3, 1959.

"one of the most inept": Mae Tinee, "Inept Movie Tells Sexy, Sordid Tale," *Chicago Tribune*, June 15, 1959.

"outrageous bilge": Richard L. Coe, "Well, 'Night' Has Fallen!," *Washington Post*, March 12, 1959.

"various scenes and lines": Anthony Slide, *"Banned in the USA": British Films in the United States and Their Censorship, 1933–1960* (New York: I. B. Tauris, 1998), 124–25.

"in which the birth": Thomas, "Movie-Makers Aim."

"emotional arguments": *Motion Pictures Classified by National Legion of Decency* (New York: National Legion of Decency, 1959), 188.

"grace and charm": *Variety*, July 30, 1958.

"great weakness": Geoffrey Warren, "'Question of Adultery' Airs Moral Problem," *Los Angeles Times*, April 27, 1959.

"a field day": "Record Reviews," *Cash Box*, January 10, 1959.

"the bikini belongs": Bruce Agnew, "Outlook for the Beach Is: More and Briefer Bikinis," *Bridgeport Post*, May 25, 1960.

"It's a funny feeling": Thomas, "Movie-Makers Aim."

Repeatedly denying: Earl Wilson, "Reporter Finds Julie London in Rare Confessional Mood," *Reno Evening Gazette*, November 26, 1960.

"That's about what it was": Julie London, interview by Binny Lum, Australian radio, April 1964.

8: The House That Julie Built

"entire mess": William Ewald, *"Francis Langford Presents* Patchwork," *Beaver Valley Times*, March 16, 1959.

"If you can work": Hedda Hopper, "London Outlook: Fair Weather," *Chicago Tribune*, June 14, 1959.

"should have let her sing": Tube, "Telepix Reviews: 'Maggie Malone,'" *Daily Variety*, June 11, 1959.

asked the writer to pen: Rebecca Craver and Adair Margo, eds., *Tom Lea: An Oral History* (El Paso: Texas Western Press, 1995), 107–8.

Shooting began: "Tom Lea Turns Actor in Best Seller," *Victoria Advocate*, October 16, 1958.

The two-hundred-strong company: Arthur Pollock, "Focus on a 'Wonderful Country,'" *New York Times*, April 26, 1959.

"crème de la crème": Lisa Breen, interview with author, May 9, 2014.

"choking stink": Lee Server, *Robert Mitchum: "Baby, I Don't Care"* (New York: St. Martin's Griffin, 2001), 338.

Mitchum advised: Alan K. Rode, *Charles McGraw: Biography of a Film Noir Tough Guy* (Jefferson, NC: McFarland, 2008), 131.

"bars and hookers": Server, *Robert Mitchum*, 338.

"rather be down at the bar": Don Bagley, interview with author, January 22, 2012.

"was awful on those sets": Craver and Margo, *Tom Lea*, 108.

"a creep": Linda Wheeler, interview with author, November 26, 2011, and January 7, 2012.

"one of the best times": "The Face on the Cutting Room Floor," *Milwaukee Journal*, November 21, 1959.

"so badly off": Wilson, "Reporter Finds."

"ventured an opinion": Gail Cottman, *Cal State College Times*, May 27, 1966 (TLS).

"All my lovely big screen shots": "Cutting Room Floor."

Lea blamed Mitchum: Craver and Margo, *Tom Lea*, 108.

Parrish's widow: Server, *Robert Mitchum*, 340.

"many of today's pictures": John L. Scott, "'Wonderful Country' Big, Moody Western," *Los Angeles Times*, October 8, 1959.

"immensely appealing": *Variety*, September 30, 1959.

"something would happen": Hopper, "London Outlook."

"sense of humor": Stanley Green, *HiFi Review*, November 1959.

"swingin'est London yet": "Album Reviews," *Cash Box*, July 25, 1959.

"well-conceived session": "Album Reviews," *Cash Box*, December 12, 1959.

Not even a telegram: Julie London, telegram to Bobby Troup, October 18, 1958 (TLS).

"The upstairs master bedroom": Photograph, November 1, 1958 (author's collection).

"Not this time!": Lisa Breen, interview with author, May 9, 2014.

"marriage has been postponed": "Julie London, Troup Take Out License," *Schenectady Gazette*, December 31, 1959.

Back at the house: "Julie London Is Wed by Pianist Bobby Troup," *Los Angeles Times*, January 1, 1960.

Among those who sent regrets: Undated note to Julie London from Johnny Mercer, typed on the back of the party invitation (Troup/London papers).

9: Julie at Home

"The thing that moved her": Hamilton, *Vamp*.

Sitting on *the piano:* Transcript of Julie London interview done by Pete Martin (The Hollywood Museum Collection, box 77 [Pete Martin material], USC Cinematic Arts Library).

"made everyone feel welcome": Don Bagley, interview with author, January 12, 2012.

"Have a drink": Emil Richards, e-mail to author, July 16, 2011.

warm feeling: Bill Reed, "Don and Julie," *People vs. Dr. Chillidair* (blog), July 26, 2010, http://people-vs-drchilledair.blogspot.com/2010/07/don-and-julie.html.

Julie was ecstatic: Murray Garrett, interview with author, October 27, 2011.

"We talked a little": Don Bagley, e-mail to author, December 22, 2011.

At over sixty-three hundred: Architectural plans by Paul R. Williams for 16074 Royal Oak Road (author's collection).

"everyone was happy": Jimmy Rowles, liner notes to *Julie at Home*, by Julie London (Liberty, LRP-3152, 1960), LP.

"intimate, warm feeling": "Special Merit Spotlights," *Billboard*, April 18, 1960.

"was so excited": Emil Richards, e-mail to author, August 2, 2011.

"insure the excitement": Albert Johnson, "Interviews with Hubert Cornfield and Paul Wendkos," *Film Quarterly* 15, no. 3 (Spring 1962): 39–46.

"the type of girl": Lydia Lane, "Dishonesty Is the Worst of Policies," *Oakland Tribune*, November 29, 1959.

several takes were "necessary": UPI photograph, November 1959.

"The studio was dissatisfied": Bawden, "Two Careers."

"strong dramatic ability": Independent Exhibitors Film Bulletin, February 1, 1960.

"to a degree": Geoffrey Warren, "'The Third Voice' Interesting Thriller," *Los Angeles Times*, January 28, 1960.

"vividly acted": Harrison's Reports, January 30, 1960.

"eerily fascinating": A. H. Weiler, "Screen: Intricate Murder in Mexico," *New York Times*, March 7, 1960.

"superior exploitation": Variety, January 27, 1960.

The only movie: "Lillie Langtry Biopic," *Variety*, July 6, 1960.

"Both José and I": "Julie London, Ferrer Form Own Company," *Bridgeport Post*, July 3, 1960.

"second fiddle": "Yes, But She Won't Like It," *Santa Ana Register*, September 18, 1960 (TLS).

once helped another gambler: Joyce Haber, "From Nightclubs to Nursing with Julie," *Los Angeles Times*, November 11, 1973.

"eat up her salary": Linda Wheeler, interview with author, January 7, 2012.

"Between rehearsals": Clint Eastwood, "Beauties Brighten Lives of Drovers," *Syracuse Herald-American*, July 25, 1965.

"commercial value": Murray Garrett, interview with author, October 27, 2011.

So when she accepted: "Day Bows Out at Harrah's: Julie London in Top Spot," *Nevada State Journal*, April 15, 1960.

"Bobby . . . keeps telling me": Harold Heffernan, "Shy Julie London Still Freezes Before Audience," *Toledo Blade*, May 19, 1960.

The days in Rio: Luiz Antonio and E. E. Raide, "Julie London Voltou Para Cantar," *Mundo Ilustrado* (Rio de Janeiro, Brazil), October 1, 1960.

Julie's visit: Hedda Hopper, "20th Busy with Many Films Rolling," *Los Angeles Times*, September 12, 1960.

"armed with bottles of Scotch": Bones Howe, interview with author, August 2, 2012.

During every show: Tom Williams, interview with author, May 14, 2014.

"not only a great talent": Murray Garrett, e-mail to author, October 23, 2011.

"a certain point": "Like a Lioness on a Leash," *TV Guide*, July 15, 1961.

"Slight she might be": Ronald Avery, "How Julie London Cried Herself a Bankroll," *Inside Story*, January 1960.

"a couple of bruises": "Julie's Vocals Still Soft-Toned Ultimate," 1962 clipping (TLS).

"far-out nightingale": "Songbird Sounds Off," *TV Radio Mirror*, 1962.

"what every other girl": "Like a Lioness."

"aren't many good scripts": Don Alpert, "Julie Wants, Doesn't Get," *Los Angeles Times*, November 19, 1961.

"one of the finest people": Linda Wheeler, interview with author, January 7, 2012.

"The way for a woman to detract": Freeman, "Man's World."

"NOTHING is too much": Mike Connolly, "A Song or Two Nets Julie London $10,000," *Hollywood Reporter*, December 9, 1960 (TLS); emphasis in original.

"She manages to achieve": Harriet Van Horne, "Gershwin Years Sing Out," *New York World-Telegram*, January 16, 1961.

"During her show": Zan Stewart, "Jack Sheldon: Middle-Aged Man with Robust Horn," *Los Angeles Times*, July 4, 1987.

"the best accompanist": Julie London and Bobby Troup, interview by Karen Schoemer, Encino, CA, April 20, 1998.

"room-hushing": Mor, "Night Club Reviews," *Variety*, August 16, 1961.

"not always as accurate": Mimi Clar, "Limelighters Top Stereo Show at Bowl," *Los Angeles Times*, September 26, 1961.

"wrapped up in glamor": Quin, "Night Club Reviews," *Variety*, November 8, 1961.

"Some of the people": Humphrey, "Julie Sounds Good."

Studio publicity indicated: Julie London publicity clipping files, USC Cinematic Arts Library.

"shadowy figures": John L. Scott, "'The Raft Story' Odd Biographical Picture," *Los Angeles Times*, January 25, 1962.

"inconclusive interlude": *Variety*, December 6, 1961.

couldn't even recall: Feather, "Troups Move."

10: There'll Be Some Changes Made

"good, wholesome scripts": James Bacon, "Singer Julie Objects to Sexy Movies," *Eureka Humboldt Standard*, April 26, 1961.

"consummate good taste": Scul, "Night Club Reviews," *Variety*, March 7, 1962.

"Yeah, that's okay": Linda Wheeler, interview with author, November 26, 2011.

"My father felt [Julie] needed a change": Lenny Waronker, interview with author, July 12, 2012.

"instantly liked each other": Thomas "Snuff" Garrett, interview with author, November 2 and 21, 2011.

"Give me a good melody": Richard Oliver, "Snuff's Philosophy: Marry the Song to the Artist," *Billboard*, December 15, 1973.

"I listened to both sides": Gilbert Garcia, "Happy Trails," *Phoenix New Times*, September 3, 1998.

"We both liked late-night sessions": Thomas "Snuff" Garrett, interview with author, November 2 and 21, 2011.

"our time was our own": Ibid.

the most impressive: Buzz Cason, interview with author, February 28, 2013.

stole from Nina Simone's 1959 hit: Salisbury, *Sunday Spectacular*.

"I'm sure [Ross] told me": Thomas "Snuff" Garrett, interview with author, November 21, 2011.

"didn't like that [drawing]": Ibid.

first stockholders' report: Liberty Records Annual Reports to Shareholders, for years ended January 31, 1961, and January 31, 1962.

unlikely merger: Lee Zhito, "Avnet Electronics Buying Liberty Co.," *Billboard*, April 21, 1962.

she gave birth: "Child to Julie London," *New York Times*, May 2, 1962.

"the most beautiful woman": Chuck Berghofer, interview with author, July 1, 2013.

"It was mainly just her": Ibid.

"pleading kind of love": Will Leonard, "On the Town," *Chicago Tribune*, August 19, 1962.

"They loved her": Chuck Berghofer, interview with author, July 1, 2013.

Taking a cue: Thomas "Snuff" Garrett, interview with author, November 21, 2011.

"spine and [the] soul": Hamilton, *Vamp*.

"I was so tired": Troup, *Jazz Book*.

a point confirmed: Pat Launer, "Here's to Hugh," *In Theater*, March 27, 1998.

"trying to feel": Thomas "Snuff" Garrett, interview with author, November 7, 2011.

it took hours: Thomas "Snuff" Garrett, interview with author, November 2, 2011.

"a round note from a flat note": Bob Barnes, "Alvin's Notes Are Flat but Bankroll's Heavy," *Toledo Blade*, January 7, 1962.

"one brand to another": David Hale, "TV Smokescreens Hid Julie London's Light," *Fresno Bee*, August 16, 1964.

Julie's LP sales: Gene Budig, "Singer Worried," *Lincoln Sunday Journal and Star*, November 10, 1963.

"just dreadful": Bobby Troup, interview by Binny Lum, Australian radio, April 1964.

"listen to Julie London": Ralph J. Gleason, "Watching Julie Sing," *San Francisco Chronicle*, February 11, 1963.

Julie was rarely affected: Linda Wheeler, interview with author, November 26, 2011.

"terribly neurotic": Dick Kleiner, "Can This Man Be the Susskind That We All Knew Long Ago?" *Alton Evening Telegraph*, January 23, 1963.

"sincere acting": Hank Grant, *Hollywood Reporter*, February 15, 1963 (TLS).

"Marilyn was the sexpot": Cecil Smith, "Marilyn's Story," *Los Angeles Times*, February 10, 1963.

"if the script says": Freeman, "Man's World."

"disappearing necklines": "Laziest Girl in Hollywood," *Chicago Tribune*, February 9, 1963.

"an undersung genius": Tony Scherman, *Backbeat: Earl Palmer's Story* (Washington, DC: Smithsonian Institution Press, 1999), 125.

"not come out until Friday": Oliver, "Snuff's Philosophy."

swaying was about the limit: Linda Wheeler, interview with author, July 19, 2012.

"modern-day songs": Thomas "Snuff" Garrett, interview with author, November 2, 2011.

"ballad caress": "Record Reviews," *Variety*, May 1, 1963.

That wish came true: "Twin Boys for Julie London," *San Francisco Chronicle*, May 29, 1963.

"The cutest thing": Cynnie Troup, interview with author, June 12, 2012.

"Andy Williams approach": Thomas "Snuff" Garrett, interview with author, November 7, 2011.

"importance of the whole package": Kelly, *Liberty Records*, 34.

never going to work in Chicago again: Tom Williams, interview with author, May 14, 2014.

"that old sock appeal": "Expectant Julie Not Wanted by Collegiates," *Deseret News and Telegram*, March 18, 1963.

"wary of personal appearances": Pat Stalnaker, "A Chat with Cynnie—Miss Troup Likes It Here," *Daily Aztec*, September 30, 1963.

"I thought I was working": Kelly, *Liberty Records*, 163, 167–69.

"Al could sell anything": Ibid., 169, 197.

"It got to a point": Lenny Waronker, interview with author, July 19, 2012.

"No decent merchandise": Kelly, *Liberty Records*, 516–17.

Bennett purchased the label: Lee Zhito, "Bennett and 3 Conclude Deal Buying Liberty," *Billboard*, October 19, 1963.

11: Live . . . in Person!

"people are drinking": Pat Stalnaker, "Julie Admits Being Nervous; Tells Dislike for Nightclubs," *Daily Aztec*, October 8, 1963.

One new option: Larry Kart, "Why Entertainment Acts from Bruce to Beaubo Give It the Old College Try," *Chicago Tribune*, March 2, 1986.

"The kids are down with colds": Budig, "Singer Worried."

"sulky, haunting": "Julie: Sulky, Haunting and Swinging Here," *Daily Iowan*, November 12, 1963.

"red-blooded": H. D. M., "When She Sang 'Cry Me a River,' Everybody Cried for Julie," *University of Alabama Crimson-White*, November 21, 1963.

personally chosen her: Julie London, interview by Martin Block, *Guard Session* radio program, 1966.

"sleek, don't-give-a-damn": Don Sider, "Julie London Sighs, Sings, So Seductively," *St. Petersburg Times*, November 25, 1963.

"I got a beautiful script": Cecil Smith, "The TV Scene," *Los Angeles Times*, July 29, 1964.

"she needed a new book": Don Bagley, interview with author, January 12, 2012.

"We started out": Ibid.

"Julie knew a lot": Ibid.

"encouraged arrangers": Ibid.

"it would be kind of interesting": Julie London, interview by Binny Lum, Australian radio, 1964.

"Once in a while": Don Bagley, interview with author, January 22, 2012.

"wanted the same kind": Don Bagley, interview with author, January 12, 2012.

"Julie hired [Lucas]": Ibid.

"those big hotels": Reed, "Don and Julie."

"keep proving": Hale, "TV Smokescreens."

"communicate with an audience": John Bornholdt and Curt Sylvester, "Julie Sings Past Mix-Ups," *Daily Iowan*, November 12, 1963.

"solid songsters": Lary, "New Acts," *Variety*, January 22, 1964.

"the lyric more than anything": Julie London and Bobby Troup, interview by Karen Schoemer, Encino, CA, April 20, 1998.

only cared about the money: Murray Garrett, interview with author, October 27, 2011.

"The Vegas show": Don Bagley, interview with author, January 12, 2012.

"would have flown her": Ibid.

"laid-back": Buzz Cason, interview with author, February 28, 2013.

"more than anything": Gehman, "New Life."

"didn't treat us like employees": Cal Sexton, interview with author, January 7, 2013.

"make the most of her opportunities": Jose [Joe Cohen], "Night Club Reviews," *Variety*, April 1, 1964.

"The physical rubbing asses": Don Bagley, interview with author, January 12, 2012.

"often augmented": Lee Evans, e-mail to author, July 15, 2012.

"that house band": Don Bagley, interview with author, January 12, 2012.

"When we got to New York": Reed, "Don and Julie."

"Who is this guy?": Bucky Pizzarelli, interview with author, January 9, 2013.

"The guys would help her": Linda Wheeler, interview with author, November 26, 2011.

Garrett flew out: Thomas "Snuff" Garrett, interview with author, November 7, 2011.

"superb change of pace": "Record Reviews," *Variety*, August 26, 1964.

"Did I play on that?": Don Bagley, interview with author, January 12, 2012.

"slow, haunting idea": "Top Singles of the Week," *Variety*, May 20, 1964.

"good jazz players": Don Bagley, interview with author, January 12, 2012.

a deal to book Julie: "Julie London Will Take Tour of Orient," *Los Angeles Times*, May 6, 1964.

"gentle and clever": Ross Barbour, *Now You Know: The Story of the Four Freshmen* (Lake Geneva, WI: Balboa Books, 1995), 163.

"They used them for a while": Don Bagley, interview with author, January 22, 2012.

Tickets for Julie's shows: "Nipponese Have Big Yen for Julie London in Tour with Bobby Troup Quintet," *Variety*, June 10, 1964.

"the best band in Tokyo": Don Bagley, interview with author, January 12, 2012.

"big production": Dennis Budimir, interview with author, September 24, 2012.

"Some of the people we know": Sharon Lawrence, "Fans of Sultry Julie May Be in for Letdown," *Desert Sun* (Palm Springs, CA), January 4, 1965.

She was content: Cynnie Troup, interview with author, September 6, 2012.

"We mostly just worked": Don Bagley, interview with author, January 12, 2012.

"As long as there are good things": Hale, "TV Smokescreens."

"knew what she wanted": Don Bagley, interview with author, January 22, 2012.

"better harmonies": Don Bagley, interview with author, January 12, 2012.

"something put together": Thomas "Snuff" Garrett, interview with author, November 21, 2011.

"sang beautifully": Gene Cipriano, interview with author, December 12, 2013.

returned home with $24,000: Julie London 1965 fees and royalties statement (author's collection).

"She was exquisite": Harry Hawthorne, e-mail to author, March 12, 2014.

"the nearest thing": Don Bagley, interview with author, January 12, 2012.

"ended up doing": Kelly, *Liberty Records*, 323.

Atmosphere and audiences: Stan, "Night Club Reviews," *Variety*, May 19, 1965.

"She is a great leveler": "Julie London Travels to Australia," *Age* (Melbourne, Australia), May 3, 1965.

12: For the Night People

Bock sold: "Liberty Buying World Pacific and Affiliates," *Billboard*, May 22, 1965.

Stacy was the catalyst: Leonard Feather, liner notes to *Feeling Good*, by Julie London (Liberty, LRP-3416, 1965), LP.

The minor-key swinger: Bobby Troup, interview by Binny Lum, Australian radio, 1964.

"adored very few people": Linda Wheeler, interview with author, October 20, 2011, and January 7, 2012.

"no forgiving": Cynnie Troup, interview with author, June 12, 2012.

"engaging pair": Kevin Tighe and Bob Bayles, *Bobby Troup: The Maestro of Route 66* (Van Nuys, CA: RonBob, 2016), 3.

"generous, funny": Ronne Troup, quoted in Tighe and Bayles, *Bobby Troup*, ix.

"inside of herself": Robert Fuller, interview with author, April 4, 2016.

"forever grateful": Linda Wheeler, interview with author, November 26, 2011.

"whatever Dick Bock": Bud Shank, quoted in James Gavin, liner notes to *All Through the Night*, by Julie London (Capitol Jazz, 50999 5 01573 2 7, 2007), CD.

"sultry and sophisticated": *Billboard*, February 12, 1966.

"jazz singer": Colin Bailey, interview with author, July 26, 2011.

"a few nips": Colin Bailey, quoted in Gavin, liner notes to *All Through the Night*.

"When she got in a low-cut gown": Linda Wheeler, interview with author, November 26, 2011.

Bailey ran into Julie: Colin Bailey, interview with author, July 26, 2011.

"on a plane by herself": "Julie London Special Promises Top Viewing," *Chicago Defender*, July 16, 1966.

earned more than $125,000: Julie London's 1965 fees and royalties statement (author's collection).

"the living room floor": Tom Williams, e-mail to author, September 9, 2012.

"when the lights are dimmed": John S. Wilson, "Julie London at Royal Box," *New York Times*, February 15, 1966.

"Jesus Christ": Cynnie Troup, interview with author, May 18 and June 12, 2012.

"Every time I looked around": Bucky Pizzarelli, interview with author, January 9, 2013.

She rarely left: Cynnie Troup, interview with author, June 12, 2012.

governmental committee: "2 Recording Stars Testify at Inquiry," *New York Times*, February 19, 1966.

"why a booking agent": John Segraves, "Julie's Little Voice Is for a Little Room," *Washington (DC) Star*, March 14, 1966 (TLS).

"Nothing seemed to go right": John Pagones, "On the Town," *Washington Post*, March 27, 1966.

low-end motel: Cynnie Troup, interview with author, June 12, 2012.

"We would go nightclubbing": Tom Williams, interview in *The Lady's Not a Vamp*, BBC Television, 2006.

"Bobby's group": Steven Cerra, "Julie London, Bobby Troup and the China Trader," *Jazz Profiles* (blog), June 13, 2011. http://jazzprofiles.blogspot.com/2011/06/julie-london-bobby-troup-and-china.html.

"it helped enormously": Percy Shain, "Bobby & Julie to the Rescue," *Boston Globe*, February 6, 1972.

"In today's show business world": John L. Scott, "Julie London—a Real Soft-Sell Singer," *Los Angeles Times*, May 28, 1966.

"I go in first": John Bryan, "Julie's Kind of Scene," August 7, 1966, clipping (TLS); emphasis in original.

"one class act": Don Bagley, interview with author, January 12, 2012.

"wise enough": Don Bagley, e-mail to author, December 22, 2011.

"head over heels": Joe Sidore, interview with author, September 26, 2012.

"listened to her": Joe Sidore, interview with author, September 26, 2012, and February 21, 2013.

"We had done 'Bill Bailey'": Don Bagley, interview with author, January 22, 2012.

The sparse sound: Joe Sidore, interview with author, September 26, 2012.

"second showroom": Maynard Sloate, interview with author, April 11, 2016.

13: Lonesome Road

shell of solitude: Dave Pell, interview with author, March 17, 2014.

"Julie was always a pleasure": Joe Sidore, e-mail to author, May 1, 2013.

"art of nuance": Arnold Shaw, liner notes for *Nice Girls Don't Stay for Breakfast*, by Julie London (Liberty, LRP-3493, 1966), LP.

"I had suggested": Don Bagley, interview with author, January 22, 2012.

"That was a big deal": Don Bagley, interview with author, January 12, 2012.

Another tribute: Letter from Buddy Ebsen to Julie London, February 17, 1967 (TLS).

At the end of 1966: "Singles Production Trimmed by Liberty," *Billboard*, December 10, 1966.

"throaty commentary": "Smoky Illusion," *Age* (Melbourne, Australia), October 5, 1967.

"soft, sentimental and gripping": "Special Merit Picks," *Billboard*, February 11, 1967.

"low-keyed, sultry voice": John L. Scott, "Julie Gives Her Fans an Earful," *Los Angeles Times*, February 16, 1967.

Julie introduced: Thomas Bähler, "An Article About Experiencing 'Getting What You Want,'" Thomas Bähler website, July 22, 2011, www.thomasbahler.com.

"She was a blast": John Bähler, e-mail to author, September 26, 2012.

"If some of her numbers": Whit, "Night Club Reviews," *Variety*, February 22, 1967.

"a blue woolly": James Kilpatrick, "Julie London Sings Copyright Blues," *Oakland Tribune*, April 24, 1967.

"Whatever creative talent": "Copyright Law Revision," Hearings Before the Subcommittee on Patents, Trademarks, and Copyrights of the Committee on the Judiciary, United States Senate, April 11, 1967 (Washington, DC: US Government Printing Office, 1967).

portable phonograph: Roy Reed, "Julie Scores," *New York Times*, April 12, 1967.

"I never thought": Dick West, "Julie's Record Proves a Point," *Kingsport Times*, April 12, 1967.

"provocative song stylings": John L. Scott, "Julie Returns to Blue Room," *Los Angeles Times*, August 16, 1967.

"overflow crowd": George H. Jackson, "Tropicana Stars Julie London," *Los Angeles Herald-Examiner*, August 15, 1967 (TLS).

"let the boys": Linda Wheeler, interview with author, November 26, 2011.

"nocturnal swingers": Forrest Duke, "Night Club Reviews," *Variety*, August 30, 1967.

"goof off": Dick Kleiner, "Show Beat," *Lima News*, December 3, 1967.

"I sing low and sexy": Bacon, "Sexy Movies."

"It was always fortunate": Linda Wheeler, interview with author, January 7, 2012.

"major failure": Jose [Joe Cohen], "Night Club Reviews," *Variety*, October 4, 1967.

Mel Fuhrman recalled: Kelly, *Liberty Records*, 400.

"understandably tense": Lee Evans, e-mail to author, July 15, 2012.

"extremely handsome": Linda Wheeler, interview with author, November 8, 2012.

"very strange": Lisa Breen, interview with author, May 9, 2014.

"absolute attention": William U. Madden, "Julie London Captures Audience at Blue Room," *New Orleans States-Item*, January 19, 1968 (TLS).

"in a class by herself": Clarence Doucet, "Julie London's Message Given with Eyes, Voice," *New Orleans Times-Picayune*, January 19, 1968 (TLS).

"marvelous reading": Unidentified clipping (TLS).

"cool projection": Bill, "The Julie London Show," *Variety*, February 7, 1968.

"called for delivery": Al Stoffel, e-mail to author, September 13, 2012.

"old time glamour": Ibid.

"I get bugged": Troup, *Jazz Book*.

she told jazz critic: Feather, "Troups Move."

"echo and the like": Joe Sidore, e-mail to author, May 1, 2013.

"pulsating as flickering candlelight": *Rocky Mountain News*, February 1968 (TLS).

"It's a very good record": Leonard Feather, "The Blindfold Test: Julie's Keen on Carmen, Jeri (London in No Fog)," *Record Whirl*, April 1956.

"He's the best": Charles Witbeck, "Julie London Has a Lot to Like in Role of Nurse Dixie McCall," *Bridgeport Post*, February 25, 1972.

"very effective": Forrest Duke, "Night Club Reviews," *Variety*, April 24, 1968.

"every inch": Maynard Sloate, interview with author, April 11, 2016.

"Liberty was the larger": Al Stoffel, e-mail to author, September 13, 2012.

14: Wild, Smooth, and Sultry

"all kinds of music": Troup, *Jazz Book*.

"creative orchestrator": Lyle Ritz, e-mail to author, October 24, 2012.

"she enjoyed": Linda Wheeler, interview with author, November 26, 2011.

"a bill of goods": Bud Dain, quoted in Kelly, *Liberty Records*, 517.

"Many of the promises": Al Stoffel, e-mail to author, September 13, 2012.

"voting age and older": John L. Scott, "Julie London Opens at New Nightclub," *Los Angeles Times*, September 28, 1968.

"She mesmerized the audience": Tedd Thomey, "In Person," *Long Beach Press-Telegram*, October 3, 1968.

"sexy spoof": "Record Reviews," *Cash Box*, October 26, 1968.

"a whole new feel": "Special Merit Spotlight," *Billboard*, October 26, 1968.

"sleek, sophisticated": *Cash Box*, November 23, 1968.

"organized abandon": Robert Sobel, "Julie London Sultry, Provocative in Act," *Billboard*, November 23, 1968.

"I've known you": Earl Wilson, "It Happened Last Night," *Times Recorder* (Zanesville, OH), November 19, 1968.

"low-key evening": William Rice, "On the Town," *Washington Post*, November 29, 1968.

"Julie purrs": Will Leonard, "On the Town," *Chicago Tribune*, December 8, 1968.

"It was pretty addictive": Linda Wheeler, interview with author, January 7, 2012.

"in great voice": Ron Batiste, "3 Big Names in Jazz Make Crowds Spin in Las Vegas," *Billboard*, March 15, 1969.

throwing up a lot: Haber, "Nightclubs to Nursing."

nothing but scorn: Bobby Troup, quoted in Kelly, *Liberty Records*, 331.

"A most tasty treat": "Album Reviews," *Cash Box*, February 8, 1969.

"sensitive approach": Bill Rumfelt, "Easy Listening," *Evening Telegram* (Rocky Mount, NC), March 30, 1969.

"written for her": Ed Allen, "Julie London Sounds Great Crooning Other People's Tunes," *Lima News*, March 12, 1969.

"younger, bigger": Al Stoffel, e-mail to author, September 13, 2012.

"world changed": Robb Baker, "Jackie DeShannon Soft, Dreamy Like Her Record Counterpart," *Chicago Tribune*, March 15, 1970.

"affectingly sad": *Variety*, June 11, 1969.

"favorite bunny": Telegram from Troup family, June 20, 1969 (TLS).

"lugging in the oxygen": Bawden, "Two Careers."

"personal showcase": John L. Scott, "Julie Makes Tropicana a Personal Showcase," *Los Angeles Times*, August 14, 1969.

"experimental diffusion": Will, "Night Club Reviews," *Variety*, August 20, 1969.

"When it comes to working": Robe, "Night Club Reviews," *Variety*, December 3, 1969.

"jaded, 'worn woman'": Doug McClelland, "Julie, a Style for All Seasons," *Record World*, December 13, 1969.

"nothing romantic": Bawden, "Two Careers."

waved from a convertible: Linda Wheeler, e-mail to author, September 8, 2012.

"To get the wallop": James A. Perry, "Audience Loves Julie Despite Voice Problems," *New Orleans States-Item*, January 2, 1970 (TLS).

the remainder: "Ailing Julie London Cuts Date in N.O. Short," *Variety*, January 14, 1970.

a blow that affected Julie: Linda Wheeler, e-mail to author, September 8, 2012.

The house was listed: Variety, May 15, 1970 (TLS).

"rather dull": Robert Hilburn, "The Lounge Is THE Place on Las Vegas Scene," *Los Angeles Times*, July 26, 1970.

"just stop": Linda Wheeler, interview with author, November 26, 2011.

"that kind of voice": Tony Russell, interview with author, February 11, 2012.

"In this era": John L. Scott, "Julie London Suited to Nocturnal 'Listening,'" *Los Angeles Times*, October 30, 1970.

"supper-club singer": Tone, "Night Club Reviews," *Variety*, November 4, 1970.

"open-fronted gown": Will, "Night Club Reviews," *Variety*, March 10, 1971.

"This kind of work": Julie London, interview by Binny Lum, Australian radio, April 1964.

15: *Emergency!*

"It came out of the blue": Vernon Scott, "Julie London, Husband, Work for Jack Webb," *Elyria Chronicle Telegram*, July 12, 1972.

The subject was unlikely: Richard Yokley and Rozane Sutherland, *"Emergency!" Behind the Scene* (Sudbury, MA: Jones and Bartlett, 2008), 8–10.

The pitch combined: Tom Williams, interview with author, May 14, 2014.

Sheinberg was convinced: Yokley and Sutherland, *"Emergency!,"* 16–17.

Cecil Smith, "What Am I Doing Here?," *Los Angeles Times*, February 1, 1972.

"Jack has a genius": Haber, "Nightclubs to Nursing."

mellowing influence: Tighe and Bayles, *Bobby Troup*, 3.

To familiarize themselves: Yokley and Sutherland, *"Emergency!,"* 82.

"two-dollar shirt": Robert Fuller, interview with author, April 4, 2016.

Four days before: Ibid.

"time to fight": Cecil Smith, "Paramedics Is Theme of NBC's New Series," *Los Angeles Times*, November 22, 1971.

"a tough boss": Scott, "Work for Jack."

"blistered the set": Hano, "She's on Hand."

He wanted all the actors: Robert Fuller, interview with author, April 4, 2016.

"I'd rather perform": Shain, "To the Rescue."

a complicated sequence: "No Weight Problems for Julie London," *Evening Herald* (Rock Hill, NC), January 24, 1972.

The stress: Moyer and Alvarez, *Just the Facts*, 258n.

"We got started": Marilyn Beck, "'Emergency' Has Unusual Family Ties," *Youngstown Vindicator*, December 26, 1971.

"I never expected to be here": Cecil Smith, "What Am I Doing Here?," *Los Angeles Times*, February 1, 1972.

soap opera: Yokley and Sutherland, *"Emergency!,"* 17–18.

"Kel and Dixie": Robert Fuller, interview with author, April 4, 2016.

"get up together": Smith, "What Am I."

"We really have a ball": Witbeck, "A Lot to Like."

"brought over albums": Kevin Tighe, e-mail to author, March 4, 2013.

accompanied his new friends: Kevin Tighe, interview with author, November 26, 2012.

"dime-novel dialog": Bill, "Television Reviews," *Variety*, January 19, 1972.

Kelly Brackett had been named: Shain, "To the Rescue."

"talked like a sailor": Cynnie Troup, interview with author, June 12, 2012.

"every bad word": Randolph Mantooth, interview by Tom Blixa, WTVN Radio, Columbus, OH, May 23, 2013.

"a mentor": Denise Ames, "One-on-One with Randolph Mantooth," *Tolucan Times*, December 12, 2013.

"My natural style": Hano, "She's on Hand."

"dry dog shit": Julie London, letter to Jack Landry, ca. 1970s (TLS).

where she could make: Letter from the producers of *Match Game* to Julie London, ca. 1970s (TLS).

"four-day party": "Star Bowling the Alley 'Cats' Meow," *Port Neches Midcounty Chronicle Review*, June 3, 1973.

"appeal in the action": Aleene MacMinn, "Julie London: She Can Settle Down Now Thanks to 'Emergency!,'" *Los Angeles Times*, June 16, 1974.

"silly financially": Ibid.

"In a club": Haber, "Nightclubs to Nursing."

"Maybe I'll sing again": "Ask Them Yourself," *Family Weekly*, May 11, 1975.

"That moment": Feather, "Troups Move."

hospital whites: Bob Bain, interview with author, March 13, 2013.

"another world": Robert Fuller, interview with author, April 4, 2016.

"I've looked the same": Windeler, "Doctor Ordered."

"Whenever there's a scene": Andee Beck, "Julie London Searching for Rainbow's End," *New York Times*, February 1, 1977.

16: "We Said We'd Never Say 'Goodbye'"

"I don't do that anymore": Linda Wheeler, interview with author, November 26, 2011.

"a very large world": Troup, *Jazz Book*.

"don't get tired": Windeler, "Doctor Ordered."

"Julie made a lot": Thomas "Snuff" Garrett, interview with author, November 21, 2011.

"front door was never locked": Tom Williams, e-mail to author, January 2, 2013.

"orphanage on the hill": Tom Williams, interview with author, May 14, 2014.

"making an entrance": Jill Schoelen, interview with author, November 18, 2013.

"enormously gifted": Jill Schoelen, liner notes to *Kelly's Smile*, by Jill Schoelen (Onward and Upward Inc., 2009), CD.

"don't spend time": Linda Wheeler, interview with author, November 26, 2011.

"I've got another song": Hamilton, *Vamp*.

"Bobby would have to beg her": Linda Wheeler, interview with author, November 26, 2011.

"If I worked at it": Feather, "Troups Move."

"I wanted her to sing": Thomas "Snuff" Garrett, interview with author, November 21, 2011.

"She was great at comebacks": Thomas "Snuff" Garrett, interview with author, November 2, 2011.

Julie asked her daughter: Lisa Breen, interview with author, May 9, 2014.

"couldn't come back": Linda Wheeler, interview with author, November 26, 2011.

"her standards were so way out of focus": Thomas "Snuff " Garrett, interview with author, November 21, 2011.

"tell a story": Jill Schoelen, interview with author, November 18, 2013.

Bobby was certain: Feather, "Troups Move."

"steady sipping": Enid Harlow, *Crashing* (New York: St. Martin's, 1980), 45, 54.

"screwdrivers": Lisa Breen, interview with author, May 9, 2014.

Julie tried to convince: Linda Wheeler, interview with author, November 8, 2012.

dropped the option: Enid Harlow, e-mail to author, October 25, 2012.

On December 23, 1982: Moyer and Alvarez, *Just the Facts*, 207.

It was a somber Christmas: Moyer and Alvarez, *Just the Facts*, 207–8.

escorted to Forest Lawn: Michael Seiler, "Police Eulogize Jack Webb as One of Their Own," *Los Angeles Times*, December 31, 1982.

"personal philosophy": Julie London, letter to unknown recipient, n.d. (copy in author's possession).

"You were born together": Kahlil Gibran, *The Prophet* (New York: Knopf, 1956), 15.

"came up to me": Peggy Webber, interview with author, March 7, 2013.

"never came around": Lisa Breen, interview with author, May 9, 2014.

"heart of gold": Ibid.

"the wisdom of Julie": Jill Schoelen, interview with author, November 18, 2013.

loved the attention: Linda Wheeler, interview with author, January 7, 2012.

"nooks and crannies": Ryann Breen, e-mail to author, June 6, 2016.

Kelly suspected: Jill Schoelen, interview with author, November 18, 2013.

"against her religion": Linda Wheeler, interview with author, January 7, 2012, and July 19, 2012.

"high blood pressure": Linda Wheeler, interview with author, November 26, 2011.

"conscious being": Robert J. Wityk, MD, in Joel Stein, Julie Silver, and Elizabeth Pegg Frates, *Life After Stroke: The Guide to Recovering Your Health and Preventing Another Stroke* (Baltimore: Johns Hopkins, 2006), xiii.

likely to have occurred: Stein, Silver, and Frates, *Life After Stroke*, 3–6, 14–17, 47–52.

repeating numbers: Linda Wheeler, interview with author, November 26, 2011.

"Parliaments": Arthur Krim, interview with author, November 18, 2011.

"master of the house": Troup, *Jazz Book*.

"full of shit": Tom Williams, interview with author, May 14, 2014.

beyond Julie's grasp: Linda Wheeler, interview with author, November 26, 2011.

At an intersection: Kenny Klein, "Crash Victim Identified as Actor's Daughter," *Desert Sun* (Palm Springs, CA), September 30, 1996 (TLS).

her misjudgment: Daniel Moyer, e-mail to author, March 14, 2013.

"there was a lot more going on": Cynnie Troup, interview with author, June 12, 2012.

"out of harm's way": Linda Wheeler, interview with author, January 7, 2012.

"got what was going on": Cynnie Troup, interview with author, June 12, 2012.

"a beautiful, beautiful time": Robert Fuller, interview with author, April 4, 2016.

"achingly slow": Karen Schoemer, "The Echo Chamber," *New York Times* Magazine, January 7, 2001.

"she forgets": Julie London and Bobby Troup, interview by Karen Schoemer, Encino, CA, April 20, 1998.

"He was a bit uncomfortable": Cynnie Troup, interview with author, June 12, 2012.

"He made it all possible": Peerenboom, *Jazz Roundtable.*

"cleverest, funniest": Thomas "Snuff" Garrett, interview with author, November 2, 2011.

Tighe stayed: Cynnie Troup, interview with author, June 12, 2012.

shared her mother's gift: Ibid.

"She was starting to ask for cigarettes": Linda Wheeler, interview with author, November 26, 2011.

"huge tears": Ibid.

"I'm going": Ibid.

Epilogue: Echoes

"smoother, wittier": Tom Ewing, "And Julie Was Her Name—Listening to Old Music," *Freaky Trigger,* www.freakytrigger.com, October 27, 2000.

"so cool": Mari Wilson, e-mail to author, January 12, 2014.

"gonna kill": James Austin, interview with author, March 24, 2014.

"cocktail music": Joal Ryan, "How to Swing," *Swing,* May 1997.

"smooth, conversational phrasing": Kenneth Wright, "Julie London," *Herald* (Glasgow, Scotland), October 24, 2000.

"Dionysian flesh": Joseph Lanza, *The Cocktail: The Influence of Spirits on the American Psyche* (New York: Picador USA, 1995), 81–87.

never been a fan: Julie London and Bobby Troup, interview by Karen Schoemer, Encino, CA, April 20, 1998.

"You gotta have the ego": Bawden, "Two Careers."

Sources

A Note on Sources

Some recording dates, locations, and personnel were found in copies of session contracts in the files of the American Federation of Musicians, Local 47, in Los Angeles.

Production details for a number of the films Julie London made for MGM, Universal, Warner Bros., and 20th Century Fox come from the collections at the Cinematic Arts Library at the University of Southern California and the Warner Bros. Archives, School of Cinematic Arts, University of Southern California.

Information on the Southern California residences of the Peck family was gathered from federal and state census reports, voter registration rolls, and city directories available on Ancestry.com.

Events during Julie's school days were gleaned from various articles in the *San Bernardino Sun* newspaper (1937–1941).

Julie's arrivals in and departures from Europe during the 1950s are taken from passenger lists available on Ancestry.com.

Books

Cason, Buzz. *Living the Rock 'n' Roll Dream: The Adventures of Buzz Cason*. Milwaukee: Hal Leonard, 2004.

Craver, Rebecca, and Adair Margo, eds. *Tom Lea: An Oral History*. El Paso: Texas Western Press, 1995.

Daniels, Draper. *Giants, Pigmies, and Other Advertising People.* Chicago: Crain, 1974.

Gioia, Ted. *West Coast Jazz: Modern Jazz in California, 1945–1960.* New York: Oxford University Press, 1992.

Guinn, J. M. *A History of California and an Extended History of Its Southern Coast Counties: Also Containing Biographies of Well-Known Citizens of the Past and Present.* Vol. 2. Los Angeles: Historic Record Company, 1907.

Hare, Cynthia. *Once I Was a Debutante.* Van Nuys, CA: RonBob, 2012.

Hoffmann, Frank W., George Albert, and Lee Ann Hoffman, compilers. *The Cashbox Album Charts, 1955–1974.* Lanham, MD: Scarecrow, 1988.

Jack, Gordon. *Fifties Jazz Talk: An Oral Retrospective.* Lanham, MD: Scarecrow, 2004.

Kelly, Michael "Doc Rock." *Liberty Records: A History of the Recording Company and Its Stars, 1955–1971.* Jefferson, NC: McFarland, 1993.

Lanza, Joseph. *The Cocktail: The Influence of Spirits on the American Psyche.* New York: Picador USA, 1995.

Lea, Tom. *The Wonderful Country.* Boston: Gregg Press, 1979.

Moyer, Daniel, and Eugene Alvarez. *Just the Facts, Ma'am: The Authorized Biography of Jack Webb.* Santa Ana, CA: Seven Locks Press, 2001.

Server, Lee. *Robert Mitchum: "Baby, I Don't Care."* New York: St. Martin's Griffin, 2001.

Starr, Kevin. *Americans and the California Dream: 1850–1915.* New York: Oxford University Press, 1973.

Steeples, Douglas. *Treasure from the Painted Hills: A History of Calico, California, 1882–1907.* Westport, CT: Greenwood, 1999.

Stein, Joel, Julie Silver, and Elizabeth Pegg Frates. *Life After Stroke: The Guide to Recovering Your Health and Preventing Another Stroke.* Baltimore: Johns Hopkins, 2006.

Summerfield, Maurice J. *Barney Kessel: A Jazz Legend.* Blaydon on Tyne: Ashley Mark, 2008.

Tighe, Kevin, and Bob Bayles. *Bobby Troup: The Maestro of Route 66.* Van Nuys, CA: RonBob, 2016.

Whitburn, Joel, ed. *The Billboard Albums.* 6th ed. Menomenee Falls, WI: Record Research, 2007.

———, ed. *Billboard Top Pop Singles.* 12th ed. Menomenee Falls, WI: Record Research, 2009.

Yokley, Richard, and Rozane Sutherland. *"Emergency!" Behind the Scene.* Sudbury, MA: Jones and Bartlett, 2008.

Newspapers and Periodicals

Archerd, Armand. "Julie London Still Prefers Acting." *Daily Reporter* (Dover, OH), October 24, 1957.

Ardmore, Jane Kesner. "Julie London Starts a New Life." N.d. Unpublished draft of June 1958 *Coronet* article.

———. "The Private Blues of Julie London." *Coronet*, June 1958.

Avery, Ronald. "How Julie London Cried Herself a Bankroll." *Inside Story*, January 1960.

Bacon, James. "Ex–Mrs. Jack Webb Rates as Top Singer, Actress." *Bridgeport Post*, February 3, 1957.

———. "Singer Julie Objects to Sexy Movies." *Eureka Humboldt Standard*, April 26, 1961.

Budig, Gene. "Singer Worried." *Lincoln Sunday Journal and Star*, November 10, 1963.

Butterworth, Keen. "Transfigurations of Loneliness," *Southern Review* 43, no. 3 (Summer 2007): 669–87.

"The Face on the Cutting Room Floor." *Milwaukee Journal*, November 21, 1959.

Feather, Leonard. "Troups Move into New Roles." *Los Angeles Times*, July 19, 1981.

Freeman, Donald. "'It's a Man's World'—Julie." *Chicago Tribune*, February 17, 1963.

Gehman, Richard. "New Life for Julie London." *Washington Post*, April 7, 1957.

Gleason, Ralph J. "Bittersweet Ballads in a Boudoir Manner." *San Francisco Chronicle*, January 17, 1956.

"Golden Mould: Julie London, One of the Nebulae of Hollywood." *Esquire*, November 1943.

Haber, Joyce. "From Nightclubs to Nursing with Julie." *Los Angeles Times*, November 11, 1973.

Hale, David. "TV Smokescreen Hid Julie London's Light." *Fresno Bee*, August 16, 1964.

Hano, Arnold. "She's on Hand to Provide the Basic Femininity." *TV Guide*, June 17, 1972.

"Hard-Working Dreamer." *Radio-TV Mirror*, November 1951.

Heimer, Mel. "My New York." *Titusville Herald*, February 7, 1957.

"Hollywood Is Awed over Julie London's New $225,000 Home." *Newport Daily News*, January 8, 1960.

Hopper, Hedda. "London Outlook: Fair Weather." *Chicago Tribune*, June 14, 1959.

———. "Looking at Hollywood." *Portland Press Herald*, March 11, 1949.

Humphrey, Hal. "Julie Sounds Good Like a Commercial Should." *Los Angeles Times*, October 28, 1962.

"Jack Webb Absent as His Wife Wins Divorce." *Los Angeles Times*, November 26, 1953.

Johnson, Erskine. "Hollywood Today." *Humboldt Standard*, May 24, 1958.

Lane, Lydia. "Dishonesty Is the Worst of Policies." *Oakland Tribune*, November 29, 1959.

"Laziest Girl in Hollywood." *Chicago Tribune*, February 9, 1963.

Lewis, Jean. "Julie London Had Allergy." *Palm Beach Post*, August 8, 1975.

"Like a Lioness on a Leash." *TV Guide*, July 15, 1961.

MacMinn, Aleene. "Julie London: She Can Settle Down Now Thanks to 'Emergency!'" *Los Angeles Times*, June 16, 1974.

Martin, Pete. "I Call on Julie London." *Saturday Evening Post*, August 17, 1957.

McPherson, Virginia. "Julie Drops Film Career to Make Home for Hubby." *Binghamton Press*, October 2, 1950.

"The Most ADULT Western of All." *Modern Man*, December 1958.

Oliver, Richard. "Snuff's Philosophy: Marry the Song to the Artist." *Billboard*, December 15, 1973.

Scott, Vernon. "Julie London, Husband Work for Jack Webb." *Elyria Chronicle Telegram*, July 12, 1972.

Shain, Percy. "Bobby & Julie to the Rescue." *Boston Globe*, February 6, 1972.

Smith, Cecil. "Julie London, Torn Between Singing and Acting, Tries Hand at Westerns." *Los Angeles Times*, June 2, 1957.

———. "What Am I Doing Here?" *Los Angeles Times*, February 1, 1972.

Thomas, Bob. "Movie-Makers Aim for Adult Themes." *Newport Daily News*, July 24, 1958.

Tynan, John. "Julie London: Cover Girl." *Down Beat*, January 23, 1957.

Webb, Jack, as told to Dean Jennings. "The Facts About Me." *Saturday Evening Post*, September 12, 1959.

Wilson, Earl. "Reporter Finds Julie London in Rare Confessional Mood." *Reno Evening Gazette*, November 26, 1960.

Windeler, Robert. "For Julie London and Bobby Troup, 'Emergency!' Is Just What the Doctor Ordered." *People*, January 14, 1977.

Witbeck, Charles. "Julie London Has a Lot to Like in Role of Nurse Dixie McCall." *Bridgeport Post*, February 25, 1972.

Zolotow, Maurice. "The True Story of Jack Webb: The Names Have Not Been Changed (Parts 1–4)." *American Weekly*, September 12, 19, 26, and October 3, 1954.

Video/Television/Audio Interviews

Kessel, Barney. "Julie London: A Rare Vocal Treasure." *Inside Jazz* radio program, Oklahoma, ca. mid-1980s.

The Lady's Not a Vamp. BBC Television, 2006.

London, Julie. Interview by Binny Lum. Australian radio, New York City, April 1964.

London, Julie. Interview by Bobby Troup. In *Jazz Book*, vol. 2. Armed Forces Radio Service, n.d. (ca. summer/fall 1964).

London, Julie. Interview by Fritz Peerenboom. *Jazz Roundtable*, WOSU Radio, Columbus, OH, October 22, 1971.

London, Julie. Interview by John Salisbury. *Sunday Spectacular*, KXL Radio, Portland, OR, July 21, 1968.

London, Julie. Liberty Records. Disc jockey open-end interview disc, ca. 1962.

London, Julie, and Bobby Troup. Interview by Bill Ballance. KNX Radio, Los Angeles, September 12, 1955.

London, Julie, and Bobby Troup. Interview by Karen Schoemer, Encino, CA, April 20, 1998.

Troup, Bobby. Interview by Binny Lum. Australian radio, New York City, April 1964.

Miscellaneous Print Sources

"Copyright Law Revision." Hearings Before the Subcommittee on Patents, Trademarks, and Copyrights of the Committee on the Judiciary, United States Senate, April 11, 1967. Washington, DC: US Government Printing Office, 1967.

Gavin, James. Liner notes to *All Through the Night* by Julie London. Capitol Jazz, 50999 5 01573 2 7, 2007. CD.

Liberty Records. *The Real Julie*. Publicity pamphlet, 1961.

Websites and Blogs

American Film Institute. *AFI Catalog of Feature Films*. www.afi.com/members/catalog/.

AmericanRadioHistory.com. www.americanradiohistory.com.

Ancestry.com. www.ancestry.com.

Bawden, Jim. "Amazing Julie London: She Juggled Two Careers in Films and on Records." Harkit Records, June 4, 2012. www.harkitrecords.com/julie_london_interview.html.

British Board of Film Classification. www.bbfc.co.uk.

Classic TV Archive. www.ctva.biz.

EmergencyFans.com. www.emergencyfans.com.

Harrod, James. *Stars of Jazz* (blog). http://starsofjazz.blogspot.com.

Hits of All Decades. www.hitsofalldecades.com.

Julie London: The Ultimate Fan Site. http://julielondon.org/J/Home.html.

University of California, San Francisco. Legacy Tobacco Documents Library. http://legacy .library.ucsf.edu.

Reed, Bill. "Don and Julie." *People vs. Dr. Chilledair* (blog), July 26, 2010, http://people-vs-dr chilledair.blogspot.com/2010/07/don-and-julie.html.

Scopitone Archive. www.scopitonearchive.com.

Index